BETWEEN COMPETITION AND FREE MOVEMENT

Between Competition and Free Movement

The Economic Constitutional Law of the European Community

JULIO BAQUERO CRUZ

·HART·
PUBLISHING
OXFORD – PORTLAND OREGON
2002

Hart Publishing
Oxford and Portland, Oregon

Published in North America (US and Canada) by
Hart Publishing c/o
International Specialized Book Services
5804 NE Hassalo Street
Portland, Oregon
97213-3644
USA

Distributed in the Netherlands, Belgium and Luxembourg by
Intersentia, Churchillaan 108
B2900 Schoten
Antwerpen
Belgium

Hart Publishing is a specialist legal publisher based in Oxford, England.
To order further copies of this book or to request a list of other
publications please write to:

Hart Publishing, Salter's Boatyard, Folly Bridge,
Abingdon Road, Oxford OX1 4LB
Telephone: +44 (0)1865 245533 or Fax: +44 (0)1865 794882
e-mail: mail@hartpub.co.uk
WEBSITE: http//www.hartpub.co.uk

British Library Cataloguing in Publication Data
Data Available
ISBN 1–84113–336–1 (hardback)

Typeset by Hope Services (Abingdon) Ltd.
Printed and bound in Great Britain on acid-free paper by
Biddles Ltd, www.biddles.co.uk

Foreword

The book we present to the public was originally a PhD dissertation brilliantly defended by the author before the Law Department of the European University Institute, at Florence. We were the two supervisors of this thesis, a rather passive role in this case, considering the dynamism and talents of the candidate.

The book deals with a specific problem of economic Community law: the interaction, gaps and loopholes between competition and free movement. These apparently classical problems concerning the application of free movement rules to private persons and of competition rules to public authorities are dealt with from a constitutional perspective. The subject is indeed about filling gaps in the economic constitutional law of the Community.

The author starts from what he calls an operational or workable (legal) concept of the constitution, which he draws from the traditions of constitutionalism as it has evolved beyond the liberal concept of the XIXth century, in Europe and in the United States. His definition of the constitution is as remarkable because of what he excludes from it as it is because of the elements that are conceived as essential. Considering the constitutional mandate received by the Convention created by the European Council meeting in Laeken, the synthesis proposed by Julio Baquero is particularly topical and opportune. It helps also to realise that a constitution is not in itself a manna. Its value depends on its content. It seems to be stating the obvious but it is well known that, for some, this exercise is more about limiting the ambitions of the Union than about allowing its well-ordered development on the scale of the Continent. On the other hand, the constituent power is not for the author an inherent element of the concept. The enduring acquiescence to the constitution of most of the persons living in a polity is more important than the historical democratic adoption made by their ancestors. Such a view does not deny a legitimating virtue, for example, to a European referendum.

For Julio Baquero, competition and free movement are of paramount importance in the economic constitutional law of the Community, as it is confirmed by the case law of the Court. That does not mean that other principles are not progressively finding their way, but they are perhaps different in nature, either as fundamental rights (gender equality) or as guiding political principles (economic and social cohesion), environmental rules being a blend of both. The importance of the constitutionalisation role of the Court of Justice is another caveat for the participants to the Laeken Convention. Any constitutional draft should take on board the important achievements of the case law especially for the private parties. If it is indeed admissible in a Constitution to find sections of an unequal normative value, such as so-called declaratory provisions next to positive rules, directly enforceable, it would be a legal regression to deny a constitutional rank to the basic rules of the single market. A constitutional norm is, indeed, as recalled by Julio Baquero, one that 'cannot be reviewed against other legal norms, which may be driven out of the legal order by the judiciary if in breach thereof'. In this vein, the author proposes a legal distinction for the concepts of positive and negative integration. 'Negative integration' is the set of rules included in the economic constitutional law, like, for example, the prohibition of discrimination on the ground of nationality, a principle that infuses the whole Treaty; 'positive integration', the rules laid down by legislation under the Constitution.

The later chapters of the thesis (not the second part of it, because each chapter builds on the previous one, adding a piece of reasoning in the demonstration like a large puzzle) are dedicated to the analysis of the case law of the Court, illustrating the problematic of what has been termed the 'privatisation' of free movement rules and 'publicisation' of competition, the subject of a famous controversy between Pierre Pescatore and Giuliano Marenco.

On the subject of private conduct running counter to the purpose of the free movement rules, the author concludes, after an examination of the pertinent case law, that private action may be caught by the Treaty rules on free movement only when it is not unlike State action, ie when it amounts to some sort of private legislation which restricts free movement with protective intent or effects. Other private action will be caught by the competition rules (undertakings) or by the fundamental rights jurisprudence of the Court of Justice (freedom of trade), if it clearly violates such rights. This is meant to preserve one of the principles inherent in the operational concept of constitution defended by the author: the existence of a protected sphere of autonomy for the persons living in the polity.

For the review of State action, the author would like to see the Court favouring the free movement route over the competition route in preference to the rather formalist tests applied by the Court in its jurisprudence. Protectionist measures are more frequent than purely anticompetitive ones that cannot be justified. If the free movement rules are not breached, Julio Baquero proposes that the analysis should afford a degree of deference to the legislator, whose legitimacy among the State's organs is the greatest. This approach, which modulates the appreciation of a national measure with regard to the Treaty, taking into account the State's organ concerned, is not in line with the way the Court traditionally approaches such kind of potential conflicts. There is no immunity for the organ reflecting directly the opinions deriving from universal suffrage. But one must admit that the proposed criterion has a constitutional logic, if seen in the perspective of a nascent multi-level constitutionalism, and leaves the State with room to manoeuvre in order to achieve objectives of economic policy transcending the requirements of competition policy.

The preceding sketch can only give a partial view of the richness of ideas contained in Julio Baquero's book—in the fields of legal theory, comparative law (in particular, through his references to US law, but also to legal doctrine in various languages), public law, and, of course, Community law, both institutional and economic. He has taken full advantage of his studies and research in Madrid, Bruges, Florence and Columbia. He defends original views, inviting the reader to continue the research, and to put to the test theories and opinions to which the reader cannot remain indifferent. In doing so he does not hesitate to swim against powerful currents in the present literature.

We wish the book the success it fully deserves.

Giuliano Amato and Jean-Victor Louis,
Firenze,
January 2002.

Preface

This book is based on a PhD thesis written between September 1997 and December 2000 at the European University Institute in Florence, under the joint supervision of Giuliano Amato and Jean-Victor Louis.

The viva took place on 5 March 2001. The examining board was composed of my supervisors, Gráinne de Búrca, Koen Lenaerts and Peter Oliver. I would like to thank them for their comments, criticism and suggestions. I am especially grateful to my supervisors, who were always of great help.

Also at the European University Institute, I would like to thank, among others, Sophia Aboudrar, Miriam Aziz, Annick Bulckaen, Claus-Dieter Ehlermann, Michelle Everson, Navraj Singh Ghaleigh, Christian Joerges, Makis Komninos, Pedro Machado, Agustín Menéndez, Alan Milward, Bill Nardini, Massimo la Torre, Alison Tuck, Alexandre Vaz-Pereira and Jacques Ziller.

I first became acquainted with some of the problems explored in this work during the academic year 1995–1996 at the College of Europe (Bruges), through the teachings of Joseph Weiler, Paul Demaret, Ami Barav and Alfonso Mattera.

I spent the spring semester of 2000 as an exchange scholar at Columbia University in the city of New York, where I familiarised myself with some of the problems of US constitutional law. At Columbia, George Bermann, Michael Dorf, Louis Henkin, Peter Lindseth and Henry Monaghan gave me valuable advice.

Anthony Arnull read and commented on a previous version of the chapter on free movement and the private sphere, for which I am grateful. I thank Miguel Poiares Maduro for commenting on drafts of some of the chapters. I am much obliged to Michel Waelbroeck for his comments on a draft of chapter 8.

In December 2000, after handing in the thesis, I started working as référendaire in the chambers of Gil Carlos Rodríguez Iglesias, President of the Court of Justice of the European Communities. I would like to thank him for the time he took to read the book, as well as his comments and criticism. At the Court I have also benefited from the help of Fernando Castillo de la Torre. In Luxembourg I have also had the chance to meet and discuss with Pierre Pescatore, former judge of the Court, whose work has always been a source of inspiration.

I would also like to mention the support of my parents and siblings from the beginning.

The direct experience of the activity of the Court may have partly changed my way of seeing things. Nonetheless, I have tried to preserve the spirit in which this work was written, with necessary changes and updating. The opinions expressed in this book are personal, and should not be attributed to the institution for which I work. Despite the various debts accumulated in the preparation of this work, it goes without saying that all opinions and remaining errors are mine alone.

For the sake of clarity, only the indispensable references are included. In the course of my research, to be sure, I have read and learnt from many others. Sometimes I take one author as a representative of a whole doctrinal school. The bibliography is, then, quite selective.

Primary sources are quoted in the conventional way. Citations in the text are always in the English language. All translations are my own, unless otherwise indicated. The original texts of the citations are provided in the footnotes. Those judgments of the European Court of Justice that have not yet appeared in the European Court Reports are quoted from the website of the Court (http://curia.eu.int/). The author is bound to acknowledge the unofficial character of the text of these judgments, which are provided free of charge. The law is stated as at 28 February 2002.

J. B. C.
Luxembourg,
February 2002

Contents

Table of Cases

EUROPEAN COURT OF JUSTICE AND COURT OF FIRST INSTANCE

1. Alphabetical

Numerical

OTHER JURISDICTIONS

Danish Supreme Court

French Conseil Constitutionnel

German Constitutional Court

Italian Constitutional Court

Portuguese Constitutional Court

Spanish Constitutional Court

Supreme Court of the United States

Table Legislation

EU SECONDARY LEGISLATION

OTHER LEGAL ORDERS

1

Themes, Intention and Method

THIS CHAPTER PRESENTS the themes explored in this work and the method employed to do so.

Themes and not just a theme are examined, for this enquiry is structured around a central question that leads to other questions that are as important as the first. Accordingly, the presentation of my findings does not follow a linear path, but is like a tree whose branches may be linked to a common trunk but simultaneously grow in various directions.

The initial focus of this work is the interaction, gaps and loopholes between the free movement and the competition rules of the Treaty establishing the European Community, which constitute the keystones of the economic constitutional law of the Community.

With a few exceptions, this has remained a relatively unexplored subject. The lack of attention among scholars is probably due to the increasing specialisation within the realms of Community law. While the competition lawyer tends to concentrate on competition, free movement specialists focus on free movement. As a result, the various situations involving both sets of norms and the possible conflicts and gaps between them have received insufficient attention.

At the beginning of this project, it seemed interesting to me to stand in the no-man's-land between competition and free movement, despite the risk that this might mean losing some of the detail that a more narrowly focused research could offer. Being in between, I expected, would allow me to highlight the intimate connection between both sets of norms and analyse their relationship in a constitutional fashion.

Another reason for this choice was the recognition of a growing tendency among competition specialists to treat their topic in a highly technical way, as distinct from the economic constitutional law of the Community. As the law now stands, however, the competition rules contained in the Treaty have a constitutional status and may be interpreted as shaping a *law of economic liberty* from restraints of competition and abuses of private economic power, not only a *law of economic efficiency*. Thus, an efficiency-oriented approach to the Community competition rules may not be in tune with the current normative structure.

Seen from the perspective of a simplification and restructuring of the Treaty—now confirmed by Declaration 23 of the Nice Treaty and the Laeken Declaration of 15 December 2001—this work defends the current constitutional status of the basic competition rules. The link between competition and free movement reinforces this argument. The constitutional character of the free movement rules seems, in principle, beyond dispute, since they limit the exercise of national powers and bestow rights on individuals. If the competition rules are complementary to the free movement rules, it would be somewhat bizarre to place them on a different hierarchical level.

My persistent use of the expression *economic constitutional law of the European Community* is deliberate. The concept, structure and prospects of this branch of the law are open issues. In a state of such uncertainty, the very subject matter of this enquiry calls for the elucidation of certain concepts and categories with the aim of imposing a degree of analytical rigour.

The classic concept of constitution shows both an external and internal fragmentation and is no longer adequate to reflect on a contemporary constitutionalism that is increasingly detaching itself from the nation-State. I shall then begin by elaborating an operational concept of the term 'constitution', based on the classical concept, but adapted to the new realities (chapter 2). Its relationship with the economy will be examined in chapter 3, in which chapter I also displace the concept of the *economic constitution* with the more apt notion of *economic constitutional law*. In chapter 4, the operational concept of a constitution is applied to the Community legal order in order to determine whether it includes a constitution and define its limits.

Besides providing the analytic framework for this work, these chapters aim to be self-standing. References to the constitutional law of the European Community—even of the European Union—have become commonplace and the literature is substantial and growing. Courses and seminars are constantly being offered under this title. And yet deeply seated ambiguities remain concerning the constitution of the European Community: its lack of definition is directly proportional to the frequency of its use. To be sure, the lack of scholarly consensus concerning the Community constitution is also a sign of the vitality and strength of the idea. Even so, it is legitimate and necessary to ask the following questions: when did the constitution of the Community begin; how is it built; where does it lead; where are its limits; what is its reach, its meaning; how should it be interpreted; where lies the legitimacy of this construction?

The confusion is doubtless due to the different concepts of 'constitution' used by various scholars. Disputes over the concept and function of the constitution lead to diverging interpretive approaches to the constitutional provisions, in addition to the specific Community issue of identifying the relevant 'materials'. It is in the interpretation and application of the law that these theories lead to intractable practical problems. The choice of a concept of 'constitution' and the corresponding interpretive attitude has great moment, for the life of the constitution depends more on the way its text is read than on the qualities of the text itself.

In this context, there is a pressing need to define and delimit the constitution of the Community, clarifying its basic features.

The approach presented here is in line with a rich strand of Community constitutional scholarship, but it reacts, at the same time, against other 'constitutional' approaches. Its centrepiece is the elaboration of a sharp concept of 'constitution' which distinguishes constitutional questions from other legal issues. To be sure, other approaches may also be legitimate and useful. Nonetheless, a distinctively *constitutional* perspective seems to me preferable for its results and analytic horizons.

Subsequent chapters move from the structural themes to substantial issues arising out of the economic constitutional law of the Community, the oldest layer of the Community constitution. Particular stress is given to the intimate connection between the formal and material aspects of the latter. The work then moves on to the issues of the interaction between competition and free movement. These chapters explore the concept and structure of the Community economic constitutional law (chapter 5), the general relationship between competition and free movement (chapter 6), the problem of the application of free movement rules in the private sphere (chapter 7), and that of the application of competition rules to anticompetitive State action (chapter 8).

It might be useful to introduce at this point some background ideas about the problems attendant with the interaction between competition and free movement. The basic binomial structure of the Community economic constitutional law (competition + free movement) reflects a division of the economic constitutional law along private/public lines. This division, however, no longer corresponds to the actual structure of the economy, but to an ideal division of the actors and their responsibilities regarding the economic objectives of the Treaty. Community law has had to be adapted by means of judge-made law and legislation to contemporary economic realities that do not squarely fit the private/public divide (the mixed economy, State involvement in the economy, privatisation, private regulation, etc.). Thus, the European Court of Justice has extended the scope of the application of free movement rules to certain forms of private action, and the application of the principles enshrined in the competition rules to certain forms of State action. It is in this body of case law, which is neither coherent nor settled, that one may find relevant data about the interaction between competition and free movement and, more generally, about the economic bent of the constitutional law of the Community.

The legislator bridges the gaps between both normative groups when it harmonises national rules. Such measures are generally obligatory to the States and economic actors, and are simultaneously aimed at opening markets, eliminating differences between national regulatory schemes, and ensuring effective competition by creating a level-playing field.

This is not just a problem of economic constitutional law. The line between the public and private dimensions of contemporary societies is one of the most intractable problems of constitutional law in general. The questions explored here are but instances of a broader issue that can be formulated as follows. The traditional, liberal view of constitutionalism conceived the constitution as a legal instrument guaranteeing a system of limited government and creating a sphere of individual autonomy immune to public power. In the contemporary world however, this traditional conception is showing its limitations vis-à-vis a growth of private power, economic or non-economic, national, international and global. The question thus arises whether constitutions should limit private power as well, and if so to what extent. Should such limitations be identical to those imposed on public power? Should they be more or less rigid? Is there any justification for establishing different standards? Or should there be no general limitations on private power as a matter of constitutional law, only of statutory law?

Many constitutions do not have an explicit answer to these issues but encounter them daily. The Community constitutional law contains some hints concerning public and private economic power, but they are far from comprehensive, much less clear.

These practical and theoretical problems are yet another branch attached to my central question.

A word about methodology to close this introductory chapter—even if the proper place for methodological reflection ought to be the end rather than the beginning of an enquiry. This work, as promised by its title, is about law. It takes constitutional law primarily as law, not policy or social fact. It has been written by a jurist, from a legal perspective, following the established methods of legal science. There is accordingly an emphasis on the interpretation of legal texts and case law which eschews other contemporary approaches influenced by sociology, political science, economics or a mixture thereof. Insofar as the law is built with words, legal science may want to begin near them if it does not want to miss its point from the outset. In other words, although legal science should not be reduced to hermeneutics, the latter constitutes an indispensable element of the former.

Community constitutional law is not taken in isolation, however. Reference will be made, when useful, to the constitutional law of the Member States and to that of the United States. While acknowledging several points of divergence, the constitutional system of the United States probably stands as the most relevant system extant for the Community experience. Some of the problems discussed in this work arose decades ago in the United States; the solutions adopted there constitute a source of reflection and inspiration. What is more, the law itself is not taken in isolation, and reference will also be made to economic, political and other extra-legal arguments, which are nonetheless taken as elements of the legal argumentation.

The method would ideally come close to that proposed by Robert Alexy in his major works. Such a method is based on a multi-dimensional approach to law that considers its subject-matter from three simultaneous perspectives: the *empirical* (what is valid and effective law, including both legislation and case law), the *analytical* (how is the law built, including conceptual, structural and systematic considerations) and the *normative* (how should the law be, looking for the correct solution to legal problems). The analytical is the most important and specifically juridical dimension (the *opus proprium* of legal science, in the words of Alexy), but all of them have to be combined in order to produce a legal science practically oriented towards the resolution of legal problems.[1]

This method may prove useful as a reaction to certain contemporary trends in legal studies which tend to see only fragments of discourse without trying to discern coherent structures in the law. The very attempt to study the gaps of a certain branch of the law presupposes the need for a rationally ordered and comprehensive legal system. To the extent that the law is not so ordered, one is forced to analyse the existing legal materials in search for an underlying logic.

At the end of his life, Wittgenstein wrote, 'our knowledge forms a big system. And only in this system do the details have the value that we give them.'[2] It is at least true that our knowledge *tends* towards forming a system. Without this tendency—the tendency towards finding a meaningful connection between the various particulars—reality falls apart.

The same can be said of legal reality. In one of its first decisions, the German constitutional court made a similar statement about constitutional interpretation:

> A single constitutional provision cannot be viewed in isolation and interpreted only on its own. It stands in a meaningful connection with the other provisions of the constitution, which shows an inner unity. From the whole content of the constitution result certain constitutional principles and fundamental decisions to which single constitutional provisions are subordinate.[3]

In the present field, Pierre Pescatore highlighted in 1972 that,

> the structure of the European Community and its law form a system, that is to say, a structured, organised and finalised whole. The Community thus benefits from the resources and the dynamics of the system.[4]

Similar interpretive ideas may be found throughout the case law of the European Court of Justice, and there is no need to stress the central importance that structural reasoning has always had and continues to have in Community law.

Another theme assumed greater importance as this research progressed. Judicial intervention to fill constitutional gaps amounts to some sort of interstitial constitution-making, not just interstitial legislation, and it raises general issues related to the role, legitimacy and competence of the European Court of Justice to properly discharge this function. The 'democratic difficulties'

---

[1] R Alexy, *A Theory of Legal Argumentation* (Clarendon Press, Oxford, 1989) 250–256; *Theorie der Grundrechte* (Suhrkamp, Frankfurt a.M., 1986) 23–27.

[2] L Wittgenstein, *On Certainty* (Harper and Row, New York, 1972) § 410.

[3] BVerfGE, 1, 14, 32 (1951): 'Eine einzelne Verfassungsbestimmung kann nicht isoliert betrachtet und allein aus sich heraus ausgelegt werden. Sie steht in einem Sinnzusammenhang mit den übrigen Vorschriften der Verfassung, die eine innere Einheit darstellt. Aus dem Gesamtinhalt der Verfassung ergeben sich gewisse verfassungsrechtliche Grundsätze und Grundentscheidungen, denen die einzelnen Verfassungsbestimmungen untergeordnet sind.'

[4] P Pescatore, *The Law of Integration* (Sijthoff, Leiden, 1974) 41.

presented by constitutional (or judicial) review, a classical theme in constitutional theory, are also relevant for this work. The solutions available in other legal contexts do not seem to fit the Community system, which would need a specific theory of constitutional review. While its elaboration clearly goes beyond the aims and scope of this work, my reflections on constitutional review under the Community economic constitutional law could be seen as a shy first step in this direction.

The non-linear character of the enquiry announced above may be clear by now. This work pursues at once several themes and problems—some theoretical, some practical—that overlap and interact in various ways. It may be seen more as a way of thinking about certain problems than as the final solution to them.

2

Towards an Operational Concept of Constitution

THE CONSTITUTIONAL LAW of the European Community cannot be completely original: it must be based on previous constitutional traditions, departing from them insofar as they are inapplicable to the Community. On the other hand, one should avoid the danger of giving traditions too much weight in emergent and novel realities. Community constitutionalism finds its place precisely in this tension between State constitutional traditions and the supranational attempt to overcome their limitations. Such limitations should be related to both world wars that marked the twentieth century, inasmuch as they reflected an excessively State-centred conception of sovereignty and constitutionalism.

An important part of the specific responses that European integration has given to unresolved problems of the European public order may perhaps be found in the *new supranational economic constitutionalism*, based on economic integration through the principles of free movement and competition. These principles have produced as their most recent outcome a monetary union and a single monetary policy entrusted to the European Central Bank. Such norms guarantee the *economic peace* among the States and the openness of their markets through their fusion in a single market. This is a radical change with respect to the previous situation.

The emergence of a supranational constitutional order, of which an important part is devoted to economic issues, has to be seen in the context of a series of changes that affected European constitutionalism in the aftermath of World War II—the generalised adoption of systems of judicial review of legislation and fundamental rights protection by courts standing as the most obvious example. All these phenomena aim at empowering the judiciary as the supreme and final interpreter of the constitution, thus having the task of umpiring the political process and defending the individuals vis-à-vis the public sphere.

These phenomena are reproduced on a supranational plane—consider, for instance, the European Convention on Human Rights and its system of judicial protection; or Community law, with its direct effect and primacy. The supranational reproduction of these developments adds something new from a qualitative point of view, because the relationships between the States are permanently changed. Their sovereignties are put, as it were, in brackets: they are neutralised. International law is 'constitutionalised'.

This work tries to reflect on the economic dimensions of this process. The substantive contributions of the Treaty of Rome to economic constitutionalism are analysed in their context, as one more piece of these new elements of the contemporary constitutional law.

All these phenomena tend to limit what political majorities can do, not only within a State but also within a community of States. The whole system offers a series of reinforced checks and balances that may put a brake on tyrannical majorities on all planes. The new Article 7 EU introduced by the Nice Treaty, for example, can be interpreted in this light. This provision allows the Council to impose sanctions that may even entail the suspension of the voting rights of a Member State that has breached human rights gravely and persistently.

This and subsequent chapters slowly approach this new supranational economic constitutionalism and the question of the gaps between competition and free movement, while providing the appropriate analytical framework. A first step will be to elaborate an operative concept of the constitution, adapted to these new realities.

2.2. THE IMPORTANCE OF LEGAL CONCEPTS

If one intends to analyse an issue, then implicit in this intention is a will to create meaning by using certain concepts, the meaning of which should be ascertainable from the beginning and remain constant throughout the course of our writing. Without a common understanding of legal concepts, legal discourse is fragile and ephemeral.

Jeremy Waldron has emphasised the contribution of legal concepts to create 'a form of interconnectedness (flagged by a corresponding technical vocabulary) that we might refer to not just as coherence but as doctrinal systematicity—the way that, in specific areas of law [. . .] rules of different kinds fit together in a structured and articulated whole as part of a system.'[1]

Thus, the importance of concepts such as 'contract' or 'constitution' is that they distinguish legal realities (a contract, a constitution) and particular legal disciplines (the law of contracts, constitutional law). Without accurate legal concepts we may lose track of the area in which we are moving, disregarding its principles and methods, and producing pointless analyses.

The importance of concepts for legal science having been vindicated, one can only add a few remarks about the way in which they are built.

Concepts are not ideal abstractions. They are benchmarks against which we name certain facts. Although there is a reciprocal relationship between the two

---

[1] J Waldron, ' "Transcendental Nonsense" and System in the Law', (2000) *Columbia Law Review* 16 at 25.

dimensions—that of facts and that of words—the starting point and the point of reflection should always lie with the realm of facts. In the words of Vico: 'The order of the ideas must proceed according to the order of things'.[2] Thus, if one wants to build useful legal concepts, their socio-economic substratum should be taken into account.

In order to avoid excessive abstraction, it might be useful to adopt Hillary Putnam's notion of a *stereotype*, to wit, 'conventional ideas, which may be inaccurate',[3] that standard speakers have in mind when they communicate. It is these stereotypes that generally produce meaning in everyday life.

Legal concepts, however, cannot be stereotypes like those used by the man in the street who uses words such as 'water' or 'tiger'. The division of linguistic labour, which 'rests upon and presupposes the division of *non*linguistic labor [sic]',[4] burdens the jurist with the task of defining with more precision the objects of enquiry. The legal concept of 'constitution' cannot be identical to the stereotypical concept of constitution used by the lay person in everyday life. Unlike normal stereotypes, legal stereotypes are not just a means of communication, but the technical terminology of a specific knowledge.

Therefore, one may only try to find an operational definition of constitution. As Putnam notes:

'no operational definition does provide a necessary and sufficient condition for the application of any such word. We may give an "operational definition" [. . .] but the intention is never "to make the name *synonymous* with the description". Rather "we use the name *rigidly*" to refer to whatever things share the *nature* that things satisfying the description normally possess'.[5]

The operational definition of constitution may then be a conventional legal stereotype that is used rigidly by a majority of the members of the legal community.

Legal concepts, understood as legal stereotypes, have obligatory and optional features. The operational concept of the 'constitution' only includes the obligatory elements that a legal reality must have at present in order to enjoy membership in the concept 'constitution', and not other possible additional elements.

Finally, it is clear that concepts change over time—for example, the transformation of European constitutionalism after 1945 has affected the very concept of constitution. Since the features included in the operational concept of constitution may also vary with time, one can adopt either a synchronic or a diachronic perspective in the quest for an accurate legal concept. Following Ferdinand de Saussure, I will favour a synchronic over a diachronic point of

---

² G Vico, *La scienza nuova*, P Rossi (ed) (BUR, Milano, 1996) 204: 'L'ordine dell'idee dee procedere secondo l'ordine delle cose.'

³ H Putnam, 'The Meaning of Meaning', in *Mind, Language and Reality, Philosophical Papers*, vol 2 (Cambridge University Press, Cambridge, 1975) 249.

⁴ *Ibid*, 228.

⁵ *Ibid*, 238.

view.[6] Like normal speakers, it is generally the current meaning of the concept of constitution that jurists have in mind when they refer to it, rather than the former historical concepts.

This need not mean that one should ignore the flux of time in the study of law. One must never forget that the past of a living legal system is part of the present, as is clear from the vitality of precedents and the principle of *stare decisis*. The past of the law is not history as long as a legal system remains in force.

2.3. AN OPERATIONAL CONCEPT OF CONSTITUTION

If the legal concept of constitution is clear, the jurist is able to discern which documents are constitutions—even though they may not go by such a name—and which are not—even though they may be so called. The jurist will then be sure to be approaching a constitutional text that demands a distinct constitutional reading. From this perspective, this concept defines a sort of *genre*. The belonging of a legal text to a given genre creates certain expectations about what we may find there, and also demands a certain way of approaching it. One does not read a novel like a poem. One does not read a constitution like a contract or a statute, if only because their respective functions, intention and language are markedly different.

Every legal body covers a certain normative field with a degree of intensity. In the case of the constitution, the field is quite broad—all the basic normative elements of the social fabric—and the treatment is quite general. Usually, the constitutional text is flexible, open-worded and usually ambiguous—consider the text of Articles 12 or 28 of the EC Treaty. This condensation of the normative substance in the constitution widens the possible interpretation and thus the importance of the work of the interpreter, who should give concrete meaning to the language of constitutional provisions. Our concept of constitutional law should include the case law, which determines the reach and meaning of the constitution.

The existence of a constitution depends on several elements. Some of them are legal and related to language. Others are non-legal. The authority of the constitution, in particular, can be traced to no text. It is rather to be found, as *a social not juridical datum*, in the observance of the constitution by the society over which it claims authority.

Moving towards this concept, it is important first to acknowledge its current fragmentation. Authors of all orientations generally give various definitions of constitution, without choosing among them. This is not problematic in itself, as the concept of 'constitution' can be understood in different ways by different authors. But it reveals the fragmentation of the concept, its relative malaise. The

---

[6] See F de Saussure, *Cours de linguistique générale* (Payot, Paris, 1983) 117–128.

problem becomes graver when a single author uses the word 'constitution' without assigning it a precise meaning. This vagueness is at the root of the fragmentation of the concept of constitution into disparate notions, according to the preferred perspective (objective, subjective . . .; sociological, legal . . .) or its alleged main substance (economic, political . . .).

Carl Schmitt, to give a well-known example, put forward several definitions of constitution without explicitly choosing among them, although his personal preference rested with his positive concept of constitution.[7] In the European Community context, Joseph Weiler gives no less than five 'dictionary definitions of the word "constitution," all of which are relevant to [his] enquiry' about the constitution of Europe.[8] Besides, there is usually a rich choice of adjectives to qualify the constitution—the notions of the formal, material, actual, legal, objective and subjective constitutions have become commonplace.[9] Finally, other authors would argue that everything (international society, religious congregations, neighbours' associations, commercial companies, etc.) has a constitution of sorts, thus softening our concept to the point of depriving it of any specific substance.

The agnosticism that lurks in these examples may be thought to reflect the current scepticism with regard to the basic functions of constitutionalism and democracy,[10] as applied to societies deeply transformed by changes in their economy, technology and social structure, and in the very definition of the polity and the relationships between polities. Against fragmentation, my preference is for an operational concept of constitution which serves as the point of departure for an assessment of the notion of 'economic constitution' and, subsequently, for a discussion on the economic constitutional law of the Community.

This concept would ideally be internally solid and externally comprehensive. The enduring value of an updated constitutionalism for contemporary societies would be emphasised by this restated concept. *Pace* Weiler, of the eight meanings of the word constitution given by the second edition of the *Oxford English Dictionary*, only the seventh ('the system or body of fundamental principles according to which a nation, state, or body politic is constituted and governed') is relevant to this enquiry. This definition is not sufficient, for we are looking for a legal, not a common, notion. It is undeniable that there are many other meanings to this polysemous word, but it seems to me important to have *one* legal concept of constitution.

---

[7] C Schmitt, *Verfassungslehre* (Duncker and Humblot, Berlin, 1970, first published 1928) 1–121.

[8] J H H Weiler, *The Constitution of Europe* (Cambridge University Press, Cambridge, 1999) viii.

[9] See F Snyder, 'General Course on Constitutional Law of the European Union' in *Collected Courses of the Academy of European Law* (1998) VI, Book I, 41 at 53 *et seq*.

[10] See F Rubio Llorente, *La forma del poder* (Centro de Estudios Constitucionales, Madrid, 1997) 43.

One *legal* concept, moreover, to the exclusion of the sociological concept of constitution deriving from Max Weber, who defined it as 'the empirically existing probability, varying in extent, kind and conditions, that rules imposed by the leadership will be acceded to.'[11] Such a notion has been adopted by some jurists, in particular Community scholars, with little awareness of its limited value for legal studies. Why limited value? For one thing, Weber himself made quite clear that this concept is 'not the same as what is meant by a "written" constitution, or indeed by "constitution" in any sort of legal meaning.'[12] In fact, by adopting a sociological concept of constitution the jurist abandons the understanding of the constitution as higher law. The social acceptance of the constitution is only one among the various elements of the constitution.

One should also try to avoid the danger of endowing the concept with a mystical flavour. This is why the operational concept is just an interpretive hypothesis. In many cultures, the word constitution has acquired a symbolic value, going well beyond the limits of a workable definition of constitution. One ought to escape from such conceptions, for constitutions are not manna. They can do some good to the societies that may have them, but there are no automatic gains involved in having a constitution.

With these provisos in mind, this section will be closed with the operational concept of constitution. The decision to include certain elements and exclude others will be justified in section 4.

A constitution is a distinct body of norms, principles and values which:

(i) derives its authority from the acquiescence of most of the persons living in the polity;

(ii) establishes organs which are endowed with certain responsibilities concerning the government of the polity and powers to discharge them;

(iii) creates a protected sphere of autonomy vis-à-vis public and private powers for the persons living in the polity;

(iv) provides for the possibility of democratic participation and change of government after a regular period of time; and

(v) cannot be judicially reviewed against other legal norms, which may be driven out of the legal order by the judiciary if in breach thereof.

2.4. THE CONCEPT EXPLAINED

This notion of constitution does not come from nowhere. It is inscribed within the Western legal tradition, being not just a European notion. The USA's contribution to Western constitutionalism is as important as the European contribution, and the limitation to a European notion of constitution appears as

---

[11] M Weber, *Economy and Society: An Outline of Interpretive Sociology* (G Roth and C Wiltich (eds)) (University of California Press, Berkeley, 1978) vol I, 50.

[12] *Ibid*, 51.

unwarranted as the limitation to a strictly American (US) notion.[13] Why would one want to isolate traditions which have common roots? The fact is that one finds remarkably similar definitions of constitution in both European and US authors, which proves that there are no significant differences across the Atlantic.[14]

The concept may not be easily transposed to socio-economic conditions other than those of the privileged West. In the African context, for example, Okoth-Ogendo has emphasised the need for an autochthonous concept of constitution that 'involves not only the rejection of external (specifically "western") institutions and constitutional "devices", but, more emphatically, the abandonment of the classical notion that the purposes of constitutions are to limit and control state power, not to facilitate it.' According to him, a tradition of constitutionalism has not developed in Africa because 'history cannot simply be *learned*, it may have to be *lived* as well. Constitutionalism is the end product of social, economic and political progress; it can become a tradition only if it forms part of the shared history of a people.'[15]

These cultural conundrums need not be a major problem in the context of European Community law. All the Member States enjoy advanced socio-economic conditions which have allowed, and indeed helped in the construction of their constitutional traditions. The number of interactions and debts among the various constitutional traditions of the West is bewildering. The struggle for, and achievement of, constitutionalism no doubt belongs to the shared history and also, probably, to the common future of the European peoples.

All the elements of the operational concept are needed.

The inclusion of norms, principles and values, to begin with, is needed for the constitution to have sustained depth and dynamism, constituting a system.

Regarding element (i), the extralegal basis for the authority of the constitution is found in the current acquiescence of the population rather than in an original foundational act. This choice will be understood better when the exclusion of the traditional concept of *pouvoir constituant* from the definition is explained.

Second, a constitution can hardly be said to constitute anything if it does not create organs which are given certain powers and responsibilities. The constitution creates and assigns functions and powers, it does not just guarantee a sphere of individual autonomy.

---

[13] J Gerkrath, *L'émergence d'un droit constitutionnel pour l'Europe* (Éditions de l'Université de Bruxelles, Brussels, 1997) 51, looks for 'une notion européenne de la constitution.' B Ackerman, *We the People: Foundations* (Harvard University Press, Cambridge, Mass, 1991) 3–6, attempts to build a US constitutional theory, *liberated* from European influences.

[14] J Gerkrath, *ibid*, 75; J Raz, 'On the Authority and Interpretation of Constitutions', 153–154.

[15] H W O Okoth-Ogendo, 'Constitutions without Constitutionalism: Reflections on an African Political Paradox' (in O Greenberg *et al* (eds) *Constitutionalism and Democracy* (OUP, Oxford, 1993) 65, 68 and 80.

Third, substantive safeguards of personal autonomy are essential for any constitution. A set of norms that would impose on government bare procedural constraints would only be workable in specific socio-economic and cultural circumstances, like those of the United Kingdom. There, the Queen-in-Parliament has been deemed to have unlimited legislative authority. Thus, it can adopt any law, as long as it does not bind future parliaments. Only cultural and political traditions, not concrete legal norms, have limited the legislator. This principle of the British constitution may have changed inasmuch as Community law is concerned in 1972, the year in which the European Communities Act—regulating the accession of the United Kingdom to the European Communities—was adopted. Thenceforth, any British judge or tribunal is obliged to set aside the laws of Parliament adopted in breach of Community law. This was a radical change in the British constitutional system.[16]

This single case, lacking generality, cannot provide an operational concept of constitution. The same would be true of a system lacking constitutional (judicial) review, at least as a matter of constitutional law. Such a system may work because of its specific characteristics, but it is not useful for the purposes of an operational concept of constitution.

The fourth element of the concept, the democratic element, seems inherent to any legitimate contemporary constitutional order, in spite of the fact that in abstract terms democracy and constitutionalism appear to be distinct notions. According to Walter Murphy, constitutionalism and democracy 'need each other. A majority may so restrict a minority's substantive rights and social status as to drain its formal participation rights of real effect [. . .]. Constitutionalism's perils lie in its propensity to paralyse government.'[17] Constitutionalism and democracy thus counteract the other's worst tendencies, resulting in a workable democracy and a practicable constitutional order.

Finally, the hierarchical position of the constitution on top of the legal pyramid is needed in order to make it a more permanent norm beyond the play of majoritarian politics. This position cannot be predicated of the constitution unless the judiciary has the capacity and the duty to safeguard it vis-à-vis the other powers.

This definition goes well beyond the liberal and bourgeois constitution, whose essential nucleus, according to the formulation in Article 16 of the 1789 French Human Rights Declaration, lies in the protection of fundamental rights and the separation of powers.[18] A constitution should have both elements, but

---

[16] See N MacCormick, *Questioning Sovereignty, Law, State and Nation in the European Commonwealth* (OUP, Oxford, 1999) 79–95, 107. Unlike Community Law the Human Rights Act 1998 has not limited the principle of Parliamentary sovereignty. Courts can only declare legislation incompatible with the rights in the European Convention on Human Rights, but the final decision has to be taken by Parliament. This latter may, but does not have to, modify the incompatible legislation.

[17] W F Murphy, 'Constitutions, Constitutionalism, Democracy' in D Greenberg *et al* (eds) *Constitutionalism and Democracy* (OUP, Oxford, 1993) 6.

[18] 'Toute société dans laquelle la garantie des droits n'est pas assurée, ni la séparation des pouvoirs déterminée, n'a pas de Constitution.'

it cannot be limited to them. First and foremost, it should establish institutional mechanisms that guarantee its effectiveness. Besides, being a relational institution among individuals as well as between those individuals and the polity they constitute, constitutional rights should be protected not only from the public sphere but also from other individuals. This contrasts with the traditional view of the constitution as a system of limitations on public authorities. This view, as it was pointed out in the introduction, ignores the reality of private power and the effects it may have on individual autonomy. The operational definition tries to overcome this defect by emphasising individual autonomy, regardless of the public or private origin of the threats to that autonomy.

Let us move now to what is excluded. Elements such as sovereignty, checks and balances, *pouvoir constituant* or division of powers, are absent from the operational concept of constitution. Indeed, they are either political concepts which determine the authority of the constitution according to part (i) of the definition, consequences of the definition and therefore unessential, or historical elements whose relevance may have waned.

The fact that a constitution is composed of legal norms that the judiciary must protect implies a degree of division of powers. Another consequence of the definition is the fact that constitutions are usually less easily altered than legislation, for otherwise there would be no limitation on majority government and the constitution could hardly be seen as higher law and the basis for the validity of legislation.

Concerning the *pouvoir constituant*, the idea that a constitution has to be created by such an entity is probably dated, because it puts excessive emphasis on *original* legitimacy. Edward Said has drawn a distinction between the notions of *beginning* and *origin*, 'the latter divine, mythical and privileged, the former secular, humanly produced, and ceaselessly re-examined.'[19]

In the context of constitutionalism, this distinction reveals the *pouvoir constituant* as a transcendental, divine, mythical and privileged concept once a generation lapses from the drafting of the constitution. Such a notion has to be abandoned in the quest for an operational concept of 'constitution'.

The legitimacy of the constitution cannot rest on the no longer extant will of people long dead and buried, but on a blend of its substantial content and a continued and wide popular acceptance at present. Since future generations do not have the chance to vote on the constitution and its revision may be severely limited, the concept of *pouvoir constituant* is incompatible with a constitution that may be in force for long periods of time. As Michael Dorf has argued about the US Constitution: 'The authority of the Constitution today rests on its general acceptance as authoritative rather than on its adoption in 1787.'[20]

---

[19] E W Said, *Beginnings: Intention & Method* (Columbia University Press, New York, 1985) xiii.
[20] M Dorf, 'Integrating Normative and Descriptive Constitutional Theory: The Case of Original Meaning' (1997) *Georgetown Law Journal* 1765, 1772.

In sum, constitutions do not have origins, they have beginnings. They are not laid down once and for all, but have to be continuously realised to adapt to a moving background.

The exclusion of the concept of sovereignty may also require some explanation, in view of its past importance and its persistence—or recent revival. In a constitutional polity, internal sovereignty is rooted in the condition of legitimacy implicit in elements (i) and (iv) of the definition, and is effectively limited or neutralised by fundamental rights and democratic principles. Thus, it is not an autonomous feature of the concept nor the foundation of public authority (as it was for Bodinus).

The concept of external sovereignty becomes problematic for the international society, as it implies the capacity of polities to behave independently from each other and according to their own interests, seriously hampering the legal force and effectiveness of international law. External sovereignty may also be neutralised or, as it were, internalised in more integrated, supranational, federal or divided-power systems as between their components, as will be seen in the next section.

As it has been remarked, many 'constitutions' will not be considered constitutions proper according to the operational concept, because they may lack one or more of the obligatory features. The normative value of the concept rests on this very fact. Nominal and semantic 'constitutions' will not be considered constitutions,[21] neither will the 'constitutions' of classical international organisations, like that of the International Labour Organisation. However, other bodies of legal rules or parts thereof which are not called constitutions may fulfil the criteria and properly be so called.

Additionally, a constitutional system will not exist unless all the elements of the concept are fulfilled to a minimum extent. Beyond this minimum, constitutionalism can take various forms, and there are several available technical devices in order to comply with the elements of the definition.

Finally, the comprehensive character of the constitution should be stressed. Carl Schmitt defined the constitution as 'a comprehensive decision concerning the nature and form of the political unit.'[22] This definition has to be rejected in all its elements but one. Schmitt replaced the normative value of constitutionalism with raw political power (decisionism). His anti-liberal concept of the political, based on the friend/enemy dialectic,[23] entailed the rejection of a constitution which would reflect an overlapping consensus concerning essential features of the society, leading partly to substantive norms (decisions) and partly to the institutionalisation of democratic processes that will deal with the matters upon which no durable consensus could be achieved. This feature of his

---

[21] See K Loewenstein, *Political Power and Governmental Process* (University of Chicago Press, Chicago, 1957) 147 *et seq*.

[22] C Schmitt, *Verfassungslehre*, above n 7, 20: 'Die Verfassung als Gesamt-Entscheidung über Art und Form der politischen Einheit.'

[23] See C Schmitt, *The Concept of the Political* (University of Chicago Press, Chicago, 1996).

conception is fatal to the understanding and development of a constitutional polity. The only aspect of his definition that will be salvaged is the comprehensive character of the constitution, but this comprehensiveness entails that it can neither be strictly political nor overly decisive.

A constitution is not only nor mainly a decision, nor is it only about the nature and form of the political unit. It extends to all the basic aspects of the social fabric—among others, the economy. In this sense, the possible silences in the constitution concerning fundamental aspects of a society are as important as its positive provisions.

2.5. FEDERAL CONSTITUTIONALISM AND THE SUPREMACY OF THE CONSTITUTION

Specific complexities for the operational definition of a constitution obtain in divided-power (meaning federal, confederal, supranational) systems, which I will generically call 'federal' or 'divided-power' systems, for convenience and because their common driving force lies indeed in the division of powers among different levels of government. As a matter of theory, the distinction between a federation (or federal state) and a confederation is clear. The establishment of a federation would imply the creation of a new sovereign entity of international law, whose norms would be directly applicable to the individuals in the States that constitute it. In contrast, a confederation would not be sovereign and its norms would only bind the States.

In their actual dynamics, the conceptual distinction between federation and confederation becomes blurred in a continuum of possible relationships between levels of government, to the exclusion only of the extreme cases where the federal principle is absent: the unitary state, the international community of sovereign states.

These issues of federal constitutionalism are key to understanding and assessing the hypothetical (economic and general) constitutionalism of the Community. The abstract analysis in this chapter may help to address the specific Community problems in chapter 4.

For some, only the federation or its members are true States. If one sees the constitution as necessarily linked to the nation-State, it would follow that in divided-power systems either the federal constitution is not a constitution proper or the member units do not have real constitutions. This misconception, refuted long ago by Rudolf Smend as a merely juridical theory,[24] is a direct consequence of the idea that two sovereign States cannot coexist within the same territory. Those who see the State as the materialisation of some transcendental essence will probably adhere to this view. But if the State, and the

---

[24] R Smend, 'Verfassung und Verfassungsrecht' in *Staatsrechtliche Abhandlungen* (Duncker & Humblot, Berlin, 1968) 224.

political community, is seen as an instrument at the service of social welfare, the question will not be so important: a degree of flexibility has to be admitted as regards the way of structuring the polity and its constitution.

This problem can be solved if we admit that the constitution of all the member units and that of the federation have to be read as parts of the integrated text of a single constitution, a text of texts which has no unitary physical reality, but has to be continuously assembled by the interpreters on different planes.

In federal systems it is only logical to infer that the different levels of government cannot have a comprehensive constitution, for they will only be complete within their sphere of powers. The constitution of a federation therefore comes to life through the joint operation of the 'constitutions' of the different levels of government. Only this composite constitution is comprehensive, only it *is* a constitution. And its parts should be seen less as incomplete or unfinished constitutions than as fragments of the actual constitution.

The dynamics of this sort of systems may lead to a situation where the federal constitution gradually absorbs most of the constitutional substance, or to a process of convergence towards the model of the federal constitution, reducing the relative weight of the states' constitutions. Such is, to a certain extent, the current situation in the US, where the federal constitution, through the expansion of federal powers and the doctrine of incorporation of the Bill of Rights via the 14th Amendment, leaves very little constitutional space to the states' constitutions. To be sure, the opposite process may also occur. The essence of a federation, however, lies in finding an equilibrium in this tension.

This shows that divided-power systems present an additional conundrum regarding the coordination and definition of the corresponding spheres of power, which is essential to determining the fields of activity of the various levels of government and the validity and hierarchy of legal sources within such levels. These issues are political, and their best solution comes through the coordination of the political branches at the various levels of government. If and when political coordination fails, however, a legal conflict may arise if two norms, one federal, the other State law, overlap and regulate the same subject matter differently. Such direct conflicts between federal and State law are normally solved through a principle of federal law supremacy over state law, a rule of conflict which stands as one of the 'essential characteristics of a federal constitution', flowing 'necessarily from the idea of federalism itself.'[25]

Even within the logic of supremacy, one is yet to determine the fields within the purview of each level of government, which is sometimes an intractable problem. In theory, no direct conflict would arise if all powers were defined as exclusive by the constitution. If there were no concurrent or shared powers, all that would have to be determined would be which of the conflicting norms has been legitimately enacted by the competent organ. The question of conflict and supremacy remains hidden, couched in terms of a problem of powers.

[25] K C Wheare, *Modern Constitutions* (OUP, Oxford, 1966) 22.

Even so, few powers can be seen as exclusive in practice. Often it would not be sensible, for federal systems are also created to share responsibilities, not only to divide them. Besides, there are horizontal competences, such as that related to market regulation (for example, the commerce clause of the Constitution of the United States or Article 95 EC). These competences, because of their generality, cut across other subjects, so that even if they were 'exclusive', normative conflicts would not be avoided. In sum, not all normative conflicts can be analysed as issues related to the division of powers.

The constitution may but need not contain a norm regarding the problem of conflict.[26] The actual solution will depend in any event on the recognition by the member units of the supremacy of federal law within the boundaries that it itself defines, either through their acceptance of such an express constitutional provision or of a doctrine established by the federal judiciary.[27]

Here we face a political element of each divided-power system: the tension between different levels of government translated into a tension between fragments of the constitution. This tension can only be solved through a political settlement that may subsequently be rationalised in legal terms. This settlement provides federal systems with an extralegal foundation not unlike the condition of authority of the constitution included in part (i) of the operational definition, being an analogous element concerning the establishment of a federation among previously sovereign States. This pact cannot be enough, in contrast to the Schmittian conception,[28] as a foundation for the federal constitution. Such constitution does not only bind its member units. Since it also affects the populations of those units, the peoples have to accept it to give it legitimacy and legal authority.

This classical account is open to doubts and questions. May the rule of conflict not be that of supremacy? Could a different kind of system be conceived? Would it be practicable and preferable?

2.6. NEIL MACCORMICK'S OVERLAPPING LEGAL ORDERS

Neil MacCormick has devoted a very interesting article to this issue, aiming for a 'more diffuse view of law', in which the 'acknowledgement of continuing unilaterally irrevocable obligations is not necessarily incompatible with the existence of a power under the rules of the national system to act validly to revoke these obligations by unilateral act. *Provided this power is not used*, the systems can remain in overlapping relations without any necessary assumption of sub- or supraordination of one to the other as a totality.'[29]

[26] As do Article VI, Section 2, US Constitution or Article 31, German Constitution.
[27] The Virginia Court of Appeals, for instance, only submitted to the Supreme Court's review of state laws under the supremacy principle after the Civil War. See G Gunther and K M Sullivan, *Constitutional Law* (13th edn, Foundation Press, New York, 1997) 60–65.
[28] See C Schmitt, *Verfassungslehre*, above n 7, final chapter.
[29] N MacCormick, 'Beyond the Sovereign State' (1993) *Modern Law Review*, 1, 8 (emphasis added).

This conception merits particular attention. In a somewhat confusing way, MacCormick admits a unilateral power to ignore federal law. The system would work, according to MacCormick, provided this power is not used.

But what power is such an unused power? And if it is indeed used, shall we assume that the relevant legal systems could not remain in overlapping relations without supraordination nor subordination? What sort of balance is possible accepting those premises?

MacCormick is not referring to supremacy as a mere rule of conflict, but to supraordination 'as a totality', something that is related to sovereignty, not to supremacy. Note also that this 'power' that 'is not used' is reminiscent of the Schmittian conception of the sovereign as 'he who decides on the exception'. For Carl Schmitt, 'the authority to suspend valid law—be it in general or in a specific case—is so much the actual mark of sovereignty.'[30] This power not to be used would then be the actual mark of sovereignty, a rather paradoxical starting point for a theory which is intended to go 'beyond the sovereign state'.

His argument then has a surprising turn in that 'there is no compulsion to regard 'sovereignty,' or even hierarchical relationships of supraordination and subordination, as necessary to our understanding of legal order in the complex interaction of overlapping legalities which characterises our contemporary Europe, especially within the European Community.'[31] He then asks rhetorically:

> Can we think of a world in which our normative existence and our practical life are anchored in, or related to, a variety of institutional systems, each of which has validity or operation in relation to some range of concerns, none of which is absolute over all the others, and all of which, for most purposes, can operate without serious mutual conflict in areas of overlap? If this is possible practically as it clearly is conceptually, it would involve a diffusion of political power centres as well as of legal authorities. It would depend on a high degree of relatively willing cooperation and *a relatively low degree of coercion* in its direct and naked forms.[32]

In his conclusion, MacCormick evokes the practical concerns of putting such an innovative system to work.[33] Such issues have busied several Community scholars in the last years, producing a number of proposals, one of which will be examined in chapter 4.

There are certain weaknesses in MacCormick's views. There is, to begin with, a degree of confusion in MacCormick's argument. Note first that he offers no clear rule of conflict in case conflicts arise, and if conflicts can arise, sooner or later they surely will. Mauro Cappelletti and David Golay, writing in 1986, presented the problem as follows:

---

[30] C Schmitt, *Political Theology: Four Chapters on the Concept of Sovereignty* (MIT Press, Cambridge, Mass, 1988) 5 and 9.
[31] N MacCormick, 'Beyond the Sovereign State', above n 29 at 10.
[32] *Ibid*, 17 (my emphasis).
[33] *Ibid*, 18.

It is inevitable that [. . .] the laws of the federal or transnational governments will sometimes conflict with those of a member state. When this occurs, as people cannot reasonably be expected to follow two conflicting commands, the law of one sovereign must apply at the expense of the law of the other, and in the federal or transnational union, if the union—and integration—are to be meaningful, it must be the federal or transnational law that, if validly enacted, is supreme.[34]

What would the system proposed by MacCormick look like? Could one imagine a system without a rule of conflict or with one that made the law of the members prevail over that of the federation? Could we conceive of a system in which the final word would be left to the discretion of each of the member units?

We can indeed conceive of all these systems in theory and also their foreseeable consequences in practice: decay, fragmentation and, eventually, dissolution.

A system based on the supremacy of federal law prevents this from happening by furthering the uniformity and integrity of the various legal systems. It may also lead, admittedly, to the deconstitutionalisation of the legal orders of the member units, but the hazard is not so great as in the other conceivable systems.

First it is already more controlled in numerical terms, as it may only come from one centre instead of two or more possible member states. Second, the federal political process channels and protects the interests and constitutional integrity of the member units. This function can be seen in the system of representation (States and population are represented in different chambers) and political organisation (federal political parties, in which federal and local interests are present, guarantee the continuity of the member units).[35] It may well be that if the members deconstitutionalise, they themselves will not see the point in trying to preserve state constitutionalism if it has been entirely or partially replaced, with their acquiescence, by federal constitutionalism. The converse is not true, as the interests of the confederation itself and those of the other members are not represented nor safeguarded in the political processes nor, for that matter, in the courts of any of the member states.

To be fair, it seems to me that supremacy would also be MacCormick's own choice had he chosen to be somewhat more concrete. His mysterious 'relatively low degree of coercion' seems to imply the supremacy of federal law in case political coordination at the level of law-creation fails and a conflict at the level of law-application ensues.

The crucial question is the following: considering that supremacy is the only solution that is capable to preserve the integrity and coordination of the legal systems involved, what sort of supremacy should we prefer?

---

[34] M Cappelletti and D Golay, 'The Judicial Branch in the Federal and Transnational Union its Impact on Integration' in M Cappelletti *et al* (eds) *Integration Through Law: Europe and the American Experience* (vol 1, Book 2, de Gruyter, Berlin–New York, 1986) 263.

[35] See H Wechsler, 'The Political Safeguards of Federalism: The Role of the States in the Composition and Selection of the National Government' (1954) *Columbia Law Review*, 543, and L D Kramer, 'Putting the Politics Back into the Political Safeguards of Federalism' (2000) *Columbia Law Review*, 215.

One may indeed conceive of constitutional orders which are nor autonomous not hierarchically ordered. In such systems, the elements of the composite constitution would coexist without a system of *coercive* supremacy—which is what is ordinarily meant by supremacy. Non-coercive supremacy would not be imposed, but rather based on voluntary acceptance through argumentation between the actors in charge of the creation and application of legal norms. This system is preferable to one based on coercion, for it is truer to the spirit of a federation and it would enhance the *legal* legitimacy of federal law.

But federal constitutionalism cannot dispense, at the very least, with this sort of supremacy. There is no higher law without supremacy, be it coercive or non-coercive, in federations. The normative value of the constitution is put into question if constitutional law does not generally prevail as higher law over conflicting non-constitutional norms. A federal constitution without supremacy over state law would be as illusory and impracticable as a constitution of a unitary state which does not prevail over conflicting ordinary law.

The absence of a principle of supremacy of federal law would give rise to competing rules of conflict in each system. We would be left with political coordination at the level of law creation and chaos at the level of its application. Legal systems would overlap and interact not only without subordination. They would also do so without legal certainty and coherence. The eventual fragmentation in the application of the law would lead to a degree of decay in the political process. Who wants to reach an agreement the enforcement of which would depend on haphazard overlappings and interactions?

This system would be very much like the international legal order 'at work'. Was not the Community, with its law and institutional mechanisms, created in part to avoid the shortcomings of classical international law?

In more recent work, MacCormick has nuanced his views, arguing that direct effect and supremacy of Community law over State law,

> secures for the overall system both coherence and integrity. It achieves this far better than if we adhered to the alternative that says there can be piecemeal amendment and alteration to the rule of recognition in respect of enforceable Community rights, casting doubt on the extent of their domestic enforceability on a case-by-case basis. This would be all the more deleterious given the normative framework within which the European Court of Justice operates.[36]

The evolution is remarkable, but not so much as it could seem. MacCormick insists in that it would be a system of 'legal pluralism under international law'— with the possibility of recourse to international arbitration.[37] The truth is that such pluralism takes place under Community law itself, and according to its own institutional and legal mechanisms, something that MacCormick prefers to continue to ignore. He accepts supremacy as a rule of conflict—for pragmatic reasons—but he does not yet want to wholly neutralise sovereignty.

---

[36] N MacCormick, *Questioning Sovereignty*, above n 16, 91.
[37] *Ibid*, 121.

Beyond these theoretical considerations, the reader will at least agree that in divided-power systems the actual value of the federal constitution greatly depends on its supremacy. Here I have been discussing the problem in abstract terms, obviously not unaware of the Community problems. The assertion, justification and general recognition of the supremacy principle are indeed crucial for the economic constitutional law of the Community and the analysis of the gaps between competition and free movement. Their actual scope, appropriate level of analysis and relationship with other parts of the legal system depend to a great extent on the fate of the supremacy principle and the health of the relevant case law of the Court of Justice.

3

The Constitution and the Economy

3.1. INTRODUCTION

THE HISTORICAL INTERACTIONS between constitutionalism and the economy are quite clear. Specific socio-economic conditions are needed to impose limits to the public sphere through constitutionalism. Constitutionalism was bourgeois, capitalist and liberal at its inception because those were the economic and social realities that gave it its original shape. As it variously emerged from the American independence and the French revolution, constitutionalism was meant to make societies more open and establish different frameworks of government.

This process did not stop in nineteenth century bourgeois and liberal constitutionalism. Once constitutions were in force, their normative contents interacted in various ways with both the economy and society. Instead of remaining there, constitutionalism started a long process of evolution and resistance through which it was transformed and adapted to various changes in the societies where it had to work.

It is important to recognise this reciprocal interaction between the constitution and the socio-economic framework in which it operates. Economic and social data determine whether a polity may have a constitution and what kind of constitution it is going to have. After it is enacted, however, the influences cut both ways, as the constitution and the legislative processes it creates will put limits on the economic process and drive it in certain directions. This interaction explains the changes constitutionalism underwent from the bourgeois-liberal-capitalist constitutionalism of the nineteenth century to its contemporary forms.

Conceptually, however, the interaction between constitutionalism and the economy is not so clear, partly because of the traditional conception that constitutions are only about politics. Politics and the economy are inextricably linked. Besides, although many contemporary constitutions explicitly deal with economic issues, the appropriate degree of constitutional involvement in economic matters, that is, the decision on what should be left to ordinary economic legislation or governmental action and what should be dealt with in the constitution, is a contentious matter.

This chapter is devoted to exploring some of these conceptual issues. It starts with the examination of the notion of 'economic constitution', an ambiguous concept due to German ordo-liberal scholars (*Wirtschaftsverfassung*),[1] but

---

[1] See D J Gerber, 'Constitutionalizing the Economy: German Neo-liberalism, Competition Law and the "New" Europe' (1994) *American Journal of Comparative Law*, 25; K W Nörr, 'Economic Constitution: On the Roots of a Legal Concept' (1993) *Journal of Law and Religion*, 343.

increasingly used in other legal traditions,[2] including Community law.[3] After close examination, it seemed to me preferable not to use such a concept and refer instead to *economic constitutional law*. This choice is related to the interpretive option for a particular conception of the constitution. The following sections explore other questions of the relationship between constitutionalism and the economy, the role of courts in this field and the recurrent theme of the economic neutrality of the constitution.

3.2. ECONOMIC CONSTITUTIONAL LAW *VERSUS* THE 'ECONOMIC CONSTITUTION'

The 'economic constitution' is not a concept, but several concepts. In its weak form, the economic constitution simply means 'economic constitutional law'. In its German ordo-liberal form, it has a stronger meaning that is not necessarily legal and does not coincide with economic constitutional law. This second meaning does not refer to any distinct legal reality, creating confusion and turning, as it were, against certain basic conceptions and functions of constitutionalism.

The critique of the concept of 'economic constitution' is limited to its original ordo-liberal version, defined in *The Ordo Manifesto of 1936* as 'a general political decision as to how the economic life of the nation is to be structured' (note in passing the strong Schmittian flavour of this definition).[4] This concept, originating from the economist Walter Eucken, and transplanted into the realms of the law by Franz Böhm, is supposed to enjoy a logic of its own, representing, as a reaction to communist or fascist models, an economic ideal based on the protection of property, contract and free markets (the so-called private law society) as quasi-absolute values.

This ordoliberal notion has a relation of mere *adjacency* with constitutionalism, being an economic concept reflected in various norms which can in turn be economic or legal, constitutional or statutory, since 'a general political decision' may take various forms among the available legal sources. Thus, it is common among ordo-liberal scholars to consider many pieces of legislation as part of the

---

[2] O de Juan, *La Constitución económica española* (Centro de Estudios Constitucianles, Madrid, 1984); G Bognetti, *La costituzione economica italiana* (Giuffre, Milano, 1993); H Rabault, 'La constitution économique de la France', (2000) *Revue française de Droit constitutionnel*, 707.

[3] Early examples are C F Ophüls, 'Grundzüge europäischer Wirtschaftsverfassung' (1962) *Zeitschrift für Handelsrecht*, 136, and L-J Constantinesco, 'La constitution économique de la CEE' (1977) *Revue trimestrielle de droit européen*, 244. More recently, M Poiares Maduro, *We the Court: The European Court of Justice and the European Economic Constitution* (Hart, Oxford, 1998) and W Sauter, 'The Economic Constitution of the European Union' (1998) *Columbia Journal of European Law*, 27.

[4] F Böhm, W Eucken and H Grossmann-Doerth, 'The Ordo Manifesto of 1936', in A Peacock and H Willgerodt (eds) *Germany's Social Market Economy: Origins and Evolution* (Macmillan, London, 1989) 24.

'economic constitution'. It is precisely this or an equally vague version of the concept of 'economic constitution' that seems to be used by some Community scholars. They would consider, for example, that the Regulation on merger control is part of the Community 'economic constitution'.

It may be more accurate to refer to the economic provisions of the constitution or economic constitutional law.[5] A German constitutional scholar actually defines the economic constitution as 'the sum of the constitutional structural elements of the economic order',[6] which after all coincides with economic constitutional law (*Wirtschaftsverfassungsrecht*). It is mainly in this sense that the concept has been adopted in the countries that have received it from Germany,[7] with the exception of some Community law scholars. The only objection to this weak version of the notion is the confusion that it may create with the ordo-liberal 'economic constitution'.

Unlike the German ordo-liberal concept, this notion of economic constitutional law is more flexible. It has no logic of its own, partaking of that of the constitution, and only enshrines certain limits regarding the economic structure (not being a *general* decision). It is a legal concept, and not an economic concept transplanted into legal science. Thus, it is part and parcel of constitutional law, entirely adopting its principles and methods. Only *ratione materiæ* may it be distinguished from other parts of the constitution.

The ordo-liberal 'economic constitution' is at once too broad and too weak a concept. It is too broad, for it presupposes a 'general decision'; it is too weak, because it does not have to be 'constitutional law', putting the emphasis on the *economic* element of the notion. 'Economic constitutional law' is a narrower concept, including some decisions and establishing some processes for the elements which are not defined in the constitution; it is stronger, for it has to be *constitutional* law proper.

This terminological choice also reflects a deeper stance aimed at safeguarding the integrity of the operational concept of constitution, which is endangered by concepts such as 'economic constitution', 'social constitution', 'financial constitution', 'political constitution' and 'what-have-you-constitution'. Such repeated restrictions of reference produce a material or internal fragmentation of the concept of constitution. Together with the formal or external fragmentation of the constitution, these conceptual phenomena tend to deprive the constitution of its

---

[5] See M García Pelayo, 'Consideraciones sobre las cláusulas económicas de la Constitución' in M Ramírez (ed) *Estudios sobre la Constitución española de 1978* (Libros Pórtico, Zaragoza, 1979).

[6] R Schmidt, 'Staatliche Verantwortung für die Wirtschaft', in J Isensee and P Kirchof (eds) *Handbuch des Staatsrechts des Bundesrepublik Deutschland* (Müller, Heidelberg, 1988) vol III, 1141, 1148: 'die Summe der verfassungsrechtlichen Gestaltungselemente der Ordnung der Wirtschaft.'

[7] J J Gomes Canotilho, *Direito Constitucional* (5th edn, Almedina, Coimbra, 1992) 480: 'conjunto de disposições constitucionais que dizem respeito à conformação da ordem fundamental da economia'; A Menéndez, *Constitución, sistema económico y Derecho mercantil* (UAM, Madrid, 1982) 29: 'conjunto de normas constitucionales [. . .] que consagran los principios y reglas por los que ha de regirse la actividad económica.'

completeness and centrality for the legal order as a whole. This material fragmentation may result in practical problems regarding the coherence between different branches of the legal order, the creation of partial legal orders with partial
constitutions and spheres which are immunised from constitutional constraints.

In addition, they may also appeal to non-democratic sources of legitimacy.
Democracy would be limited to the so-called political constitution. In the economic field, the dangerous substitution of democratic political legitimacy by
technocratic economic 'legitimacy' (actually 'expertise') or the autonomous
logic of the economy may already be implicit in the notion of 'economic constitution'.

History shows the risks of such constructions. 'Economic constitution'
referred some decades ago to a government structured through the representation of economic interests, not citizens. Corporatism was a potentiality of the
Weimar constitution of 1919 (never quite developed in practice, though) and
some other constitutional systems of that era. These considerations, as will be
seen in chapter 4, are not without consequence for the vexed questions of comitology and technocratic 'governance' in the European Union, which resound
with corporatist themes. Thus, the critique of the German ordo-liberal concept
of economic constitution may not only preserve the comprehensive character of
the constitution, but also its linkage to democratic principles and values.

This choice of terminology and perspective may also make a difference
regarding the interpretive approach to the relevant legal texts. Cocozza has
rightly seen that the currency of the concept 'economic constitution' depends on
its capacity to designate a specific part of the constitution devoted to economic
matters, which should be interpreted according to a method other than that
applied to the rest of the constitution.[8]

Here lies the main reason to reject the ordoliberal concept of economic constitution. The division of constitutional law into several independent branches with
autonomous methods of interpretation seems unwarranted precisely because it
would upset the comprehensiveness which is so central to the operational concept, preventing the constitution from ensuring a degree of coherence between the
different branches of the legal order. In terms of legal construction, an 'economic
constitution' approach to constitutional gaps and loopholes would tend to bridge
them sparingly and always with reference to values such as efficiency and economic growth, ignoring other constitutional values and principles. This would
create inconsistencies with other parts of the constitution. In contrast, an
approach based on the concept of economic constitutional law would use constitutional methods of interpretation, in particular inferences from the structure of
the constitution as a whole, taking into account non-economic values and not
lightly assuming a default rule of general economic liberty in case of a gap.

[8] F Cocozza, 'Riflessioni sulla nozione di "costituzione economica"' (1992) *Il diritto dell'economia*, 71, 73–74.

There is, finally, a linguistic proviso regarding the current use of the expression 'economic constitution' in the German constitutional doctrine, for which the concept *Wirtschaftsverfassung* 'secures the status of a central concept.'[9] Its use in German could perhaps be less confusing than in other languages. *Verfassung* means constitution, but, for historical reasons, the current German Constitution is called *Grundgesetz*. There is, then, no confusion between *Wirtschaftsverfassung* (economic constitution) and *Grundgesetz*. An expression such as *Wirtschaftsgrundgesetz* is not used. Since there is no possible confusion between both expressions, scholars actually refer to the *Wirtschaftsverfassung des Grundgesetzes*,[10] which in English would be rendered as the nonsensical expression 'economic constitution of the constitution'.

3.3. ECONOMIC CONSTITUTIONAL LAW AND ITS TRANSFORMATIONS

Economic constitutional law consists of the constitutional rules that deal with economic matters. It is *constitutional* law in that these rules are included in a constitution which accords with the operational concept. It is also *economic* law, for the organisation, structure and processes of the economy are its subject matter. In other words, in a vertical division of the legal order, economic constitutional law belongs to constitutional law. In a horizontal division of the legal order, economic constitutional law belongs to economic law, being supreme and conditioning the remaining economic law.

The economic provisions of a constitution vary within the structural limits imposed by the operative concept of the constitution.

Constitutions drafted in the second half of the present century usually contain an explicit treatment of some economic issues, the importance of which for the structuring of society and the effective preservation of liberty is beyond doubt. The influence of economic theory on contemporary constitutions, due to the current prominence of economics among the social sciences, is substantial. The Marxist external critique of liberal democracy and capitalism, to which constitutionalism is closely linked, is a good example. Marx and his followers unveiled the economic content of law, seeing the legal system as a superstructure that hides subjacent economic conflicts and relationships. Marx criticised bourgeois law as a law of inequality, precisely because it tends to treat equally that which is deeply unequal, instead of treating unequally what is not equal.[11] Pashukanis was the first to apply this critique to constitutionalism, arguing that '[t]he constitutional state (*Rechtsstaat*) is a mirage, but one which suits the bourgeoisie very well, for it replaces withered religious ideology and conceals

---

[9] K W Nörr, 'Economic Constitution: On the Roots of a Legal Concept', above n 1.

[10] See P Badura, 'Grundprobleme des Wirtschaftsverfassungsrechts' (1976) *Juristische Schulung* 107.

[11] K Marx, 'Critique of the Gotha Programme' in K Mark and F Engels, *Collected Works* (vol 24, London, 1989) 87.

the fact of the bourgeoisie's hegemony from the eyes of the masses. [. . .] Power as the "collective will", as the "rule of law", is realised in bourgeois society to the extent that this society represents a market.'[12]

Keynesian economics may also have had some influence on these developments, through an internal critique of liberalism and a transformation of economic policies, to which the constitutional order had to adapt and give way by substitution, amendment or interpretation. The most important change took place in the United States, with the radical change of the Supreme Court vis-à-vis the New Deal, a theme that will be examined below.

In the long run, all these movements prompted a transformation of constitutionalism. The basic constitutional framework of societies could not stay untouched after the demise of classic capitalism with the Great Depression of the 1930s. The same may be said of political liberalism (and, to a certain extent, of liberal constitutionalism), which suffered a serious crisis with World War II. Constitutionalism changed markedly in response to pressing social demands. After World War II, a new constitutionalism came to life on both sides of the Atlantic.

These transformations were internal to the concept of constitution, and did not transform the liberal 'political constitution' of the nineteenth century into an 'economic constitution'. They all are constitutions and share the same basic elements. Liberal constitutions, for example, are as economic as more recently drafted constitutions. Their silence concerning economic issues merely reflects the legal internalisation of certain economic views. The liberal market economy gave shape to a form of constitutionalism in much the same way that the mixed-economy did afterwards or the 'regulated economy' is doing nowadays. This silence expressed as much as many of the contemporary constitutions expressly including economic provisions.[13]

Thus, constitutionalism has never been nor can it be neutral in economic terms. This idea is essential to understand the relationship between the constitution and the economy, and the transformation brought by Community law in such a relationship. Economic interests are always hidden beneath the letter of the constitution. Charles Beard, pioneer of the economic analysis of the constitution, argued that the US Constitution 'was essentially an economic document based upon the concept that the fundamental private rights of property are anterior to government and morally beyond the reach of popular majorities.'[14]

Other constitutional documents reflect other economic interests, or a balance among various economic and non-economic interests. But the value of the US and other constitutions lies precisely in their ability to stand as normative doc-

---

[12] E B Pashukanis, *Law and Marxism: A General Theory* (Pluto Press, London, 1989) 146.

[13] See M Bassols Coma, *Constitución y sistema económico* (2nd edn, Tecnos, Madrid, 1988) 23–24.

[14] C A Beard, *An Economic Interpretation of the Constitution of the United States* (The Free Press, New York, 1986) 324.

uments, having a life of their own regardless of which group or groups were influential in writing their interests in the constitution at the time of its drafting. The relationship between the constitution and the economy is never fixed and one-dimensional, but complex and changing. Neither the economy nor the constitution completely determine each other. There is a process of reciprocal inter-action.

The themes of economic constitutional law have also been enlarged with time. Particularly important contemporary themes, in addition to those of the liberal age, are those of private economic power, the guarantee and reach of the social state and social rights, and the globalisation of markets and politics. When constitutions are silent as regards these questions, transformative inter-pretations of existing materials are once again needed to bridge the inter-temporal gap between an old document and the problems presented by its present application.

From an economic point of view there are at least three ideal kinds of consti-tutions, roughly corresponding to three successive moments in the historical transformation of the modern State. To be sure, most constitutions stand between these ideal categories, which are primarily of analytical interest.

First are those liberal-bourgeois constitutions lacking specific provisions regarding economic matters, besides the customary protection of private prop-erty and individual liberty. They give substantial leeway to government in its choice of economic policy (unless limits are *read* into the constitution by the judiciary). In this case, neither the public nor the private sphere are constitu-tionally limited regarding their use of economic power. Limits may come from the legislature in the form of statutory law, but they are not guaranteed by the constitution. This silence can be explained in that the intervention of the public sphere in the economy was not too significant in any case. The issue of the lim-its of such intervention only became important after the radical change of eco-nomic policies that followed the Great Depression of the 30s.

Far from being neutral vis-à-vis the economy, these constitutions reflect a clear economic option.[15] The understanding of the US Constitution during the Lochner era may well exemplify this category. *Lochner*, an important case to be analysed in detail below, stands for several decades of case law in which the Supreme Court took the 'existing distribution of wealth and entitlements under the baseline of the common law'[16] as neutral and pre-political, and judicially barring any political attempt to transform society.

Arguably even New Deal post-Lochner constitutionalism did not depart very radically from this model, being no more than a corrective to it. The Supreme Court's persistent opposition to the New Deal until *West Coast Hotel*[17] may

---

[15] See B H Siegan, *Economic Liberties and the Constitution* (University of Chicago Press, Chicago, 1980) *passim*.
[16] C R Sunstein, 'Lochner's Legacy' (1987) *Columbia Law Review* 873, 875.
[17] 300 US 379 (1937).

serve to explain the watered-down version of the original New Deal project that President Roosevelt finally had to put into effect. Welfare rights, proposed by Roosevelt as a second Bill of Rights, were not constitutionally proclaimed.[18] In part as a result of the Supreme Court's initial resistance, the US Welfare State was never constitutionalised in the way that the social state was in some European countries. This provides the constitutional law of the United States with a marked continuity with regard to its liberal economic character.

Secondly, one finds constitutional systems with a number of express provisions referring to the economy, the effectiveness of which may be so marginal that they hardly pose any limits on the government of the economy and private economic power. These limits may be so loose (eg there is a rejection of both a completely liberal and a completely public economy, and certain matters are reserved to legislation) that it is difficult to conceive a situation in which the constitution could effectively limit the exercise of economic power.

These are generally constitutions enacted after World War II, and adapted to the mixed economy. They stand undecided in the tension between the market and public intervention, being the constitutional translation of the Cold War era. This lack of definition, reflected in the tensions and contradictions of their text, is what renders their economic provisions highly ineffective. The Italian, German or Spanish constitutions provide suitable examples of this type, for they place public and private economic initiative at the same level, and leave a very wide range of options open to the political arena in order to modulate the structure of the economy. It is indeed in the legislation, not in the constitution, that one may find the basic legal framework regulating the economies of these countries.

Thirdly, there are constitutions containing enforceable provisions that limit the exercise of economic power by government and, less frequently, by individuals. Since a constitution needs to be safeguarded by the judiciary, the bite of the economic provisions will nevertheless always depend on the willingness of judges to oppose the economic views of a democratic legislator and the extent to which they will be able to do so. The importance of the judiciary's role of imposing limits to the exercise of economic power is here as paramount as it is generally for the end of limiting government and preserving a constitutionally protected sphere of individual autonomy.

The Portuguese constitution, originally of socialist inspiration, was an example of this category, but after the amendments of 1982 and 1989 it may have fallen into the second category. The constitutional reform of 1989 critically allowed for the privatisation of public enterprises, by repealing the principle of irreversibility of nationalisations originally enshrined in Article 83 of the Constitution. As Gomes Canotilho notes, 'the constitutional amendments of 1982 and 1989 eliminated the abstract ideological option of "socialist

---

[18] See C R Sunstein, 'The Beard Thesis and Franklin Roosevelt' (1987) *George Washington Law Review* 114, 115–116.

decision".'[19] It is perhaps interesting to note that the changes in Portuguese economic constitutional law were justified by the growing divergence of the real economy from the socialist ideal expressed in the constitutional text and also by the need to adapt to the surrounding environment in view of the economic constitutional model imposed by Community law.[20] This example shows that an important part of the substance of the economic constitutional law of the Member States has been replaced by Community law.

The economic constitutional order that results from the Treaty of Rome may also be a good example of this third category of constitutions with an economic bite. According to the interpretation given by the European Court of Justice, economic integration and the constitutional provisions in pursuance thereof (competition and free movement) constitute effective limits on the conduct of governments, legislature and private actors.

Inasmuch as the 'themes' of the economic constitutional law of the Community go beyond the traditional contents of economic constitutionalism, and that its impact is on a supranational plane, it could be argued that Community law constitutes a new model of economic constitutional law.

3.4. THE ROLE OF THE JUDICIARY

The importance of courts for constitutionalism in general and particularly for economic constitutionalism lies in the fact that the text of a constitution does not provide an answer to the three central questions of any constitutional system: does the judiciary review the action of public and private economic powers vis-à-vis the constitution? What should it review? According to what standards?

The first question is concerned with the very existence of an economic constitutional law—do we put anything, in this area, beyond the reach of majority rule?

The second asks about its reach, namely, which among the various forms of economic activity in the polity, public and private, will be subjected to judicial scrutiny according to constitutional rules and principles, and which will remain free of it?

In respect of the strength of the economic model imposed by the constitution, the final question asks about the concrete limits the constitution imposes on economic processes, legislation and governmental action.

---

[19] J J Gomes Canotilho, *Direito Constitucional* (5th edn, Almedina, Coimbra, 1992) 472: '[a]s revisões costitucionais de 1982 [. . .] e de 1989 [. . .] eliminaram a opção abstracta-ideológica da «decisão socialista»'.

[20] See E Paz Ferreira, 'A Constituição Economica de 1976: "Que reste-t-il de nos amours?" ' in J Miranda (ed) *Perspectivas Constitucionais nos 20 Anos da Constituição de 1976* (vol 1, Editora Coimbra, 1996) 383.

The answers to these questions will be given by the courts in charge of the interpretation and application of the constitution. They may take different attitudes through time. There is, besides, the problem of applying a constitution many years after it was drafted—which may be solved by a flexible theory of constitutional interpretation—and the recurrent problem of the so-called 'counter-majoritarian difficulty'.

The classical formulation of the counter-majoritarian difficulty is provided by Alexander Bickel: 'when the Supreme Court declares unconstitutional a legislative act or the action of an elected executive, it thwarts the will of representatives of the actual people of the here and now; [. . .] the charge can be made that judicial review is undemocratic.'[21]

There is some force to this charge, but if one gets too enthusiastic about it, the dubious charge could also be made that constitutionalism itself is undemocratic. It is indeed meant to be so in order to provide democracy with a degree of stability by differentiating between the constitution as a result of constitutional politics, which provides for a stable framework of government that may only be changed by a reinforced majority through a special procedure, and legislation as a result of 'politics as usual'.

Constitutional review should preserve this more stable framework of government against the possible excesses of political processes.[22] This leads us to the idea that, in any constitutional system, the judiciary has perforce to find its place and role between an absolute deference to the political branches of power (constitutionalism renounced) and an extreme judicial enforcement of constitutional provisions, which would render lead to the government of judges ('gouvernement des juges'). The fact that the role of the judiciary lies precisely in this tension makes it difficult to propose a single theory for the judicial interpretation of the constitution. The solutions to the problem of judicial review have always been the product of practice.

Constitutional and other courts usually feel unable or unwilling to derive practical consequences from the uncertain wording of economic constitutional provisions. Various courts have elaborated the concept of the economic neutrality of the constitution, meaning that the constitution does not expressly imply any decision concerning the economic system of the polity in the ordo-liberal sense. The consequence is that the public sphere (governments or legislatures) have very wide limits regarding economic policy. This concept can be linked to the process-based theories of the constitution, inasmuch as it softens the consequences of a specific substantive part of the constitution devoted to economic matters and only procedural limits are imposed (certain matters may be reserved to legislation; the legislative procedure should be followed).

---

[21] A M Bickel, *The Least Dangerous Branch: The Supreme Court at the Bar of Politics* (Bobbs-Merrill, Indianapolis, 1962) 16–17.

[22] See B Ackerman, 'The Storrs Lectures: Discovering the Constitution', (1984) *Yale Law Journal* 1013, 1049–1051.

Examples are legion. In a decision of 1954, the German constitutional court announced that 'the "constituent power" has not opted for a specific economic system. This omission enables the legislature to pursue economic policies deemed proper for the circumstances, insofar as the Basic Law is observed.'[23] The Spanish *Tribunal Constitucional* has spoken in much the same terms, expressly referring to the concept of 'constitución económica'.[24] One finds similar pronouncements in Portuguese constitutional case law[25] and in certain rulings of the French *Conseil constitutionnel*, in which the more socially oriented Preamble to the 1946 Constitution appears to be neutralised by the precedence given to the liberal 1789 Human Rights Declaration.[26]

The constitutional law of the US may be a good example of this tendency. The process-based theory of judicial review (introduced by Justice Stone in the famous footnote 4 of *Carolene Products* and theorised by John Hart Ely),[27] with its emphasis on rights of participation and the protection of politically weak groups ('discrete and insular minorities'), was the constitutional theme that replaced the economic 'substantive due process' discourse after the demise of *Lochner* in the 1930s. The emphasis shifted to the political interpretation of the constitution, and its economic dimension became under-enforced. This was due to the adoption of a very soft criterion of review (rationality review).

Thus, in *Nebbia*, a due process case, the Supreme Court held that a State is 'free to adopt whatever economic policy may reasonably be deemed to promote public welfare, and to enforce that policy by legislation adapted to its purpose. The Courts are without authority either to declare such policy, or, when it is declared by the legislature, to override it.'[28] Also revealing is the decline of the limits on federal power under the commerce clause. In *US v Darby*, Justice Stone himself declared that '[t]he motive and purpose of a regulation of interstate

---

[23] BVerfGE 4, 7, 17–18 (1954): 'der Verfassungsgeber nicht ausdrücklich für ein bestimmtes Wirtschaftssystem entschieden hat. Dies ermöglicht dem Gesetzgeber, die ihm jeweils sachgemäß erscheinende Wirtschaftspolitik zu verfolgen, sofern er dabei das Grundgesetz beachtet.'

[24] First mentioned by L Díez Picazo in his dissent to judgment 37/81 (*Jurisprudencia Constitucional*, 1981, vol II, 293, 321): 'la constitución económica contenida en la constitución política no garantiza necesariamente un sistema económico ni lo sanciona.' Taken by the Court in judgment 1/82 (*Jurisprudencia Constitucional*, 1982, vol III, 1, 15).

[25] See E Paz Ferreira, 'A Constituição Economica de 1976: "Que reste-t-il de nos amours?"', above n 20, 397–398, citing judgment 108/88 of the Portuguese Constitutional Court (*Acordãos do Tribunal Constitucional*, 1988, vol 11, 83; especially the dissent by Vital Moreira against the 'neutralisation' by the Court of Article 83 of the Portuguese Constitution, on the irreversibility of nationalisations, 127: 'As normas da parte económica da Constituição não são diferentes das demais normas constitucionais. Não são mais 'fracas', nem estão mais à disposição do legislador e do intérprete que as demais.').

[26] See Decision 81–132 (*Loi de nationalisation*), *Recueil des décisions du Conseil Constitutionnel*, 1982, 18. The right to private property is not breached unless the legislature commits *a manifest error in the appreciation of the public necessity* which justifies a public taking under Article 17 of the Human Rights Declaration, which in turn cannot be rendered inapplicable by para 9 of the 1946 Preamble (establishing that national public service should become collective property).

[27] *United States v Carolene Products Co*, 304 US 144 (1938); J H Ely, *Democracy and Distrust: A Theory of Judicial Review* (Harvard University Press, Cambridge, Mass. 1980).

[28] 291 US 502 (1934).

commerce are matters for the legislative judgment upon the exercise of which the Constitution places no restriction and over which the courts are given no control.'[29] Only with the 1995 *López* case did the Supreme Court find again a federal criminal statute unconstitutional under the commerce clause, arguing that Congress had gone beyond its commerce power.[30] But the mainstream of the case law shows an almost absolute deference to the federal political process.

This case law does not have a parallel in Community law. As we shall see, the Treaty and the interpretive attitude of the Court are based on the existence of certain limits—narrower than those imposed by national constitutions—to the economic process and the legislative framework of economic activity.

3.5. OLIVER WENDELL HOLMES JR. AND THE ECONOMIC NEUTRALITY OF THE CONSTITUTION

When a constitution is said to be neutral on an issue, what is normally meant is that its determination is left to forces external to the constitution. As we have seen, this idea is related to a constitutional preference of process over substance, so that the constitution should establish legitimate processes, but remain indeterminate about their concrete outcomes.

This section presents a critique of the doctrine of the economic neutrality of the constitution. The point of departure will be Justice Holmes' famous dissent in *Lochner*,[31] a 1905 decision of the US Supreme Court, dissent that stands as an important historical and intellectual source of the doctrine. This section analyses his dissent in a wider context.

The facts in the case were straightforward. In accordance with established case law, the Supreme Court was striking down regulations of working hours for New York bakers on the grounds that they were a paternalist intervention in breach of the contractual liberty enshrined in the substantive interpretation of the due process clause.

Holmes dissented:

> This case is decided upon an economic theory which a large part of the country does not entertain. [. . .] [A] Constitution is not intended to embody a particular economic theory, whether of paternalism and the organic relation of the citizen to the state or of laissez faire. It is made for people of fundamentally differing views, and the accident of our finding certain opinions natural or familiar, or novel, and even shocking, ought not to conclude our judgment upon the question whether statutes embodying them conflict with the Constitution of the United States.[32]

---

[29] 312 US 100 (1941).
[30] 514 US 549 (1995).
[31] 198 US 45 (1905).
[32] *Ibid*, 75–76. See also *Otis v Parker*, 187 US 606, 608–609 (1903).

His stance may be traced back to the doctrinal position of James Bradley Thayer, a Harvard Professor whose influence owed much to Holmes and other Supreme Court Justices who had been his pupils. In a 1893 article, Thayer defended the idea that the Supreme Court should be deferential to Congress on democratic grounds unless the legislation reviewed were totally unreasonable.[33] Such views are not dissimilar to Sunstein's more recent defence of judicial minimalism, which argues that by deciding as little as possible or leaving issues completely undecided, the Supreme Court reinforces and leaves space to democratic processes.[34]

Holmes' short doctrinal dissent, that in time became the opinion of the Court's majority, hides not only an idea of economic constitutional law, but an idea of the constitution itself. It is only superficially neutral in economic terms. Behind the veil of 'neutrality' is hidden a wide deference to governmental economic regulation and a marked unwillingness to carry out a balancing test in order to determine whether or not contractual freedom had been duly limited with a lawful purpose. In *Lochner*, it seemed clear that the New York legislation was proportionate, but Holmes's reaction and the subsequent demise of *Lochner* by the Court, implying an abandonment of constitutionalism in the field, seem exaggerated.

In fact, the very idea that a constitution, let alone the judiciary, may in any meaningful way be neutral is already a disguised decision in favour of one or another system of government—in the particular case of Holmes, one in which the economic power of the legislature goes unchecked by the judiciary. He was clearly after the affirmation of certain public powers aimed at the common good but barred by the legal paradigm at that time. But the presentation of his solution as neutral is just a rhetorical device.

A constitution cannot be economically neutral any more than it can be apolitical. Choosing between the different degrees of intensity of judicial review of economic regulation, or choosing not to review at all, always involves an ideological decision as to the scope and the force of the constitution. According to Sunstein, the main problem with Holmes' position is that, taken to its extreme, it 'would amount to an abandonment of constitutionalism altogether.'[35] However, as much can be said about Sunstein's own minimalism.

Beyond the limitations of 'neutrality' or 'minimalism', one should acknowledge the existence of some constitutional principles of an economic nature that may be found in most constitutions. Federal constitutions, for example, include certain provisions designed to prevent the member units from dividing the market into separate markets. These provisions effectively limit government power

---

[33] J B Thayer, 'The Origin and Scope of the American Doctrine of Constitutional Law' (1893) *Harvard Law Review*, 6.

[34] C R Sunstein, 'The Supreme Court 1995 Term: Foreword: *Leaving Things Undecided*' (1996) *Harvard Law Review*, 6 and *One Case at a Time: Judicial Minimalism on the Supreme Court* (Harvard University Press, Cambridge, Mass. 1999).

[35] C R Sunstein, 'Lochner's Legacy', (1987) *Columbia Law Review*, 873 at 905.

over the economy, but do not directly impair the exercise of private economic power. An economic constitutional law that would only control public action would not guarantee individual economic autonomy, for the latter could be limited by other individuals or private economic groups. Competition law, which usually takes the form of statute law but in Community law enjoys a constitutional status, is devoted to the control of the exercise of economic power by undertakings and individuals.

Following Hayek, it seems unwise to draw a sharp distinction between economic and political autonomy, for it is difficult to distinguish economic action from political action.[36] Besides, if constitutions are the result of certain socio-economic circumstances that move people to bind themselves to certain institutions, norms and principles, it might be important to preserve the core of such socio-economic circumstances from the constitution itself. Otherwise, constitutional law runs the risk of being reduced to the protection of procedural rights, regardless of the social and economic order they produce. It may well be that political rights and the protection of minorities are more pressing and important constitutional tasks than the protection of economic rights, but this need not mean that the economic dimension of the constitution is to be ignored. Political autonomy presupposes a degree of economic autonomy, without which democracy would be illusory. Since political, economic and social rights are inextricably linked, they all deserve effective protection, perhaps to various extents and according to various levels of scrutiny.

In this context, the judiciary owes the legislature and the executive a degree of deference. But this cannot lead to an abandonment of economic constitutional law. Deference should be based on decisions whose principles have a degree of generality.[37] Courts should not second-guess the choices of the government and legislator: they can only annul them, a fact that already entails a degree of deference. Moreover, judicial decisions should not dictate one line of conduct on matters of economic policy (something that would lead to the government of judges). But limits should also be found to deference and self-restraint if the integrity of the constitutional order is to be preserved.[38]

It is difficult to find a balance in this tension between the government of judges and the abandonment of the constitution in the abstract. This chapter aimed at introducing certain persistent problems of economic constitutional law that will be explored in the Community context.

---

[36] F A Hayek, *The Constitution of Liberty* (Routledge and Kegan Paul, London, 1960).

[37] H Wechsler, 'Toward Neutral Principles of Constitutional Law', in *Principles, Politics and Fundamental Law: Selected Essays* (Harvard University Press, Cambridge, Mass. 1961) 27.

[38] See W J Nardini, 'Passive Activism and the Limits of Judicial Self-Restraint: Lessons for America from the Italian Constitutional Court' (1999) *Seton Hall Law Review*, 1.

4

Community Constitutionalism Revisited

'DOCTRINES', VICO ONCE wrote, 'should begin when the subjects they deal with begin.'[1]

In this connection, Joseph Weiler has argued that European integration has not produced,

> a European legal order of constitutionalism without a formal constitution, but the opposite: it is a constitutional legal order the constitutional theory of which has not been worked out, its long-term, transcendent values not sufficiently elaborated, its ontological elements misunderstood, its social rootedness and legitimacy highly contingent.[2]

The constitution of the European Community has been and is being erected through a series of constitutional moments (an expression due to Bruce Ackerman) authored by the Member States. The first of these moments took place in 1951, with the signing in Paris of the Treaty establishing a European Coal and Steel Community. The following moments are well known. In the near future the process may be completed by a more stable and perfect constitution. For the time being the Community only has a bundle of *constitutional materials*.

Constitutional theories about the Community have been in the main focused on this process of constitutionalisation. There lie the seeds of a constitutional theory that may only emerge—according to Vico's insight—after a fully-fledged Community constitution gives final shape to the currently existing constitutional materials. Joseph Weiler may be asking more than what can be presently achieved. The values, ontological elements and legitimacy of the Community are not misunderstood or insufficiently elaborated. They may be *somewhat* contingent and open to question. But these values and constitutive elements are contingent in reality, not only in the theory that reflects on that constitutional reality. An incomplete constitution that is always in flux can only produce incomplete and provisional constitutional theories. To announce permanent values, definite structures and necessary conditions of legitimacy would be a

---

[1] G Vico, *La scienza nuova* (P Rossi, (ed) BUR, Milano, 1996) 225: 'Le dottrine debbono cominciare da quando cominciano le materie che trattano.'

[2] J H H Weiler, *The Constitution of Europe* (Cambridge University Press, Cambridge, 1999) 8.

risky leap for any such theory, and for the future development of the process of integration itself.

In the coming decades we may witness a political re-founding of the European Union that could radically change its present structure. Such a re-founding may lead to a more federal and integrated system—'a more perfect Union'—or else limit the federal elements of the Community. Such a re-founding, besides, could limit itself to a 'restructuring' or codification of the constitutional materials. Declaration No 23 of the Nice Treaty calls for 'a deeper and wider debate about the future of the European Union.' This debate 'should address, *inter alia*, the following questions': the delimitation of powers between the Union and its States, the status of the Charter of Fundamental Rights of the European Union, 'a simplification of the Treaties with a view to making them clearer and better understood *without changing their meaning*', and 'the role of national parliaments in the European architecture'. An intergovernmental conference will be convened in 2004 to address such issues, after the 'preparatory steps' taken by a sort of Convention which will be similar to the one that drafted the Charter of Fundamental Rights. All these novelties have been recently confirmed by the Laeken declaration of 15 December 2001. The Convention on the future of the European Union first met on 28 February 2002, and will make its proposals by the end of the year.

With such a menu and the new method for the preparation of reforms, the results of the process are quite unpredictable. Some aspects of this declaration point to a process aimed at perfecting what already exists, not to a re-founding, but the eventuality of a radical change cannot be excluded.[3] Consider the effect that such a departure could have on the constitutional theories of integration.

Difficult times for theoretical reflection, then, but some things may still be said with an acceptable degree of certainty about many aspects of the Community constitution, particularly about its economic constitutional law, perhaps its oldest and best established element. The constitutional doctrine of the Community finds a safer harbour in this and other established fields.

It could be said that the main gap in European constitutional law is the constitution itself. Upgrading the treaty into a constitution may, in a way, be seen as no more than a legal fiction, for want of something better. But it is a fiction that has proven normatively warranted, workable and quite advantageous to most of the actors concerned. This Community constitution 'by default', as it were, deserves a true constitutional approach.

Such an approach started rather early, as is shown, for example, in the works of Pierre Pescatore.[4] This doctrinal effort both influenced and was influenced by

---

[3] See, for example, the speech by the Joschka Fischer, German foreign minister, at the Humboldt University of Berlin, 12 May 2000, *From Confederacy to Federation—Thoughts on the Finality of European Integration*, repeatedly proposing to 'reestablish Europe' in the next decade).

[4] See P Pescatore, 'La Cour en tant que juridiction fédérale et constitutionnelle' in *Dix ans de jurisprudence de la Cour de Justice des Communautés européennes* (Institut de Droit des Communautés Européennes de l'Université de Cologne, Cologne, 1965).

the constitutional interpretive attitude of the Court and its members, some of whom were and are constitutional scholars. As in Vico's dictum, Community constitutional theories started just after the reality of the Community began to have constitutional substance (*Van Gend en Loos* dates from 1963; *Costa v ENEL* from 1964). The practical and theoretical erection of a 'law of integration'—elaborated by Pescatore—which was to be qualitatively distinct from international law, already implied the process of constitutionalisation. The stress on the specificity of Community law, most notably by Leontin-Jean Constantinesco, writing in 1966, also pointed clearly in the direction of a constitutional perspective.[5] This approach was developed by other scholars.

Other more recent tendencies use the label 'constitutional' for analyses which are not constitutional in a the strong sense. Take as an example a 1997 article authored by Norbert Reich. He makes clear that he uses the notion of European constitution 'to describe the dynamic of establishing, guaranteeing and implementing individual and collective rights as subjective rights [. . .] for EC citizens [*sic*] during the process of European integration.'[6] He then argues that the States' constitutional systems 'usually contain a hierarchy of sources of law whereby fundamental rights enjoy the highest place in the constitution and reside above legislative and administrative acts. *Such a hierarchy does not exist at Community level.*'[7]

In these excerpts we find the quintessence of a form of Community pseudo-constitutionalism. The conception of the European constitution as a 'dynamic of establishing, guaranteeing and implementing' rights fails to grasp what is specifically *constitutional* about the Community. Rights can also be established outside the constitution, as a matter of secondary law. The Community's constitutional law cannot be found in such a process.

The second contention is at odds with the legal reality of the Community. Community law is based on a hierarchy of legal sources. This hierarchy is well established and, unlike the principle of supremacy of Community law, does not depend on its observance by national courts in order to be effective. We shall return to this question below. Let us just recall for now that Article 230 includes among the grounds for the review of Community acts the '*infringement of this Treaty or of any rule of law relating to its application.*' Hence it has always been clear that secondary law must be respectful of primary (constitutional) law, including, since the 1970's, fundamental rights protected by the Court of Justice as general principles of Community law.

---

[5] L-J Constantinesco, 'La spécificité du droit communautaire' (1966) *Revue Trimestielle de droit européen*, 1, 9: 'Après leur entrée en vigueur, les traités instituant les Communautés européennes doivent être considérés comme des actes constitutifs des Communautés possédant en quelque sorte un caractère constituant. Comme tels ils cessent d'appartenir au droit international classique.'

[6] N Reich, 'A European Union for Citizens: Reflections on the Rethinking of Union and Community Law' (1997) *European Law Journal*, 131, 132.

[7] *Ibid*, 139 (my emphasis).

Doctrinal examples such as this could be multiplied, but there is little point in devoting more space to their critique. One is tempted to say that *they are not even wrong*, since they do not work descriptively and would be disastrous as a prescriptive matter.[8] They reveal, however, the tensions and radical uncertainties at the heart of Community constitutionalism, and the resistance of national mentalities. The actual danger posed by these theoretical vagaries is minimal, as in all probability they will only have a marginal influence on reality. Their usefulness lies in the fact that they offer a view of the Community legal order which goes against the legal materials and the classical accounts thereof. The constitutional jurist is thus given the precious chance to define a theoretical position through a mixture of continuity and antagonism to certain works and lines of thought. In this context, my choice was to build on the classical accounts of Community and general constitutionalism, and depart from more recent contributions that lead to a stalemate, if not to a dead-end, in theoretical and practical terms.

4.2. EUROPEAN COMMUNITY (NOT UNION) CONSTITUTIONAL LAW

Constitutionalism has not yet grafted to the European Union as a whole: it is confined to its Community pillar. Nevertheless, certain authors refer to the 'constitutional law of the European Union', an expression that can be misleading. One has to agree with Francis Snyder that 'nowadays it is difficult, if not impossible, to understand EC law from the technical legal standpoint except in the broader legal context of the EU'.[9] One may also argue that the Union is a single composite organisation. But it does not follow that the European Union has a constitution, if only because the legal principles that provide Community law with a constitutional flavour only apply to the Community pillar. As Weiler has put it, '[c]onstitutionalism, more than anything else, is what differentiates the Community from other transnational systems and, within the Union, from the other "pillars".'[10]

The few and frail elements which link the Union and the Community pillars (mainly, the 'common' institutional framework, amendment procedure and accession) do not suffice to endow the Union pillars with a constitutional character similar to that of the Community.[11] The argument that 'the general rules [direct effect, supremacy, implied powers] apply with respect to the relation

---

[8] For another example, see P Lindseth, 'Democratic Legitimacy and the Administrative Character of Supranationalism' (1999) *Columbia Law Review*, 628 (criticising the constitutional approach and arguing that the Community is best understood as an administrative entity to be analysed according to the principles of administrative law).

[9] F Snyder, 'General Course on Constitutional Law of the European Union', *Collected Courses of the Academy of European Law*, vol VI Book I, 1998, 41, 50.

[10] J H H Weiler, *The Constitution of Europe*, above n 2, 221.

[11] See J-V Louis, 'Le modèle constitutionnel européen: de la Communauté à l'Union' in P Magnette and E Remacle (eds) *Le nouveau modèle européen*, (vol 1, Éditions de l'Université de Bruxelles, Brussels, 2000) 31, 38–39.

between Union law and national law' and that 'Union law acts issued under the competences of the CFSP and CJH directly apply in all legal systems—and indeed with supremacy *if* a Union norm conflicts with a national norm'[12] may be exaggerated and is probably mistaken. Nowhere in the Union pillars may one find support for this view—one finds indeed quite the opposite, as in Article 34(2)(b) and (c) EU, establishing that framework decisions and decisions taken under Title VI EU 'shall not entail direct effect.' In any case, since the jurisdiction of the Court does not extend to these pillars, it would not be possible for it to develop and safeguard such constitutional principles.

In sum, even if they are part of a unitary legal system of sorts, the Union pillars presently lack a constitution and are qualitatively distinct from the Community pillar, the only one that presents 'constitutional materials'. The fact that they have to respect in full, and build on, the *acquis communautaire* and that they may need, according to the Treaty, 'to be revised with the aim of ensuring the effectiveness of the mechanisms and the institutions of the Community' (Article 2, indent 5, EU), is revealing of the provisional character of the Union pillars, whose likely fate is their inclusion in a single pillar (whose features will be similar to those of the Community pillar, regardless of its eventual name) in the near future.[13]

4.3. COMMUNITY CONSTITUTIONALISM

The first constitutional moment of the Community, as has already been noted, is the Paris Treaty establishing a European Coal and Steel Community. That Treaty and further moments have their starting point in the Schuman declaration. On the eve of the tenth anniversary of the German invasion of the Netherlands, Belgium and France (10 May 1940), Robert Schuman, then French minister of foreign affairs, pronounced a very important official declaration. He was inviting Germany and other European States to unite their productions of coal and steel as a first step towards 'a European Federation indispensable for the preservation of peace.' Peace was to be guaranteed on the continent by making war between France and Germany 'not only unthinkable, but materially impossible.' The declaration also affirmed that 'Europe will not be made all at once, or according to a single plan [*une construction d'ensemble*]', rather 'through concrete achievements which first create a de facto solidarity.' These concrete achievements would start in key sectors of the economy (the production of coal and steel).[14]

---

[12] A von Bogdandy and M Nettesheim, '*Ex Pluribus Unum*: Fusion of the European Communities into the European Union' (1996) *European Law Journal*, 267, 283–284.

[13] See J-V Louis, 'Le modèle constitutionnel européen: de la Communauté à l'Union', above n 11, 39.

[14] Reproduced in Bull EC 5–1980, 15: 'une Fédération européenne indispensable à la préservation de la paix'; 'non seulement impensable, mais matériellement impossible.' 'L'Europe ne se fera pas d'un coup, ni dans une construction d'ensemble : elle se fera par des réalisations concrètes créant d'abord une solidarité de fait.'

The debate launched by the Nice Treaty about the future of the Union is a debate about the grand theme that was not to be addressed through the functionalist method propounded by the Schuman declaration. After half a century of 'concrete achievements' the time has perhaps come to address the question of the 'construction d'ensemble' that corresponds to such achievements. It is a debate about the constitution of the European Union.

The economic orientation of the project of integration was also clear in the last paragraph of the declaration: 'In contrast to international cartels, which aim at dividing up and exploiting the national markets by means of restrictive practices and the maintenance of high profits, the proposed organisation will ensure the fusion of the markets and the expansion of production.'[15] This entailed the need both to control undertakings through competition rules and to prevent State protectionism through the guarantee of the free movement for the relevant economic factors. The Schuman declaration, reproduced almost verbatim in the preamble to the Treaty of Paris establishing a European Coal and Steel Community (1951), is a fundamental constitutional document containing the basic political and economic values and finality of the process of European integration. These values and principles will pass to the substance of the Paris Treaty, and will also find their way to the Rome Treaty.

The subsequent pragmatic stress on economic goals hides the fact that the Treaties were and remain means to the further goal of peace and stability among the European nations. The parallel emphasis on the States as being masters of the Treaties (*Herren der Verträge*), an oft repeated platitude loaded with nationalist rhetoric, is similarly ignorant of recent European history—in particular, of the aim to create a Community of States and peoples, not only of States.

Confronted with this change of perspective, if they are to preserve the main values and finality of the process of integration, the States can only be masters of their creation jointly and together with the European peoples, not as separate sovereign entities. The reasons and ideals underlying the emergence of the European Community, even if new generations may not perceive them so clearly, remain crucial for a constitutional understanding of the Community, for any constitution feeds on elements which are beyond the legal texts.[16] In spite of some sort of collective amnesia, a constitutional conception of the Community needs to take these values and principles into account.

Karl Loewenstein saw the essence of constitutionalism in 'the adequate containment of political power by the interaction of either the several power holders or the power addressees themselves.'[17] In this sense, the Community has effectively contributed to the taming of both public and private, political and

---

[15] Reproduced in Bull EC 5–1980, 15: 'A l'opposé d'un cartel international à la répartition et à l'exploitation des marchés nationaux par des pratiques restrictives et le maintien de profits élevés, l'organisation projetée assurera la fusion des marches et l'expansion de la production.'

[16] See J H H Weiler, *The Constitution of Europe*, above n 2, 238–263.

[17] K Loewenstein, *Political Power and Governmental Process* (University of Chicago Press, Chicago, 1957) 7.

economic power in the continent. It has been successful in preventing a war among its members by creating a community of interests among them—this, of course, within the framework of NATO, but one should tend to see NATO, the Community and the Council of Europe as mutually reinforcing institutions of a new European order. In the Community context, the Member States have thus decided to be bound to each other and to their common creation. Thereby they have radically changed the nature of their relationships prior to the signing of the Treaties or their accession thereto, relinquishing a non-negligible portion of their autonomy and powers by channelling them through the Community institutions and decision-making process. The powers of the Community itself are also contained by the constitution of the Community.

4.4. THE TREATY AS AN INTERNAL AND EXTERNAL COMMUNITY CONSTITUTION

Advocate General Lagrange argued in 1956, with respect to the Treaty establishing a European Coal and Steel Community, that,

> our Court of Justice is not an international court, but the court of a Community created by six States on a model which is more closely related to a federal than to an international organisation, and [. . .] although the Treaty, which the Court has the task of applying was concluded in the form of an international treaty and although it unquestionably is one, it is nevertheless, from a material point of view, the charter of the Community, since the rules of law which derive from it constitute *the internal law of that Community.*[18]

There is no explicit reference to constitutionalism in these words, but two elements are present that would later lead to the discovery of constitutional law in the Treaties. Lagrange's effort was aimed at distinguishing the Court from international courts and Community law from international law, while recognising that the Treaty was formally concluded under international law. Thus, the Treaty appears as the *charter* of the Community, something more than an international agreement. This charter includes enforceable rules of law and constitutes a coherent and self-contained legal system ('the internal law of the Community'), but remains something less than a constitutional order.

This rhetoric became explicit in a 1986 judgment, *Les Verts*. The Court first referred to the Treaty establishing the European Community as 'the constitutional charter of a Community based on the rule of law.'[19] This statement was confirmed in Opinion 1/91,[20] a crucial pronouncement to which we return below.

---

[18] Case 8/55 *Fédéchar* [1956] ECR 245, 277.
[19] Case 294/83 *Les Verts* [1986] ECR 1339, para 23.
[20] Opinion 1/91 *EEA* [1991] ECR I–6079, para 21.

It has become commonplace among Community scholars to refer to this case law as authority for the contention that the Treaty is a constitution. Rhetoric is important for the law, but one has to distinguish between what is said or written and what is done with words. The Treaty could not be qualitatively transformed merely as a result of words. It should also be borne in mind that the concept of constitution is flexible and polysemous, so one has to determine first to what concept of constitution the Court was referring.

The Court was only able to adopt a constitutional rhetoric once the Treaties, or a part of them, could be seen as a constitution or as constitutional materials—by virtue of the juridification and constitutionalisation of the Community legal order effected in the early 1960s. The Treaty is not a constitutional charter because the Court is saying it. The Court says so because in judgments such as *Van Gend en Loos*, *Costa v ENEL* and *ERTA* it had extracted and developed the constitutional seeds contained in the Treaty. *Les Verts* and Opinion 1/91, in a way, do nothing else than recall and give their name to a series of jurisprudential developments that were by then well established and had been implicitly ratified in subsequent Treaty revisions.

The essence of this process of constitutionalisation consisted in a true constitutional interpretive approach to the text of the Treaty, and it had one important consequence: the Community and the States had to take Community law seriously.

With the assertion and recognition of the supremacy principle by the judiciaries of the Member States, the Treaty came to be regarded as something more than 'the internal constitution of the Community', as the Court had already described it Opinion 1/76.[21] The 'internal constitution' kind of discourse still resembles that of Advocate General Lagrange in *Fédéchar*. In *Les Verts* the Court recognised that the Treaty has become the constitution of the Community.

There is a difference in rhetoric as well as in substance. The reach and reality of the Community constitution is now linked to the question of the assertion and recognition of the supremacy of Community law over State law. We have already pointed out that the constitution of divided-power systems depends on the effectiveness of the supremacy of the law common to the member units over the singular laws of each unit. The constitutional character of the Community constitution thus depends on the effectiveness of the principle of supremacy, asserted by the Court as early as 1964 and generally recognised by the States' political and judicial institutions. Only insofar as supremacy is effective does the Community constitution work not only as an 'internal constitution of the Community', but also as part of the common constitution of the Community and its States, integrated with the national constitutions, but above them in its sphere of application.

The Court itself has linked the adoption of a constitutional rhetoric to previous developments in its case law. Opinion 1/91, on the European Economic Area, affirms that the Treaty,

---

[21] Opinion 1/76 *Laying-Up Fund* [1977] ECR 741.

albeit concluded in the form of an international agreement, none the less constitutes the constitutional charter of a Community based on the rule of law. As the Court of Justice has consistently held, the Community treaties established a new legal order for the benefit of which the States have limited their sovereign rights, in ever wider fields, and the subjects of which comprise not only Member States but also their nationals. [. . .] The essential characteristics of the Community legal order which has thus been established are in particular its primacy over the law of the Member States and the direct effect of a whole series of provisions which are applicable to their nationals and to the Member States themselves.[22]

The reasoning is based on the classical jurisprudence of the 60s, which is cited by the Court. The idea implicit in this paragraph is that the Treaty is a constitution in the material sense, and that it is not only the internal constitution of the Community legal order, but that it pierces the veil of the States through direct effect and supremacy, thereby being applicable to the States and 'their nationals.'

It was highlighted in chapter 2 that Carl Schmitt considered that the constitution of a federal union may begin with a treaty among its members. Karl Loewenstein agreed. He wrote that the constitution of a federation,

> is the treaty of a permanent union by which the heretofore sovereign member states agree to divest themselves of certain sovereign rights, in favor of the central state, in compensation for the protection of their existence by the totality of all members and the benefits derived from participating in a larger state society.[23]

In the Community context, this sort of idea could clash with a *democratic* constitutionalism—that is, with the operative concept of the constitution— inasmuch as a simple pact between States would not be enough to establish a legitimate constitution without the acceptance of the people or peoples. This issue will be examined in subsection B of the following section.

The terseness of Opinion 1/91 could nevertheless be questioned nowadays, for it is almost a decade old and the Court has never subsequently used so clear a constitutional discourse. Only in Opinion 2/94, of 1996, did it refer in passing to the possibility of an accession of the Community to the European Convention on Human Rights as a step 'of constitutional significance',[24] thus requiring a Treaty amendment, not only an extension of the powers of the Community via Article 308 EC. While it is true that the political environment has been anything but propitious for this kind of judicial pronouncements and that the Court has not seized various opportunities of rendering decisions of constitutional import (Opinions 1/94 and 2/94, for instance), neither Opinion 1/91 nor the other constitutional cases that preceded this decision, have been overruled. It is then reasonable to presume that the principles stated in Opinion 1/91 remain good law.

---

[22] Opinion 1/91 *EEA* [1991] ECR I–6079, para 21.
[23] K Loewenstein, *Political Power and Governmental Process*, above n 17, 281.
[24] Opinion 2/94 *ECHR* [1996] ECR I–1759, para 35.

Again, calling something a constitution does not mean much in itself. The important test is to examine whether the Treaty, as interpreted by the Court, fulfils the elements of the operational concept of constitution.

A. Direct Effect and Supremacy

According to the operational concept of a constitution, the Treaty constitutes a distinct body of norms, principles and values the enforcement of which is effectuated by the Community judiciary, composed of the Community and national courts. This body is heterogeneous and does not have a formal unity. Thus, it is better to refer to Community 'constitutional materials'.

According to Article 220 EC, the Court 'shall ensure that in the implementation and application of this Treaty the law is observed.' The amendment of this provision by the Nice Treaty, which is not yet in force, includes an explicit reference to the Court of First Instance—as if it were not a part of the Court of Justice according to Article 7 EC. It also clarifies that each institution shall act each 'within its jurisdiction'. This amendment is quite unhappy if compared with the traditional wording of this provision.[25]

As regards national courts, the Court held in *van Gend en Loos* (1963) that,

> the task assigned to the Court of Justice under Article [234 EC], the object of which is to secure uniform interpretation of the Treaty by national courts and tribunals, confirms that the states have acknowledged that Community law has an authority which can be invoked by their nationals before those courts and tribunals.[26]

Accordingly, direct effect ensures the normative character of the Community legal order and the efficiency of the Treaty as a legal norm. To oblige national judges to apply Community law was the solution adopted by the Treaty in the absence of a more developed Community judiciary. But even if a federal judiciary existed, national judges would still be obliged to apply Community law by virtue of the supremacy principle. Besides, the nature of the legal order—with national administrations carrying out through delegation most of the measures adopted in the fields covered by Community law and the predominant use of the Directive as a legal source—is well adapted to a jurisdictional system in which national courts are also Community courts. In this system, preliminary rulings guarantee a degree of uniformity.

The principle of direct effect was complemented a year later by that of supremacy (*Costa v ENEL*). Direct effect is not a characteristic of some Community norms, but of any effective legal norm that is capable of judicial

---

[25] See P Pescatore, 'Guest Editorial: Nice—Aftermath', (2001) *Common Market Law Review* 265, 269.

[26] Case 26/62 *van Gend en Loos* [1963] ECR 1, 12.

adjudication.[27] Even though both concepts are clearly related, supremacy and direct effect remain distinct categories with different practical effects.[28] Direct effect implies supremacy, but the latter has a wider significance, since all Community law, irrespective of its direct applicability, is supreme over all national law, constitutional law included.[29] As a consequence of supremacy, the breach by a Member State of both directly effective and not directly effective Community law may give rise to State liability.[30] Finally, national legislation has to be construed in accordance with Community law.[31]

It is important to recall at this juncture the reasoning in *Costa v ENEL*:

By contrast with ordinary international treaties, the EEC Treaty has created *its own legal system* which, on the entry into force of the Treaty, became an *integral part of the legal systems of the Member States* and which their courts are bound to apply.

By creating a Community of unlimited duration, having its own institutions, its own personality, its own legal capacity and capacity of representation on the international plane and, more particularly, real powers stemming from a limitation of sovereignty or a transfer of powers from the States to the Community, the Member States have limited their sovereign rights, albeit within limited fields, and have thus created *a body of law which binds both their nationals and themselves*.

The law stemming from the Treaty, an independent source of law, could not, because of its special and original nature, be overridden by domestic legal provisions, however framed, without being deprived of *its character as Community law* and without the legal basis of the Community itself being put into question.[32]

The Court noted once again the specificity of Community law with respect to international law. It also held that the Treaty is an independent source of law and that Community law constitutes an integral part of the national legal systems. The supremacy of Community law is held to be an existential need for this system of law. Without supremacy, Community law ceases to be 'communautaire'—it no longer is the common law of the members of the Community.

It is important to make clear that the Court did not coercively impose these principles onto national courts. It could not be otherwise, because the Treaty does not confer authority on the Court to review national law through preliminary rulings nor does Community law have effective coercive means, besides the mechanism of Article 228(2) EC, to ensure direct effect or supremacy—which will probably not be used against a violation of direct effect or supremacy by a national court.

[27] See P Pescatore, 'The Doctrine of "Direct Effect": An Infant Disease of Community Law' (1983) *European Law Review* 155, 177.
[28] D Simon, *Le système juridique communautaire* (PUF, Paris, 1997) 260.
[29] Cases 9/65 *San Michele* [1967] ECR 37; 11/70 *Internationale Handelsgesellschaft* [1970] ECR 533.
[30] Cases C–6/90 & C–9/90 *Francovich* [1991] I–5357; C–46/93 & C–48/93 *Brasserie du Pêcheur/Factortame III* [1996] ECR I–1029; C–392/93 *British Telecommunications* [1996] ECR I–1631.
[31] Case C–106/89 *Marleasing* [1990] ECR I–4135.
[32] Case 6/64 *Costa v ENEL* [1964] ECR 585, 593–594 (my emphases). The English translation is incorrect: '*issu d'une source autonome*, le droit né du traité ne peut se voir *judiciairement* opposer un texte interne *quel qu'il soit* sans perdre *son caractère communautaire* et sans que soit mise en cause *la base juridique* de la communauté elle-même' (my emphases).

The assertion of supremacy was based on argumentation and persuasion, and was generally welcomed by national courts,[33] in spite of some initial problems—some difficulties persist, as will be shown later in this chapter. It was also perceived by the States, which did not amend the Treaty in order to deprive these principles of authority or entered the Community in the knowledge that such principles were part of the legal order. One should recall that when the Member States wanted to amend the Treaty to limit the effects of some judgment, they have done so.[34] In truth, direct effect and supremacy suit the States rather well. According to de Witte,

> all states have an interest that the rules which they made in common, or which were adopted by the institutions that they set in place, should stick. The fact that *their* national laws should occasionally be set aside is the price to be paid for the guarantee that *all* national laws shall be in conformity with EC law, thus protecting the achievements of the integration process.[35]

The supremacy of Community law recurs time and again as the crucial question to determine whether part of the Treaty is endowed with a constitutional character. It is not the internal constitutional character of the Treaty that makes it supreme. It is rather the acceptance of its asserted supremacy over State law (including State constitutional law) that makes it constitutional.

B. Extralegal Foundations, Internal Supremacy

Under criterion (i) of the definition, the Treaty, as the constitution of the Community, derives its authority from extralegal sources. After decades of existence and in spite of minor signals of popular indifference or dissatisfaction (for example, in Denmark concerning the Maastricht Treaty or in Ireland as regards the Nice Treaty), there is no ground to believe that a general acquiescence over the Community does not exist among an important majority of the peoples of the States. The approval of several recent revisions of the Treaty by national Parliaments is a clear, if indirect, sign of acquiescence. The general observance of the Treaty rules by national administrations, judges and individuals is another sign of acquiescence.

Nonetheless, it seems clear that the Union—and the Community constitutional system—can evolve in many ways, and there is no consensus regarding its finality and future. At a certain point—the moment in which constitutionalisation is

---

[33] See J-V Louis, 'Droit communautaire et droit national' in *Commentaire Mégret-Le droit de la CE* (2nd edn, Presses de l'Universite libre de Bruxelles, Brussels, 1995) 549–605; B de Witte, 'Direct Effect, Supremacy, and the Nature of the Legal Order' in P Craig and G de Búrca (eds) *The Evolution of EU Law* (OUP, Oxford, 1999) 178, 194.

[34] Protocol No 2 to the Maastricht Treaty was intended to limit the financial consequences of Case C–262/88 *Barber* [1990] ECR I–1889; the Act of Accession of Spain and Portugal excluded the applicability of Case 189/80 *Merck* [1981] ECR 2063 to trade with these States.

[35] B de Witte, 'Direct Effect, Supremacy, and the Nature of the Legal Order', above n 33, 195.

completed with a 'construction d'ensemble'—the peoples should be given the chance of directly deciding for themselves, and the result should enter into force among the States whose peoples approve it. Insofar as the process remains slowly incremental, however, acquiescence may be enough and the only practicable option for providing the incomplete Community constitutional order with a degree of legitimacy.

Thus, the sort of legitimation that has been used so far may be enough for the current 'constitutional materials', but perhaps it would not be sufficient for the adoption of the formal constitution of a more perfect Union.

Even though they are connected, the question of the extralegal foundation of the Community constitution is different from that of the democratic legitimacy of its decision-making processes, which will be examined in subsection D.

C. Community Law and Individual Autonomy

The Treaty has established institutions endowed with powers and tasks, according to element (ii) of the concept. It also guarantees a sphere of autonomy for the persons living in the Community, limiting the effects that both the Community and individuals can have on other individuals within the scope of the Treaty. These guarantees, of course, complement those that citizens already have at the national level. In this context, the human rights jurisprudence of the Court springs to mind. Besides, the four freedoms and the competition rules undoubtedly enhance economic freedom, even if they are not to be seen as fundamental rights.[36]

As regards fundamental rights, it is well known that the Court has held that they are to be protected as general principles of Community law within the framework of the structure and objectives of the Community. Such protection is inspired by the constitutional traditions of the States and international instruments to which they are parties. While the European Convention on Human Rights has a special significance in this regard, the Court devises its own uniform standards of protection. Such standards are uniform, and the case law of the Strasbourg Court on the margin of appreciation of the States does not seem to have a place in the Community framework. Community protection under Community standards generally operates in the fields coming under Community competence, regardless of whether Community or State implementing measures are at issue.[37]

---

[36] T Kingreen, *Die Struktur der Grundfreiheiten des Europäischen Gemeinschaftsrechts* (Duncker and Humblot, Berlin, 1999) 115: 'Sie sind [die Grundfreiheiten] Schutznormen genenüber transnationalen Benachteiligungen, nicht aber Grundrechte, die vor jeder unverhältnismäßigen Beeinträchtigung der Wirtschaftlichen Handlungsfreiheit schützen.'

[37] See Cases 29/69 *Stauder* [1969] ECR 419; 11/70 *Internationale Handelsgesellschaft* [1970] ECR 1125; 4/73 *Nold* [1974] ECR 491; 44/79 *Hauer* [1979] 3727; 60 and 61/84, *Cinéthèque* [1985] ECR 2605; 12/86 *Demirel* [1987] ECR 3719; and 2/92 *Bostock* [1994] ECR I–955.

This protection could be reinforced by a written charter of fundamental rights. The elaboration of such a charter was opened by the Cologne European Council of 3 and 4 June 1999.[38] The Charter of Fundamental Rights of the European Union was drafted by a Convention convened to that effect. The Convention was composed of 62 members (15 representatives of the Heads of State or Government of Member States, 1 representative of the Commission, 16 members of the European Parliament and 30 members of national Parliaments). The Charter was solemnly proclaimed on 7 December 2001. One of the questions to be discussed in the context of the debate on the future of the Union launched by the Nice Treaty is precisely that of the legal status of the Charter, which for the time being is not a binding instrument, although it could have an interpretive value.[39]

The other option to give a more solid base to the protection of fundamental rights in the Community legal order was the accession of the Community to the European Convention on Human Rights. This option was put to rest in 1996, with Opinion 2/94.[40] The Opinion had declared that a Treaty amendment conferring a specific competence concerning fundamental rights to the Community was necessary before accession took place. Such an amendment has not yet taken place, but the Laeken declaration refers to the accession as a complement to the Charter.

This discussion goes beyond my main focus. It is enough to state that these rights appear to fulfil the requirement of section (iii) of our operational definition.

D. The Democratic Element

An apparent weakness of the Community constitution is the democratic element, which founds the legitimacy of public authorities to act within the constitutional framework. This subsection will examine the election of public authorities in the Community, public deliberation and certain aspects of the decision-making process.

There are certain democratic elements in the Community system. The Treaty allows for the possibility of peaceful and democratic change of government after a reasonable period of time through a framework of public deliberation.

Changes in the composition of the Council ('representatives of each Member State at ministerial level', according to Article 203 TEC) depend on the changes

---

[38] See Bull EU 6–1999, 13 and 35.

[39] Advocate General Tizzano, in Case C–173/99 *BECTU* [2001] ECR I–4881, para 28, has argued that, 'in proceedings concerned with the nature and scope of a fundamental right, the relevant statements of the Charter cannot be ignored; in particular, we cannot ignore its clear purpose of serving, where its provisions so allow, as a substantive point of reference for all those involved—Member States, institutions, natural and legal persons—in the Community context.'

[40] Opinion 2/94 (ECHR) [1996] ECR I–1759.

in national governments, hence on national political processes. One of the conditions for accession to the Community is a democratic form of government (Articles 49 and 6 EU).

According to Article 214 EC, the Commission is appointed every five years by the national governments with the approval of the European Parliament (according to the Nice Treaty, not yet in force, the Council will appoint the Commission, by qualified majority, with the approval of Parliament). Since 1979, the Parliament has been elected through direct universal suffrage every five years (Article 190 EC). Judges and Advocates General of the Court of Justice are appointed 'by common accord of the governments of the Member States for a term of six years' (Article 223 EC).

Only the European Parliament is endowed with direct democratic legitimacy. The remaining institutions have an indirect legitimacy, linked to national political processes. It is worth recalling, however, that in many constitutional systems the democratic legitimacy of the executive and the judiciary is also indirect, deriving from the legislature. Some national executives thus have a second-degree legitimacy, shared by the Council. The Commission has a more direct legitimacy because of the European Parliament's intervention in its nomination. This was reinforced with the entry into force of the Amsterdam Treaty, as the nomination of the Commission's President is now subject to express parliamentary approval. The Nice Treaty will adopt a 'Community' system of election for the Commission, through qualified majority in the Council. Curiously enough, the members of the Court of Justice will still be elected by common accord of the governments of the Member States. In comparison with the Commission, then, the Court will have an enhanced legitimacy as regards the States, but perhaps less legitimacy regarding the peoples.

Public deliberation on European issues, an important source of legitimacy, is a weak element of the Community, because true European parties, which channel political life, are lacking. However, it is something of a logical leap to conclude that because '[t]he European level of politics lacks a matching public', '[t]he achievement of the democratic constitutional State can for the time being be adequately realised only in the national framework.'[41]

A framework of public deliberation exists, even though it is national political life which currently channels most debates on European affairs, with the attendant distortion. In other words, the democratic European polity is structured through the national political processes, at least while the European political process remains fragmented and does not catch the public eye. Perhaps politics comes first and public deliberation follows, so that they will only grow together. Since the visibility of a European public space is closely related to the importance of the matters dealt with at the European level, the achievement of the Economic and Monetary Union may contribute to the creation of a European framework of public deliberation.

---

[41] D Grimm, 'Does Europe Need a Constitution?', (1995) *European Law Journal*, 282, 296–297.

These democratic elements cannot be neglected but are not totally satisfactory. There is a clear democratic difficulty in the Community. The Member States are aware of its frail legitimacy.[42] This difficulty ensues both from the strengthening of national executives over legislators without an equal countervailing force in the European Parliament, and from the stochastic interaction between national political processes without a central and ordered Community political process. These problems should however not be exaggerated or deemed to be insoluble. The Parliament has increased and will go on increasing its powers in the future, and a more perfect democratisation is possible. This practicable European democracy, if it is not to be redundant, depends on the ability to create political structures to empower the peoples at the European level through a European political process which is not just a corollary of the national political processes.

Other difficulties have to do with the Community decision-making process, in particular with the so-called 'comitology'. Certain authors have argued that comitology, an administrative excrescence of the Community's institutions and decision-making process, embodies a so-called 'deliberative supranationalism' that would legitimate democratically the activities of committees.[43] Comitology unbound through constitutional constraints is, in contrast with these views, deeply anti-democratic—if by democracy we understand a degree of participation of the citizenry in public affairs and the regular possibility of a majoritarian change of government. Comitology betrays the decision-making process constitutionally established in the Treaty, undermines the Community institutional balance, and badly wants effective limits.[44]

In this sense, the recent Comitology Decision fails to establish such limits.[45] It obviously fails as regards the wider aspects of comitology not covered by the Decision (all the other dimensions of the Community decision-making process which are linked to comitology but do not strictly involve a formal delegation of implementing powers by the Council to the Commission).[46] But it also fails as regards such implementing powers. This is quite significant, for after all it is a *Council* Decision adopted under Article 202 of the Treaty, which merely requires the opinion of the Parliament to be requested.

[42] The Declaration No 23 annexed to the Nice Treaty is significant in that the intergovernmental conference 'recognises the need to improve and to monitor the democratic legitimacy and transparency of the Union and its institutions, in order to bring them closer to the citizens of the Member States.'

[43] See C Joerges and J Neyer, 'From Intergovernmental Bargaining to Deliberative Political Processes: The Constitutionalisation of Comitology', (1997) *European Law Journal*, 273, 292–299.

[44] See G de Búrca, 'The Institutional Development of the EU: A Constitutional Analysis' in P Craig and G de Búrca (eds) *The Evolution of EU Law* (OUP, Oxford, 1999), 69–75.

[45] See Council Decision 99/468/EC, laying down the procedures for the exercise of implementing powers conferred on the Commission, OJ 1999 L 184/23; *corrigendum* in OJ 1999 L 269/45; see also the declarations in the Council minutes in OJ 1999 C 203/1. The Decision replaces the former 'Comitology Decision', Council Decision 87/373 OJ 1987 L 197/33.

[46] See J H H Weiler, 'Epilogue: 'Comitology' as Revolution—Infranationalism, Constitutionalism and Democracy' in C Joerges and E Vos (eds) *EU Committees: Social Regulation, Law and Politics* (Hart, Oxford, 1991) 339, 340.

The main problem with the Decision is the absence of a principle or reserve of legality. This principle is a keystone of any constitutional system, as it distinguishes legislation from administration, reserving a domain for the legislator. Its absence in the Community legal order, related to the absence of a hierarchical ordering of the sources of secondary law, undermines the democratic value of conferring more powers to the Parliament through the generalisation of the co-decision procedure, inasmuch as the Council and Commission may manage to reduce legislation to a minimum and defer most of the important decisions to implementation by committees, where Parliament is absent and private interests have an enhanced voice. The solution is not in giving Parliament a voice within the committees, but in establishing a precise domain reserved to the Parliament.

Lenaerts and Verhoeven argue that the '*Köster* case law, which imposes a marginal test in the light of the distinction between what is essential and what is ancillary, seems both appropriate and sufficient.'[47] This distinction may be too vague to be considered sufficient. If the steps towards democracy in the Community are to be meaningful and comitology is to be bound, a more concrete principle of legality is urgently needed in Community law, preferably at the constitutional level.

Concerning the wider comitology problem, it seems to me that expert discussion and decision-making have to be integrated in a traditional democratic context. Since experts do not enjoy democratic legitimacy of their own, political responsibility wanes. To introduce specific societal interests in an expert discussion does not make it democratic. One should not forget in this context the historical offspring of the corporatist State, based on not dissimilar principles of 'virtual representation'. These problems were already mentioned in the critique of the concept of 'economic constitution'.

Regarding the ideas of Joerges, who continues to hold that comitology stands as the embodiment of deliberative supranationalism,[48] account should be taken of the fact that his defence of comitology would prevent the Community from evolving further in its democratic path. An argument, thus, for maintaining the status quo.

Well, the Community plainly poses such problems, which can only be solved by further democratising its decision making-process—not only its institutions. An important step could be to establish an operational reserve of legality. The technical legitimacy of expert committees, besides, could at most be supplementary of the democratic legitimacy of the Community, which can only be based on the double link to the States and their peoples.

It could be noted, finally, that the technocratic theories that have been criticised here constitute, in the field of democratic legitimacy, the *pendant* of the

---

[47] K Lenaerts and A Verhoeven, 'Towards a Legal Framework for Executive Rule-Making in the EU? The Contribution of the New Comitology Decision', (2000) *Common Market Law Review*, 645, 661; see Case 25/70 *Köster* [1970] ECR 1161, para 9.

[48] C Joerges, '"Deliberative Supranationalism"—A Defence', *European Integration online Papers*, 2001 (http://eiop.or.at/eiop/texte/2001–008a.htm) 10.

pseudoconstitutional theories of the Community and of the ordoliberal conception of the 'economic constitution'. 'Economic constitution' as something quite
distinct from general constitutional law, a pseudoconstitutional approach to
Community law that ignores its primacy and its internal hierarchy, and a
defence of 'comitology' as 'deliberative supranationalism' can be seen as various
aspects of one doctrinal position.

E. Internal Hierarchy

Concerning element (ii) of the definition, it is also clear that, within the
Community legal order, the rules of the Treaty, including general principles
such as fundamental rights, cannot be reviewed against other legal norms nor be
changed through institutional practice.[49]

The Treaty is only subject to the amending procedure established in Article
48 EU, a provision that comes under the jurisdiction of the Court, being an
island of Community law in the Union pillars. This means that the intergovernmental element that generally prevails in the EU Treaty has to operate under the
Community rule of law regarding the amendment procedure.

The Treaty constitutes the basis for the validity of all secondary law, which
can be driven out of the legal order by the judiciary if in unavoidable conflict
with it.

The Community litigation system provides for various ways of challenging
secondary legislation in breach of the Treaty. Not only does all secondary legislation need a legal basis in the Treaty, which 'must be based on objective factors
which are amenable to judicial review';[50] besides respecting those formal
requirements (legal base, competent organ, procedure to adopt the measure),
secondary law should respect substantive provisions of the Treaty. Thus, the
provisions of the Treaty (norms and principles) are considered as 'the first of
the norms of the whole legal order, the fundamental norm, *lex superior*'.[51] The
Court has assumed, for reasons of coherence, an exclusive jurisdiction concerning the validity of secondary legislation.[52] Hence all national courts, even those
which are not of last resort, are forced to refer to the Court a question on validity under Article 234 EC before declaring a Community norm invalid.

Schul I, among other cases,[53] provides a clear example of how the Treaty
works as a constitution vis-à-vis secondary legislation. Article 2(2) of the sixth
VAT Directive was challenged as in breach of Article 90 EC. The Court held

---

[49] Case 68/86 *United Kingdom v Council* [1988] ECR 855, para 24.

[50] Case 45/86 *Commission v Council* [1987] ECR 1493, para 11.

[51] E García de Enterría, *La Constitución como norma y el Tribunal Constitucional* (3rd edn,
Civitas, Madrid, 1983) 49–50.

[52] Case 314/85 *Foto Frost* [1987] ECR 4199.

[53] See Case 41/84 *Pinna* [1986] ECR 1, annulling a provision of a Regulation for breach of the
Treaty Case 218/82 *Commission v Council* [1983] ECR 4063, para 15.

that 'the requirements of Article [90] of the Treaty are of a mandatory nature and do not allow derogation by any measure adopted by an institution of the Community.'[54] Nevertheless, the Court ruled that the contested provision of the Directive was valid if construed 'in a manner consistent with the requirements of the Treaty.'[55]

This is a usual technique in constitutional law. If a statutory provision can be construed in accordance with the constitution it will not be struck down as long as it is interpreted that way. Unnecessary declarations of the unconstitutionality of legislation will thus be avoided by the judiciary.

4.6. THE EXTERNAL VIEW OF COMMUNITY CONSTITUTIONALISM

This section examines the external perspective of the Community constitution. Such a perspective is not the only one, nor the most correct, but it cannot be ignored. It differs from the internal perspective in its perception of the foundation (the *Grundnorm* or basic norm) of the Community legal order. For the internal perspective, such foundations are to be found in the pact between the States, ratified, in some way or another, by their peoples. Such a pact would give the Community an original legitimacy. For the external perspective, Community law has its basis in the constitutions of the Member States, in particular in the clauses which permit the 'transfer' of powers to the Community.

This conflict of perspectives is mainly latent and need not give rise to actual conflicts. This conflict of perspective is however problematic regarding the supremacy principle. Much of what has been said above about the Community constitution depends on the acceptance of the supremacy principle by the national legal orders. Supremacy, an existential need for Community law, has been generally accepted by national courts.[56] However, this acceptance is not always absolute, and certain limits have been announced by some national constitutional courts with a view to preserving the integrity of their constitutional orders, mainly focusing on fundamental rights, democratic processes and competences. In general, such potential limits have not been put into effect. Their legitimacy in a divided-power system, in view of their unilateral imposition on all other members, is at least doubtful.

From an internal perspective, the question of the validity of the supremacy principle—understood as a rule of conflict between Community law and national law—has to be decided in favour of such a principle. The reasons put forward in chapter 2 are relevant here. Denying the validity of this principle implies the acceptance of fragmentation and decay. Such a process is already in

---

[54] Case 15/81 *Schul I* [1982] 1409, para 42.

[55] *Ibid*, para 43.

[56] See G C Rodríguez Iglesias and A Valle Gálvez, 'El Derecho comunitario y las relaciones entre el Tribunal de Justicia de las Comunidades Europeas, el Tribunal Europeo de Derechos Humanos y los Tribunales Constitucionales nacionales' (1997) *Revista de Derecho comunitario europeo*, 329.

place in the guise of the mechanisms of so-called 'closer cooperation'. The difference is that the possibility of 'closer cooperation' has been introduced by a Treaty amendment, and is subject to strict procedural and substantive conditions, whereas a breach of the supremacy principle is a unilateral act imposed on the other States, and amounts to a regression of the Community system to the principles of an international Community composed of sovereign States.

This is not the place to give an exhaustive treatment of this highly complex topic, but something has to be said about it, for the economic constitutional law—more precisely, its *constitutional* character—of the Community critically depends on the effectiveness of its supremacy.

The potential problems for the supremacy principle are not too many but they are not negligible either. They come from different courts, not just from the German and Danish courts, and may take the following forms:

(i)   Reserving untouchable islands of national sovereignty;[57]
(ii) Reserving for themselves the last word on certain issues, like competences or fundamental rights;[58]
(iii) Considering that they are not obliged under Article 234 EC, as courts of last resort, to request a preliminary reference from the Court when the case involves a question of Community law;[59]
(iv) Considering that the denial of such a preliminary reference by a higher court is not a breach of the rights of defence;[60]
(v)   Accepting supremacy as a principle but paying lip service to it when confronted with a Community norm in a constitutional controversy, because Community law is not part of the 'parameters of constitutionality'.[61]

All these situations would deprive Community law of its most salient constitutional characteristics by 'calling into question the very existence of the Community.'[62] It is to be noted that, rather than exerting a power of control, the relevant national courts usually threaten to do so in the future. Some tend to see

---

[57] Conseil Constitutionnel, Décision 92–312, *Recueil des décisions du Conseil Constitutionnel*, 1992, 76 (*Maastricht 2*); Décision 97–394, *Recueil des décisions du Conseil Constitutionnel*, 1997, 344 (*Amsterdam*). See also the Maastricht Decision of the Danish Supreme Court of 6 April 1998 (http://www.um.dk/udenrigspolitik/europa/domen/, visited on 11 August 1998), point 9.8.

[58] See the *Maastricht* Decision of the German Constitutional Court (BVerfGE 89, 155 [1993]; English translation in [1994] 1 CMLR 57); and the Maastricht Decision of the Danish Supreme Court, above n 57, point 9.6.

[59] Corte Costituzionale, ordinanza 536/95, *Giurisprudenza costituzionale*, 1995, 4459.

[60] In judgment 180/93 (*Jurisprudencia Constitucional*, 1993, vol XXXVI, 371), the Spanish Tribunal Constitucional held that there is no such breach if the higher court believes that there is no doubt regarding the interpretation of the norm, in a way that does not exactly square with the criteria established in Case 283/81 *CILFIT* [1982] ECR 3415.

[61] The Spanish Constitutional Court (judgment 147/96, *Jurisprudencia Constitucional*, 1996, vol XLVI, 90), considers that Community law is not a parameter by which to measure the constitutionality of national law. The principle of supremacy was accepted in judgment 28/91 (*Jurisprudencia Constitucional*, 1991, vol XXIX, 287), seemingly with regard to national courts other than the Constitutional Court itself.

[62] P Pescatore, *The Law of Integration* (Sijthoff, Leiden, 1974) 94.

these events as episodic and beneficial for the Community legal order, since they force the courts to adopt a higher standard of argumentation, and this may redound to the advantage of the quality of justice. Besides, they can be understood as part of a system of judicial checks and balances which further constitutionalises the Community legal order, by keeping an eye on the centre, controlling its centripetal tendencies and preserving the supranational structure.

This may be true, but if they were taken to the extreme, such episodes could pointlessly complicate the operation of the legal systems involved, eventually leading to a process of fragmentation and decay.

In the wake of MacCormick's article commented on in chapter II, certain authors have proposed institutional innovations to cope with the problems posed by supremacy and establish a non-hierarchical interaction between the Community and State legal orders. As an example of these proposals, we shall analyse Weiler's idea for the establishment of an European Constitutional Council that would have jurisdiction on issues of competence and subsidiarity—that is, in the fields in which the judicial application of the supremacy principle has attracted more resistance.[63]

This proposal would perhaps be incompatible with Article 292 EC, unless it were repealed or amended. This provision, one of the keystones of the Community jurisdictional system, establishes that the 'Member States undertake not to submit a dispute concerning the interpretation or application of this Treaty to any method of settlement other than those provided for therein.' It provides the Court and the judicial system established in the Treaty with an exclusive jurisdiction regarding conflicts over Community matters. Moreover, it ensures, together with Article 220 EC, that disputes will be solved by applying the law, and not according to some sort of balance of interests, arbitration or 'out-of-court settlement'. Such a system would not be compatible with the consideration of the Community as a Community based on the rule of law (*Rechtsgemeinschaft*). All problems would be solved by amending Article 292 EC, to be sure. However, the amendment or repeal of this provision is problematic, for it is one of the foundations of the judicial branch of the Community.

Besides, it is quite difficult to determine what is a competence or a subsidiarity issue. These two fields, if broadly interpreted, could take away from the Court a number of very important cases, transforming it into some sort of second Court of First Instance.

A Constitutional Council along the lines suggested by Weiler would not solve the legitimacy problems of the Court. Weiler argues that his Council would have an enhanced legitimacy because it would be composed of one judge from each State constitutional or higher court, plus the president of the European Court of Justice. This argument is not totally convincing. Legitimacy does not spring from the State origin of the judge, but from their nomination and the obligation to apply the law according to accepted legal methods. The judges of the Court

---

[63] See J H H Weiler, *The Constitution of Europe*, above n 2, 322, 354.

already apply the law, mostly according to accepted, if sometimes questionable, methods of interpretation. In contrast, the new Council would be prone to solve issues on prudential, not legal, grounds, because of its very composition and function. The legitimacy of the Constitutional Council would not be stronger than that of the Court, and its decisions would perhaps be more contested. To enhance the formal legitimacy of the latter it would suffice to establish a general procedure of consent by the Parliament to the appointees to the Court.

Fundamentally, the proposal would entail, in a more or less direct manner, the grave danger of making a State a judge in its own cause.[64] Each State would have a judge or arbitrator in the Constitutional Council. They would not be judges entrusted with ensuring that the law is respected in the interpretation and application of the Treaty. They would be representatives of the legal order of the Member State, and members of their judiciaries. Thus, it would be difficult for them to adopt a neutral perspective, different from that of the State they represent. The controversies would just be taken to another sphere, but remain direct controversies between the States.

It may perhaps be preferable to live with some latent constitutional tensions at national level than to attempt to solve them through a system that would alter the legal structure of the Community. There seems to be then no unavoidable need to create new organs or procedures to solve the practical problems posed by supremacy. A preferable option would be to make the existing ones work better. The dialogue between courts through the preliminary procedure and other informal means may already be having such an effect within the present institutional setting. Perhaps in the past the Court took an interpretive attitude that was too deferential to the decisions of the Council. Perhaps the States wanted to do too much with the Community without enhancing its democratic legitimacy. The warnings of constitutional courts may have had the desired effect, as the Court has taken a stricter approach regarding the division of powers between the States and the Community seriously.[65] Sometimes too strict, as in Opinion 1/94.[66]

An interesting example concerns the limits of Article 95 EC, the most important legal basis in Community law, as least insofar as economic law is concerned. These limits have been more clearly defined in a recent case that has annulled Directive 98/43/EC, on tobacco advertisements,[67] precisely because the Community legislator had exceeded them.[68] It is the first time that an act of secondary law is annulled for exceeding the competences of the Community—some acts were previously

---

[64] The *locus classicus* is T Hobbes, *Leviathan* (Cambridge University Press, Cambridge, 1991) 109: 'seeing every man is presumed to do all things in order to his own benefit, no man is a fit Arbitrator in his own cause: and if he were never so fit; yet Equity allowing to each party equall benefit, if one be admitted to be Judge, the other is to be admitted also; & so the controversie, that is, the cause of War, remains, against the Law of Nature.'

[65] J H H Weiler, *The Constitution of Europe*, above n 2, 321.

[66] Opinion 1/94 *WTO* [1994] ECR I–5281.

[67] OJ 1998 L 213/9.

[68] Case C–376/98 *Germany v Council* [2000] ECR I–8419.

annulled for breach of substantive Treaty provisions,[69] but never for lack of competence. The Directive could not have been adopted as a health measure, for Article 129(4) of the Treaty expressly excludes any harmonisation of State laws regarding human health. Thus, even though the Directive was annulled because Article 95 was not the appropriate legal basis, the Community probably lacked the powers to adopt such a measure under any legal basis.

This development in the case law has to be related to the more recent case law of the German constitutional court in which the latter shows deference to the Court of Justice as ultimate interpreter of Community law.

This evolution is quite significant, for the German court used to be the most outspoken national court putting potential limits on supremacy, most notably in its 1993 *Maastricht decision*.[70] In a 2000 decision rendered in the context of the bananas dispute, the German court has given a narrow interpretation of the *Maastricht decision*, clearly reaffirming the principles stated in *Solange II*.[71] The German constitutional court has declared that it will hold inadmissible any constitutional question related to Community secondary law as long as the level of protection of fundamental rights by the European Court of Justice in the field of Community law remains generally equivalent to that afforded under German constitutional law, with special regard to the essential content of fundamental rights guaranteed by the German constitution.[72]

This also softens the problem of the potential control, be it marginal, of Community competences by the German constitutional court. It will be recalled that in the *Maastricht decision* the issue of competences was raised in the context of a complaint that certain fundamental rights of German citizens were violated by the Maastricht Treaty. Of the rights allegedly violated, the complaint was only declared admissible insofar as it related to Article 38 of the German constitution, which guarantees the right to participate in a democratic system of government. The complaint was finally rejected, with certain provisos related to the democratic structure of the Union and the extent of its powers. The *Maastricht decision* was therefore about fundamental rights, the competences issue being incidental to that of rights. In this sense, the clear return of the German court to its previous position in *Solange II*, to wit, that it will declare inadmissible any question relating to Community secondary law in so far as the level of protection of fundamental rights in the Community legal order remains generally acceptable, practically means that the said court will very rarely, if ever, avail itself of an actual chance to rule on Community competences. The German constitutional court has not explicitly referred to the *Kompetenz-Kompetenz* problem in this recent decision, but the actual potential for conflict of the competence issue is neutralised by its due deference towards the European Court.

---

[69] See Case 41/84 *Pinna* [1986] ECR 1.
[70] BVerfGE 89, 155 (1993).
[71] BVerfGE 73, 339 (1986).
[72] BVerfGE, 2 BvL 1/97 of 7.6.2000, paras 58–61 (http://www.bverfg.de/).

With this decision, a point of equilibrium seems to have been reached in the interaction between the Community and German constitutional systems, without creating new institutions or procedures. This balance is valuable, for it has been found through cooperation and without coercion. Other constitutional courts will hopefully follow suit and remain deferential vis-à-vis the Court and Community law, while accepting its supremacy. This deference reflects the recognition that 'it is the proper function of the federal constitution, umpired by a federal judiciary, to strike the appropriate balance between the federation and its component entities.'[73]

The fact that the Court has changed its approach to Community competences does not have to be seen as an instance of the Court paying deference to the German or other national constitutional courts—which would detract credibility from this change—but rather as the European judiciary protecting the political rights of citizens, which are being silently limited by the States' executives. At the same time, the Community Court should not exaggerate such control, for the prerogatives of the States are rather well preserved by the Community political process. An excessive judicial intervention in these matters would distort the operation of the decision-making process, particularly for decisions taken by qualified majority. The political process is to be seen as the main guarantee that the limits of Community competences will be respected.[74] Judicial intervention should remain minimal and of last resort.

This process is still open. The threats to supremacy and the Community constitution can be seen as part of a transitional period that may lead to a clearer acceptance of both and of the ultimate interpretive authority concerning Community law, including the issues of competence and subsidiarity.[75]

These potential conflicts will remain, even if a more perfect balance is reached. The importance of achieving a more perfect position in the judicial assertion and acceptance of supremacy cannot be exaggerated. Only if supremacy is effective may the Treaty and the national constitutions be read together as a comprehensive constitution for the integrated Community and the States. The view of Pernice that 'Europe already has a "multilevel constitution", a constitution made up of the constitutions of the Member States bound together by a complementary constitutional body consisting of the European Treaties (*Verfassungsverbund*)'[76] only holds true insofar as supremacy generally prevails.

---

[73] K Lenaerts, 'Constitutionalism and the Many Faces of Federalism', (1990) *American Journal of Comparative Law*, 205.

[74] See H Wechsler, 'The Political Safeguards of Federalism' (1954) *Columbia Law Review*, 543.

[75] See J-V Louis, *L'ordre juridique communautaire* (OPOCE, Luxembourg, 1993) 192.

[76] I Pernice, 'Multilevel Constitutionalism and the Treaty of Amsterdam: European Constitution-Making Revisited?', (1999) *Common Market Law Review*, 703, 707.

5

Community Economic
Constitutional Law

5.1. FORM AND SUBSTANCE IN COMMUNITY CONSTITUTIONAL LAW

THE PREVIOUS CHAPTERS have established the conceptual and structural framework in which the economic constitutional law of the European Community and, more particularly, the gaps between competition and free movement, may be productively analysed. The present chapter moves to the economic constitutional law of the Community. It deals with the concept of internal market (section 2), the hierarchy in this branch of the law (section 3), the differences in the method of interpretation to be applied to constitutional and secondary law (section 4), a comparison with the economic constitutional law of the States (section 5) and a prospective assessment of this branch of the law (section 6).

The formal characteristics that provide Community law with a constitutional flavour are inextricably linked to various substantive provisions of the Treaty—quite often economic provisions. Even though the principles of direct effect and supremacy are characteristics of Community law as a whole, they were usually created and developed with regard to economic provisions. Hence substance and form are closely linked in Community law. A relationship could be likewise established between the decision-making process—in particular the democratic difficulties attendant to it—and the economic orientation of Community secondary law. The theme of legislative dynamics and the statutory economic framework, although quite important, goes beyond the scope of this work.

The economic constitutional law of the Community is composed of rules, principles, objectives and policies that are fleshed out in a series of concrete Treaty provisions. It is developed and complemented with measures adopted by the institutions pursuant to the Treaty. The distinction between legislation and administrative regulation, as we have seen, is unclear in Community law, because there is as such no domain clearly reserved to the legislator, nor a clear difference between the legislative and the executive powers. The distinction between constitutional law and the rest of the legal order, that between constitutional and statutory interpretation, and that between the judiciary and the other Community branches, can be drawn with more ease.

The principles and objectives are found in Articles 2, 3, 4, 14 and 16 of the Treaty, among which Articles 2 (tasks) and 3 (activities) are most important.

They are developed in Part Three of the Treaty, which includes the various Community *policies*: free movement of goods; agriculture; free movement of persons, services and capital; right of establishment; provision of services; capital and payments; transport; competition; tax provisions; approximation of laws; economic and monetary union; employment and social policy; common commercial policy; industry; economic and social cohesion, etc.

These policies include both directly applicable rules and enabling provisions that provide the Community with a competence to enact measures of secondary law. Other sections only include enabling provisions. Directly effective provisions included among the Community *policies* should not be seen just as constitutionally enshrined policies to be pursued through secondary law, but as directly applicable constitutional law.

This distinction is essential to understand the conception of the economic constitutional law of the Community that is put forward here. Article 82 EC, for example, belongs to the first category, because it clearly and unconditionally prohibits certain kinds of behaviour on the part of undertakings. Article 95 EC belongs to the second category, for it only allows the Council to 'adopt the measures for the approximation of the provisions laid down by law, regulation or administrative action in Member States which have as their object the establishment and functioning of the internal market.' This provision only establishes a head of competence for the Community, indicating the institutions and procedures to be used should this competence come into play. It also enshrines certain principles that have to guide the action of the institutions when acting in pursuant to this provision (for example, Article 95(3) EC commands the Commission to take as a base in its proposal a high level of protection concerning health, safety, environmental protection and consumer protection). Both norms belong to the constitutional law of the Community, but the absence of direct effect in the latter entails quite different legal effects. A provision of secondary law may be annulled by the Court if it was not adopted in accordance with the specifications contained in the legal basis. It may also be annulled if it violates any other norm of the Treaty. Of course, this will be more often the case with regard to directly applicable provisions, because individuals can rely upon them before national courts, and the latter are obliged to apply them. Besides, directly applicable provisions usually have a more precise normative content— this is why they have direct effect. This fact makes them more likely to be breached by secondary law.

The constitutional or higher law status of Treaty provisions is not an option for the interpreter or one among various models of interpretation, but a basic datum of the Community legal order. This work is focused on directly applicable Treaty norms, which offer valuable information about the economic constitutional law of the Community. This is not to deny the central importance of Community legislation and its interpretation, or that of the various legal bases included in the Treaty and the delimitation of Community vis-à-vis State competences. In spite of their different effects, both kinds of norms are constitutional.

Among these directly applicable constitutional norms, the free movement and competition rules appear to be the most important, in view of the generality of their reach, the strength of their wording and their direct connection with essential objectives of the Treaty. Their field of application extends to all the sectors of the economy, unless the Treaty itself provide otherwise. The main complements to these provisions are economic and monetary union (arguably, the logical outcome of the internal market) and the common commercial policy (generally seen as the external projection of the internal market). Economic and monetary union provides the Community with an element traditionally linked to State sovereignty (the single currency and monetary policy). The common commercial policy, to the extent that it is truly common, provides the Community with an international presence and effective leverage in international economic affairs.

These sets of norms (four freedoms, competition, economic and monetary union and common commercial policy) truly limit the Community and the States, constituting the foundations of the economic constitutional law of the Community and giving expression to its economic ethos. They give flesh to the objectives and principles stated in Articles 2 and 3 of the Treaty. Endowed with the formal qualities of Community law (direct effect plus supremacy), they have an important influence over the economic structure of the Community.

From an economic point of view, the ethos of Community economic constitutional law is predominantly and continuously based on the 'principle of an open market economy with free competition', an expression to be found in Treaty provisions as crucial as Articles 4, 98 and 105. This expression refers, in my view, to those objectives of the Treaty which are fleshed out in the free movement provisions (open markets) and the competition rules (free competition). Other policies, which may be based on different principles, operate, as it were, as exceptions to the 'open market economy with free competition'. This basic constitutional ethos of Community economic law is completed through secondary law, which provides for a wide but ascertainable scope for manoeuvre within the Community constitution.

A clear example of this characterisation may be found in the 1975 *Sugar* case, which concerned the common agricultural policy. This policy, based on the fixing of prices and national quotas of production by the Community institutions, constitutes a constitutional exception to the principle of free competition. In the case, the Court considered whether the common organisation of the sugar market was such that it eliminated any effective competition. After analysing the anti-competitive elements present in the system, the Court realised that there was some space left for competition, and 'if [the common organisation of the sugar market] leaves in practice a residual field of competition, that field comes within the provisions of the rules of competition.'[1] Hence, within the interstices

---

[1] Joined Cases 40–48, 50, 54–56, 111, 113 and 114/73 *Suiker Unie* [1975] ECR 1663, para 24.

of the common organisation of the market, the Treaty rules on competition were applicable and could be breached by the European sugar cartel.

There is a Community economic constitutional law *beyond*, not only *between*, competition and free movement. The latter is, nonetheless, the main concern of this work, and defines its focus. This is not to deny the importance of the social dimension of the Community legal order. However, such social counterpart to this predominantly market-oriented system is for the time being timidly represented by some provisions of the Treaty which are far less entrenched than the competition and the free movement rules. The reason for this imbalance lies in the fact that the States have not transferred to the Community the bulk of their social competence. Such a transfer would often imply Community redistributive policies—with Community taxes and a more substantial budget. The Treaty is not based on a *social* market economy, for the social dimension does not have in the Community a comparable presence to that of the market. An effective balance against the expansiveness of these market rules is rather to be found in the social elements of the States' constitutions, when read together with the Community constitution as parts of a single constitutional body. While my interest is focused on the interaction *between* free movement and competition, there can be no doubt that there is a potential ground for conflicts of the latter with the emergent Community social policies and, more importantly, with those of the States.[2] This topic will be touched upon again in connection with the economic 'neutrality' of the Community constitution.

5.2. THE CENTRALITY OF THE CONCEPT OF INTERNAL MARKET

The concept of internal market determines the interpretation and the evolution in the application of the provisions relating to it. It could be said that the objective becomes more important than the norm. Thus, because of this concept two similarly drafted norms may be applied differently.

This is exemplified by *Polydor v Harlequin*,[3] a preliminary ruling on the interpretation of Articles 14(2) and 23 of the Agreement between the Community and Portugal (prior to Portugal's accession in 1986),[4] which were worded similarly to Articles 28 and 30 EC. The context was an action for infringement of copyright against two British undertakings which imported records from Portugal without the consent of the owner of the right. The point of law was to determine

---

[2] I have explored some of these issues in my article 'La protección de los derechos sociales en la Comunidad Europea tras el Tratado de Amsterdam' (1998) *Revista de Derecho Comunitario Europeo*, 639.

[3] Case 270/80 *Polydor v Harlequin* [1982] ECR 329. See also Cases 26/76 *Metro v Commission* [1977] ECR 1875; 15/81 *Schul* [1982] ECR 1409; 9/73 *Schülter* [1973] ECR 1135, para 39.

[4] Signed in Brussels on 22 July 1972. See Regulation (EEC) No 2844/72 of the Council of 19 December 1972 (OJ, English special edition (31 December) (L 301) 166).

whether the doctrine of exhaustion of intellectual property rights—holding that such rights cannot be invoked to prevent intra-Community trade in goods which have been lawfully placed on the market by the proprietor or with its consent— could be extended to the interpretation of the similarly worded articles of the association Agreement between the Community and Portugal.

The Court considered the wording, preamble, and objectives of the Agreement, concluding that the relevant case law was only applicable in the Community context, for the Agreement did 'not have the same purpose as the EEC Treaty, inasmuch as the latter [. . .] seeks to create *a single market reproducing as closely as possible the conditions of a domestic market.*'[5]

The Court added that,

> such a distinction is all the more necessary inasmuch as the instruments which the Community has at its disposal in order to achieve the uniform application of Community law and the progressive abolition of legislative disparities within the common market have no equivalent in the context of the relations between the Community and Portugal.[6]

Thus, the protection of intellectual property rights could justify the restrictions on trade in goods questioned in the case. The different objectives and the possibility of harmonisation through the institutional setting, not present in other legal contexts, are the grounds for the Court not to extend its case law beyond the Community context. This shows that the correct interpretation of the relevant norms in the context of the Community did not spring solely from its wording, but from the interpretive influence of the internal market concept.

The concept of single or internal market was first used by scholars,[7] then by the Court and was finally constitutionalised in the 1986 Single European Act through Article 14(2) of the Treaty. This provision defined it as 'an area without internal frontiers in which the free movement of goods, persons, services and capital is ensured in accordance with the provisions of this Treaty.' This concept superseded and included the original concept of common market enshrined in Article 2 EC, and entrusted the Community institutions with the task of achieving it through policy measures by 31 December 1992.

Despite their relation, it is important to distinguish the concept coined by the Court—based on a constitutional value enshrined in primary law—from the political aim of achieving the internal market announced in the Single European Act, and materialised in secondary legislation. The latter has not yet been completely achieved and it has received repeated attention from both the

---

[5] Case 270/80 *Polydor v Harlequin* [1982] ECR 329, para 18 (emphasis added).
[6] *Ibid*, para 20.
[7] See, for example, P Pescatore, 'La notion du marché commun dans les traités instituant l'Union économique belgo-luxembourgeoise, le Benelux et les Communautés européennes', in *En hommage à Victor Gothot* (Faculté de Droit de Liège, Liège, 1962) 496, 497: 'un espace économique unifié et homogène, qui offre des conditions analogues à celles d'un marché intérieur'.

Commission and Council.[8] The former is the mandatory legal framework in which the political aim to create an internal market and all other Community and State policies have to operate. In this sense, the economic distinction between negative and positive integration, which has been adopted by many lawyers,[9] can be translated as a distinction between constitutional and statutory law.

From a legal perspective, the provisions of 'negative integration' are part of the economic constitutional law of the Community. 'Positive integration', on the other hand, refers to the economic administrative law of the Community, which has to respect the substantive provisions of the Treaty.[10] Hence the processes of deregulation and subsequent regulation at Community level may be seen as, respectively, a constitutionally mandated prohibition of any form of State protectionism (unless justified) and the legislative action aimed at harmonising market regulation.

Wolf Sauter, for instance, has referred to some sort of '*transition* from negative integration to positive integration.'[11] To be sure, the revitalisation of legislative processes is always felt in the practical application of any constitution, and something of the sort may have happened in the Community after the Single European Act and the generalisation of decision-making by qualified majority. When legislation occupies a given field, the Treaty norms are not displaced, there is no transition from one to the other. Constitutional law will perhaps find less instances of direct application—inasmuch as Community legislation is compatible therewith. Legislation complements the economic constitutional law of the Community, but it does not substitute it, if only because harmonisation very rarely is complete and has to be respectful of the said rules.

---

[8] See the Commission's report pursuant to the Council's resolution on the internal market (OJ 1992 C 334/1. No. 10), *The Impact and Effectiveness of the Single Market* (Doc 96 [520] final) and the Action Plan presented by the Commission and approved by the European Council of Amsterdam of 16–17 June 1997 (*Europe Documents*, 10 June 1997, No. 2041/42). See also the communication of 24 November 1999, from the Commission to the European Parliament and the Council, on the strategy for the internal market during the next five years (http://europa.eu.int./comm/internal_market/en/update/strategy/strat2en.pdf/, viewed on 1 March 2000).

[9] See R Bieber *et al* (eds) *1992: One European Market?* (Nomos, Baden-Baden, 1988), 13: 'negative integration, or the removal of barriers to transactions across the frontiers of different states, implies also the more exacting effort to achieve positive integration, or common policies with aims going beyond the straightforward removal of discrimination, when the barriers are not just tariffs and quotas, but differing regulations, taxes or laws.'

[10] For example (concerning free movement of goods), Case C–51/93 *Meyhui* [1994] ECR I–3879, para 11: 'It is settled law that the prohibition of quantitative restrictions and of all measures having equivalent effect applies not only to national measures but also to measures adopted by the Community institutions.' See also Case 15/83 *Denkavit Nederland* [1984] ECR 2171, para 15.

[11] W Sauter, *Competition Law and Industrial Policy in the EU* (Clarendon Press, Oxford, 1997) 229 (my emphasis).

5.3. THE QUESTION OF HIERARCHY IN COMMUNITY ECONOMIC LAW

This distortion in the assessment of the concept of internal market is related to the preference of some authors, in the wake of contributions of political scientists, to see the economic law of the Community as an isomorphous reality, neglecting the hierarchical relationship extant between its various sources. These views are not dissimilar to those of Norbert Reich, which have already been reviewed in chapter 4.

The approach to economic primary and secondary law (negative/positive integration) as homogeneous and equivalent legal realities seems to me to be questionable. Political science theories of regulation regularly fall into this misconception. Majone, for example, has written that,

> [w]ith the exception of the automatic clauses concerning the elimination of customs duties between the member states, the Treaty of Rome provides only general principles and policy guidelines, and delegates to the European institutions (especially the Commission and the Council) the task of specifying the concrete measures to be taken in order to achieve the broad objectives set out in Article 2.[12]

This assertion is not correct. One should not ignore a host of very important directly applicable Treaty provisions beyond those on customs duties.

In the wake of these theories, some jurists adopt a similarly isomorphous approach to Community legal sources. Wolf Sauter, for example, takes the view that industrial policy and competition policy are complementary and compatible, analysing both at the same level. According to him, 'there is no hierarchical order between the various intermediate objectives of the Treaty set out in Article 3 EC.'[13] This very proposition could be questioned, but it need not mean that there is no such order between the concrete provisions giving effect to the Community's various objectives and activities. Even if we assume that Community policies are compatible and the objectives equally important, it remains true that if the norms giving effect to them clash, the secondary legislation on industrial and other flanking policies will bend before directly effective provisions of the Treaty that bind the Community legislator as much as they bind the States.

Sauter by-passes the hierarchy of Community sources when he argues for the complementary character of the competition and industrial policies, considering them as pertaining to the same hierarchical level.[14] His interpretation ignores that the Treaty provision on industrial policy, like many other enabling provisions, simply empowers the Community to enact secondary law, which in turn has to respect the higher competition and free movement rules. This springs from the very wording of Article 157 EC, according to which the industrial policy of the

---

[12] G Majone, *Regulating Europe* (Routledge, London, 1996) 71.
[13] W Sauter, *Competition Law and Industrial Policy in the EU*, above n 11, 225.
[14] *Ibid*, 111–116, 159–161, 230.

Community has to be conducted 'in accordance with a system of open and competitive markets'. The legal situation would perhaps be the same in the absence of this express language in Article 157, which only states a consequence of the subordination of secondary law to the Community constitution.

Opinion 1/91 is based on such ideas. The Court compared the draft Agreement establishing a European Economic Area, including provisions similarly worded to the free movement and the competition rules, with the Community Treaty, reaching the conclusion that the system of judicial supervision to be established by the draft EEA Agreement would be incompatible with Community law. The conclusion was partly based on the specific characteristics of the economic constitutional law of the Community, together with the formal features of its general constitutional law—which were analysed in chapter 4.

The draft Agreement was seen by the Court as 'concerned with the application of the rules on free trade and competition in economic and commercial relations between the Contracting Parties.' In contrast, it said, the EC Treaty,

> aims to achieve economic integration leading to the establishment of an internal market and economic and monetary union. Article 1 of the Single European Act makes it clear moreover that the objective of all Community treaties is to contribute together to making concrete progress towards European unity.
>
> It follows from the foregoing that the provisions of the [EC] Treaty on free movement and competition, far from being and end in themselves, are only a means for attaining those objectives.[15]

The Court then considered whether the proposed system of courts could 'undermine the autonomy of the Community legal order in pursuing its own particular objectives.'[16] The fact that the EEA Agreement took over 'an essential part of the rules—including the rules of secondary legislation—which govern economic and trading relations within the Community and which constitute, for the most part, *fundamental provisions of the Community legal order*', was one of the central grounds for reaching the conclusion that 'the agreement's objective of ensuring homogeneity of the law throughout the EEA will determine not only the interpretation of the rules of the agreement itself but also the interpretation of the corresponding rules of Community law.' Thus, the draft agreement was declared incompatible 'with Article [220 EC] and, more generally, *with the very foundations of the Community*.'[17]

This Opinion holds the free movement and competition rules to be fundamental provisions of the Community legal order.

The 1999 judgment in *Eco Swiss China Time* follows the same logic. This case concerned the jurisdictional review of arbitration awards, which is limited in the Netherlands to certain grounds, among which is the possibility that the award was made contrary to public policy. One of the parties applied for the annulment

---

[15] Opinion 1/91 (EEA) [1991] ECR I–6079, paras 15, 17–18.
[16] *Ibid*, para 30.
[17] *Ibid*, paras 41, 45–46 (my emphasis).

of an award arguing that it was contrary to public policy by virtue of the nullity of an agreement under Article 81 EC, although this point of law had not been raised during the arbitration proceedings. The referring court asked for a preliminary ruling, but it had the intention not to apply Community law. According to the referring court, the competition rules are not regarded as mandatory fundamental rules in Netherlands law.[18]

In contrast, the Court stated that,

> according to Article 3(1)(g) of the EC Treaty, Article 81 constitutes *a fundamental provision which is essential for the accomplishment of the tasks entrusted to the Community and, in particular, for the functioning of the internal market* [. . .].'
>
> It follows that where its domestic rules of procedure require a national court to grant an application for annulment of an arbitration award where such an application is founded on failure to observe national rules of public policy, it must grant such an application where it is founded on failure to comply with the prohibition laid down in Article 81(1) EC.[19]

This reasoning, confirmed in *Courage*,[20] would apply with at least equal force to the free movement rules. This judgment reaffirms the view that the provisions on competition and free movement are fundamental constitutional provisions of the Community legal order, even though similar national provisions may not be themselves endowed with such a character.

The Court is not always so clear. In *Albany*, the hierarchical relation between directly applicable Treaty norms and secondary law is somewhat blurred. Albany, a textile company, refused to pay its contributions to the Textile Industry Trade Fund, arguing that the compulsory affiliation to such Fund was contrary to Articles 3(1)(g), 81, 82 and 86 of the Treaty. According to Albany, the request to public authorities by organisations representing employers and workers to make affiliation compulsory constituted an agreement contrary to Article 81, since it deprived Albany of the possibility of affiliation to another pension scheme and excluded other insurance companies from the relevant market.

The Court held that the Community includes among its activities not only a 'system ensuring that competition in the internal market is not distorted', but also 'a policy in the social sphere' (Article 3(1)(g) and (j)), which is developed in a series of Treaty provisions and the Agreement on social policy.[21] 'It is beyond question', went on the Court,

> that certain restrictions of competition are inherent in collective agreements between organisations representing employers and workers. However, the social policy objectives pursued by such agreements would be seriously undermined if management and labour were subject to Article [81](1) of the Treaty when seeking jointly to adopt measures to improve conditions of work and employment.

---

[18] Case C–126/97 *Eco Swiss China Time* [1999] ECR I–3055, para 24.
[19] *Ibid*, paras 36–37 (my emphasis).
[20] Case C–453/99 *Courage* [2001] ECR I–6297, paras 20–21.
[21] Case C–67/96 *Albany International BV* [1999] ECR I–5751, paras 54–58.

It therefore follows from *an interpretation of the Treaty as a whole which is both effective and consistent* that agreements concluded in the context of collective negotiations between management and labour in pursuit of such objectives must, by virtue of their nature and purpose, be regarded as falling outside the scope of Article [81](1) of the Treaty.[22]

The Court held that the collective agreement in hand complied with such conditions and fell outside the scope of Article 81 by virtue of its nature and scope.

This judgment is open to various interpretations. It is reasonable to think that it is important, but its reach is limited. It stands for an equivalence of the concrete Community objectives and activities involved in the case in hand. It can not be interpreted as an embodiment of the theory that puts constitutional and secondary law on the same hierarchical plane. It only interprets together two groups of constitutional provisions, those on competition and those on social policy. The Court finds that the effectiveness of the Treaty provisions on social policy requires a limited exemption from the competition rules for collective agreements. Limited, because it is only given to agreements concluded in the context of collective negotiations between management and labour aimed at certain social objectives.

Secondly, *Albany* does not change the fundamental character of competition law in the Community system. As Advocate General Jacobs highlighted in his Opinion in *Pavlov, Albany,*

is clearly limited to the special case of collective agreements between management and labour on conditions of work and employment [. . .] [I]n Community competition law there is no general exception for the social field. Contrary to many national competition law systems, the Community rules apply to virtually all sectors of the economy. That is because according to well-established case law the sectors outside the scope of the competition rules must be expressly mentioned in the Treaty.[23]

In sum, *Albany* does not change but marginally the following ideas: that (i) there is a hierarchy of Community sources, in spite of the alleged—perhaps reasonable—equivalence of the various Treaty objectives; that (ii) among constitutional rules, those having direct effect and a wide scope of application are fundamental.

5.4. CONSTITUTIONAL AND STATUTORY INTERPRETATION

The confusion between constitutional interpretation and the interpretation of secondary legislation can be graver, as it blurs in practice the hierarchical relationship between constitutional and secondary law.

---

[22] Case C–67/96 *Albany International BV* [1999] ECR I–5751, paras 59–60 (my emphasis).
[23] Joined Cases C–180/98 to C–184/98 *Pavlov* [2000] ECR I–6451, paras 96 and 101 (footnotes omitted).

In *Analir* and *Malpensa*,[24] for example, certain State conducts had been assessed by the Commission under the Community policy on the liberalisation of transport (sea and air transport, respectively). The Treaty excludes this kind of transport from the application of the Treaty rules. The Council may enact appropriate provisions (Article 80(2) EC). Liberalisation has been achieved through measures of secondary law that aimed at opening markets and establishing conditions of competition that are compatible with the public service character of many of these forms of transport. In both cases, the Council had enacted secondary legislation, and the Court, reviewing the Commission's decisions pursuant to this legislation, had to decide whether the State measures were compatible with it. In both cases, the Court does not only control the Commission's decisions with regard to secondary law interpreted according to a method of statutory interpretation—which is normally somewhat stricter and more textual than constitutional interpretation—but reads within the secondary law the Treaty rules and the case law related to them. Thus, it carries out a proportionality analysis identical to the analysis that would apply to the Treaty. This is sometimes done regardless of the text of the provision of secondary law.[25]

The problem with such an approach is that the difference between constitutional and secondary law, which is affirmed as a principle, is denied in practice through the interpretation of the norms. The material content of the free movement rules is sometimes read into the legislation. In the end the case law on free movement is applied, not the legislation—and this is quite different from conform interpretation. Thus, the differences between primary and secondary law become blurred. This may have negative effects on legal certainty, as secondary legislation is deemed to be useful because it provides for a more stable framework than that of the provisions of the Treaty.

The more recent judgment in *DaimlerChrysler* presents a different, more rigorous approach. In this case, a German Land had adopted certain measures pursuant to Regulation 259/93, on the shipments of waste.[26] The national court raised the question whether it had to examine the compatibility of the measure only with the Regulation, whose compatibility with the Treaty had been taken for granted, or whether it also had to analyse it under Articles 28–30 EC. The Court held that where a matter is regulated in a harmonised manner at Community level, any national measure relating thereto must be assessed in the light of the provisions of that harmonising measure and not of the Treaty norms which are harmonised (in the case, free movement and environment).[27]

---

[24] Case C–205/99 *Analir* [2001] ECR I–1271; Case C–361/98 *Italy v Commission* [2001] ECR I–385.

[25] Something similar happened in Case C–95/99 *Khalil* [2001] ECR I–7413, a case concerning the social security of refugees and stateless people, in which the interpretation of the Treaty was preferred to the wording of Regulation 1408/71, on the coordination of the social security systems of the Member States.

[26] Council Regulation (EEC) No 259/93 of 1 February 1993 on the supervision and control of shipments of waste within, into and out of the European Community (OJ L 30/1).

[27] Case C–324/99 *DaimlerChrysler* [2001] ECR (not yet published), paras 32–46.

5.5. A COMPARISON WITH STATE ECONOMIC CONSTITUTIONAL LAW

The novel character of Community economic constitutional law comes to light when compared with its State counterparts, which have traditionally been relegated to a secondary plane, devoid of an effective influence on the structure of the economy. In the economic law of the States, legislation is much more important than the constitution. This is reflected, as we have seen in chapter III, in the so-called economic 'neutrality' of the constitution.

In contrast, the economic orientation of the Community Treaty is much more specific than the constitutions of its States with regard to its preferences and the limits it imposes on the economy. It could actually be said that one of its central functions or consequences is that of bridging the economic gaps of the States' constitutions.

The constitution of the Community provides a more stable framework than the States' constitutions, for it has transferred to the Community a number of powers related to economic matters. At the same time, it has limited the exercise of the powers retained by the States, and it has also limited the use of private economic power through fundamental and enforceable legal rules. A strong Community economic constitutional law has taken the place of the weak economic constitutional law of the Member States.

Let us compare, as an example of this difference, the effectiveness of Article 28 EC with that of Article 139(2) of the Spanish Constitution,[28] a remarkably similar provision which is nonetheless seen by both the doctrine and the Constitutional Court as a simple principle, despite its clear, precise and unconditional formulation. Article 139(2) appears as an under-enforced constitutional provision that works most often as a principle of interpretation and quite rarely as a residuary limit to the regulation of trade by the autonomous communities. So far it seems not to create individual constitutional rights that Spanish courts must protect, and it has been only regarded as an 'institutional guarantee'.[29]

The doctrinal attempt to find inspiration in the Community experience for the interpretation of Article 139(2) of the Spanish Constitution has found little actual reflection in the constitutional case law. The Spanish Constitutional Court has affirmed that the constitution posits 'the unity of the national economic order and has as a consequence the existence of a single market. Such market unity presupposes, at least, the unhindered free movement throughout

---

[28] 'No authority shall adopt measures that directly or indirectly hinder the free movement and establishment of persons and the free movement of goods throughout the Spanish territory.' ('Ninguna autoridad podrá adoptar medidas que directa o indirectamente obstaculicen la libertad de circulación y establecimiento de las personas y la libre circulación de bienes en todo el territorio español'.)

[29] E Albertí Rovira, *Autonomía política y unidad económica* (Civitas, Madrid, 1995), 256 *et seq.* See judgments 71/82 (*Jurisprudencia Constitucional*, 1982, vol IV, 401) and 52/88 (*Jurisprudencia Constitucional*, 1988, vol XX, 658) of the Spanish Constitutional Court.

the national territory of goods, capital, services and workers.'[30] The concept of single market, not explicitly stated in the Spanish Constitution, is obviously borrowed from Community law and from the case law of the Court of Justice. The Constitutional Court, however, remains in the uncompromising realm of principles and fails to extract practical consequences from them.

Both Article 139(2) of the Spanish Constitution and Article 120 of the Italian Constitution, while being comparable to the four freedoms, are considered only to enshrine values which are more effectively protected by fundamental rights such as equality or the freedom of trade and profession. The relevant provisions thus have a residual nature vis-à-vis fundamental rights.[31] They limit the powers of the different territorial units of the decentralised State (autonomous communities, regions) to ensure the values and principles reflected in such economic rights, but their construction remains quite narrow.

To illustrate this point let us analyse a concrete case in which the Italian Constitutional Court examined the constitutionality of a Sardinian statute that imposed on holders of concessions to exploit certain mines the obligation to refine the materials in Sardinia. The legislation was attacked by the Italian Prime Minister on the grounds of a breach of Article 41 of the Italian Constitution, according to which private economic initiative is free, and Article 120, which prohibits obstacles to free movement. The Court devoted a single page to Article 120, concluding that the said provision would be applicable only if the conditions for the concession were so hard to meet that there would be no applications for concessions—which would damage the national production of energy.[32]

This interpretation may be compared with the foreseeable position in Community law towards a similar measure taken at national or regional level, which would most probably be declared in breach of Article 28 of the Treaty. It springs from *Aragonesa de Publicidad* and *Ligur Carni* that,

> when a national measure has limited territorial scope because it applies only to a part of the national territory, it cannot escape being categorized as discriminatory or protective for the purposes of the rules of free movement of goods on the ground that it affects both the sale of products from other parts of the national territory and the sale of products imported from other Member States.[33]

The same principle applies to restrictions of exports, as is proved by *Delhaize*.[34] The public security exception successfully pleaded by Ireland in a

[30] Judgment 88/86 (*Jurisprudencia Constitucional*, 1986, vol XV, 368), ground 6: 'la unicidad del orden económico nacional, que trae como consecuencia la existencia de un mercado único. Esta unidad de mercado supone, cuando menos, la libertad de circulación sin traba por todo el territorio nacional de bienes, capitales, servicios y mano de obra.'

[31] For Spain, see E Albertí Rovira, *Autonomía política y unidad económica*, above n 29, *passim*; for Italy see A Pubusa in G Branca (ed) *Commentario della Costituzione. Le regioni, le province, i comuni* (Tomo 1, Art 114–120, Zanichelli, Bologna, 1985) 444, 445.

[32] Judgment 12/63 (*Giurisprudenza Costituzionale*, 1963, 60, 70).

[33] Joined Cases C–277/91, C–318/91 and C–319/91 *Ligur Carni* [1993] ECR 6621, para 37; Joined Cases C–1/90 and C–176/90 *Aragonesa de Publicidad* [1991] ECR I–4179, para 24.

[34] Case 47/90 *Delhaize* [1992] ECR 3669, para 14.

similar case, *Campus Oil*,[35] would not be applicable to the case in hand, as it was based on the need to maintain in operation the only refinery extant in Ireland, an extreme situation clearly distinguishable from the Italian case.

The comparison shows that the structure and reach of the Community constitution is quite different from those of the States. In the Community legal order, fundamental rights have been so far protected as general principles of the law, with the inherent difficulties involved in such a construction, related to the problem of finding those rights in the absence of a single text of reference for their interpretation and application. In Community law, freedom of trade and other liberal fundamental rights have had so far a residuary function. In contrast, the four freedoms, giving the Court firmer textual ground on the Treaty, have a more important role than Community fundamental rights in the protection of values such as the unity of the market and freedom of trade. Fundamental economic rights have, contrariwise to the States constitutional systems, a residual function with regard to the protection of these values. This fact does not make the four freedoms and the competition rules fundamental rights. They protect constitutional values and principles that in other constitutional systems may be protected through fundamental rights. But their structure and aim is quite different from that of fundamental rights.

These differences probably come from the different tasks of these legal orders: creating a market from separate markets in the Community; preserving existing markets in the case of the States. The latter generally constitute integrated markets before the adoption of the constitution. They may include a rule to preserve the unity of the market, but their main intent is not to create it.[36] This economic fact, together with the specific principles and aims of the respective texts, explain and justify the different approach taken towards similar norms in different legal systems.

5.6. ECONOMIC NEUTRALITY OF THE COMMUNITY?

Community economic constitutional law cannot be termed neutral, if any constitutional law may indeed be considered as neutral, because it is more specific than the constitutional laws of its Member States as regards the constitutional determinations of economic structure and process. Indeed, one could say that it is even less neutral.

Some authors have argued that the Treaty 'does not specify *a priori*—any more than does any national constitution of the Member States—where the precise balance between the two poles of "market forces" and "government inter-

---

[35] Case 72/83 *Campus Oil* [1984] ECR 2727.
[36] E Alberti Rovira, *Autonomía política y unidad económica*, above n 31, 276–277, 300.

vention" must lie. Instead, the choice of the desired economic order, in practice, is left to the outcome of discussions essentially political in nature.'[37]

This view is questionable, if only because the range of economic options left to the Community and national public authorities is narrower than that left to State authorities by State constitutions. It suffices to mention the direct consequences of many Treaty provisions (on free movement, State aid . . .) and the indirect consequences of the establishment of the legal framework of the economic and monetary union (the convergence criteria established in Maastricht—Article 121 EC and the Protocol on this provision; the Regulations that embody the stability pact,[38] which drastically limit the behaviour of public powers). Besides, the Community constitution limits the economic behaviour in the private sphere through the competition rules—a dimension that the States normally leave to economic administrative law.

The Treaty enshrines more of a liberal market economic order than of a mixed economy, and its legislative dynamics, because of the constraints inherent in the need to reach an agreement among a growing number of quite disparate Member States, produce an even more liberal regime in practice. Perhaps the mechanism of comitology, with the higher presence of private interests that it sometimes entails, may not be unrelated to this liberal bent of the legislative process. The possible corrections or restrictions to its orientation take place at Community and national level, in accordance with the limits imposed by the Treaty itself, as the Court often holds.[39] The norms on free movement and competition presuppose a market economy, based on the legal institutions of property and contract. Without a market economy in the States there can be no free movement and competition. This is exemplified by the fact that, according to the criteria established by the European Council of Copenhagen of 1993, the candidates to accession have first to secure a market economy in the domestic sphere. Hence free movement and competition are, for the process of European integration, as important as the private law institutions of property and contract are for the liberal market economies.

Can one conflate this corrected market economy with theories of political economy such as classical liberalism and neo-liberalism, and see the Treaty as a legal translation thereof?

Perhaps, but with the important proviso that classical liberalism and neo-liberalism were theories conceived in terms of, and meant to apply to, domestic economic systems. Concerning the international economy, they usually adopted

[37] P VerLoren van Themaat and L W Gormley, 'Prohibiting Restriction of Free Trade within the Community: Articles 30–36 of the EEC Treaty', (1981) *Northwestern Journal of International Law & Business*, 577, 579.

[38] Council Regulation (EC) No 1466/97 of 7 July 1997 on the strengthening of the surveillance of budgetary positions and the surveillance and coordination of economic policies (OJ 1997 L 209/1); Council Regulation (EC) No 1467/97 of 7 July 1997 on speeding up and clarifying the implementation of the excessive deficit procedure (OJ 1997 L 209/6).

[39] See, for example, Case 120/95 *Decker* [1998] ECR I–1831, para 23.

a more pragmatic approach. Razeen Sally has pointed out that for Hume and Smith international order 'must rely on a pragmatic combination of open commerce and a network of alliances and treaties to maintain balance of political power between states; international order cannot rely on a harmony of interests.'[40] This, to be sure, in the absence of normative and institutional structures aimed at finding such harmony, through the formulation of a common interest within a stable constitutional framework. Economic neo-liberal thought was, in general, opposed to a regional system of economic integration including hard rules and institutions in charge of their enforcement such as the European Community. German ordoliberals limited economic liberalism to the nation state, proposing some sort of soft arrangement for the international and European economic order in the form of a free trade area. They thought that a customs union went too far.[41]

In contrast, the project of European integration appears as a feast of social engineering and public intervention—only the content, not the form, of the intervention has a liberal bent. This new intervention is aimed at opening, liberalising and regulating the markets it merges together. It is a mixture of constitutional and legislative elements—the fruit of a peculiar decision-making process. A major innovation of European integration may be thus found in having taken a blend of liberalism and constitutionalism to the international sphere.

From an historical perspective, the ECSC and Euratom Treaties were still heavily influenced by French *dirigisme*, whereas the economic orientation of the Community Treaty clearly is more liberal. At present, these preferences appear constitutionalised in the Maastricht version of Article 4 EC, quoted above, and the fundamental principle of *an open market economy with free competition*.

In previous sections of this chapter we have referred to the argument according to which the Community objectives concerning competition and free movement are just two among other objectives and do not have a more prominent place in the system of the Treaty. This question remains contentious, for these objectives are, at least for the Community, more important than others—perhaps because of their specific Community nature, whereas in other fields the action of the Community is only complementary to that of the States. But even leaving this issue undecided, it remains that competition and free movement are ensured through directly applicable Treaty provisions, at the highest level of the hierarchy of legal sources in Community law, while the other ends are only announced in the Treaty by provisions conferring competence on the European institutions in order to pursue them through secondary legislation. Such legislation, as we have seen, has to respect the constitutional rules of the internal market and competition, to which the Community legislator is itself bound.[42] The

---

[40] R Sally, *Classical Liberalism and International Economic Order* (Routledge, London, 1998), 57.

[41] *Ibid*, 131, 144.

[42] See, for example, Joined Cases C–363/93 and C–407 to C–411/93 *Lancry* [1994] ECR I–3957.

issue of the hierarchy of the objectives and policies of the Community is distinct from the issue of the hierarchy of the provisions fleshing out such policies, which reflect a more clear economic orientation.

Besides, the exceptions to the free movement and competition rules, like that established in Article 30, are only *exceptions*, and have traditionally been construed narrowly—although the extension of the available grounds of justification with *Cassis de Dijon* constitutes an extensive interpretation of the exceptions. The special rule in Article 86 (services of general economic interest) may deserve a less restrictive interpretation, but its objective scope of application is also narrowly defined.

Some have seen the Treaty of Maastricht as adopting a mixed economy system by '[reinforcing] pre-existing interventionist elements and [creating] new forms and mechanisms for public intervention.'[43] The Treaty of Amsterdam has also been perceived as effecting a 're-balancing of the Community economic model.'[44] This has not been said of the Nice Treaty, probably because it has not added to the Community competence.

These views are partly right, but they neglect again the fact that those policies added in Maastricht and Amsterdam (enabling provisions on environment, industrial policy, etc.) are not constitutionalised through directly effective norms, but through norms that merely announce principles and confer powers on the Community institutions. Article 152(4)(c) EC, for example, empowers the Council to enact 'incentive measures designed to protect and improve human health, *excluding any harmonisation of the laws and regulations of the Member States.*' This sort of limitation is quite common in the non-economic aspects of the Community competence (see, as another example, Article 129 EC, which excludes harmonisation of State law on employment).

Thus, although the Maastricht and Amsterdam Treaties may have slightly corrected it, the neo-liberal economic ethos of the Community, embodied in the constitutional status of free movement and competition—which, again, is not just an interpretive option but a normative datum—remains at the heart of its legal system. Besides, the actual rebalance of the Community economic model—including legislation—would probably require certain changes in the institutional and decision-making process. Without them, any addition to the competence of the Community may be illusory in practice, for the legislative process drives legislation in a given direction.

A good example may be found in *Germany v Council* (the tobacco advertisement case), to which we have referred in chapter 4. Germany was pleading for the annulment of the tobacco advertising Directive,[45] arguing that the Community

[43] M Poiares Maduro, *We the Court* (Hart, Oxford, 1998), 160.

[44] F Dehousse, 'Les résultats de la Conférence intergouvernamentale' in *Cahiers du CRISP* 1997 No 1565–1566, 4: 'un rééquilibrage du modèle économique communautaire.'

[45] Directive 98/43/EC of the European Parliament and of the Council of 6 July 1998 on the approximation of the laws, regulations and administrative provisions of the Member States relating to the advertising and sponsorship of tobacco products (OJ L 213/9).

lacked the competence to adopt an almost complete prohibition of such advertising. The Directive had been adopted on the basis of Article 95 EC (internal market), whereas the basis relating to human health (Article 152 EC) excludes any harmonisation of State legislation regarding human health (note that both legal bases were added after the Single European Act, being part of the so-called period of economic 're-balancing' of the Treaty). One may have thought, nonetheless, that Article 95 gave the Community a general regulatory competence that could offset, through secondary legislation, the liberal bent of the free movement and competition rules.

The Court, following Advocate General Fennelly, did not follow this interpretation. Secondary legislation adopted through Article 95 partakes, as it were, the general spirit of free movement and competition. It can also go beyond them, inasmuch as, while it entrenches the internal market and regulates it, it may also pursue other parallel objectives. But it cannot go against them and be used for other general purposes unrelated to the internal market. Thus, according to the Court, Articles 3(1)(c) and 14,

> read together, make it clear that the measures referred to in Article [95] of the Treaty are intended to improve the conditions for the establishment and functioning of the internal market. To construe that article as meaning that it vests in the Community legislature a general power to regulate the internal market would not only be contrary to the express wording of the provisions cited above but would also be incompatible with the principle embodied in Article [5] of the EC Treaty that the powers of the Community are limited to those specifically conferred to it.[46]

The Court bases its annulment of the Directive on the intrinsic limits of Article 95. The limits of Community competence regarding public health and their interaction with Article 95 are only recalled as an *obiter dictum*.[46a]

In sum, Community law imposes stronger and more effective constitutional constraints on economic structure and process than national constitutional law. The liberal bent of the Community constitution is slightly corrected if read in unison with other Community policies and national constitutions with which it forms the comprehensive constitution of the European polity. In spite of these various corrections, the influence of the liberal Community constitution over the common European constitution remains remarkable. This is due to the fundamental nature of the free movement and competition rules in the Community legal order, to the articulation of the relationship between Community law and State law through the supremacy principle, and to the limited nature of the Community powers and institutional means to pursue ends of a social character.

---

[46] Case C–376/98 *Germany v Council* [2000] ECR I–8419, para 83; Opinion Fennelly, para 83.
[46a] *Ibid*, paras 77–79.

5.7. THE UNCERTAIN FUTURE

The perspective of a restructuring and simplification of the Treaties coupled with the possible incorporation of the charter of fundamental human rights—solemnly proclaimed in Nice but for the time being of an uncertain legal nature—may constitute a very positive development from the point of view of the progressive development and consolidation of the constitutional features of the Community legal order, but it may also have important consequences for the Community economic constitutional law as it stands at present. Everything depends on how that restructuring and simplification is made, and what is one with the charter.

This perspective has been confirmed. As we have seen, the 'Declaration on the future of the Union' annexed to the Nice Treaty, signed on 26 February 2001, specifically calls for a debate on these issues. The Laeken declaration of 15 December 2001 explicitly raises the debate about the simplification and reorganisation of the Treaties as a constitutional debate.[47] The Convention on the future of the European Union will surely deal with this issue.

The debate launched in Nice may produce various results. Regarding the economic constitutional law of the Community, these developments could underestimate—as happened with previous proposals—the value of the economic constitutional rights enshrined in the Treaty and developed by a rich body of case law. The free movement and competition rules could be played down to the status of infra-constitutional norms open to revision through a procedure simpler than that established for constitutional amendments. This would entail a radical change in the constitutional law of the Community.

The Spinelli project (1984) already introduced this possibility. Writing in 1986, its commentators noted that the project,

> takes as its starting point the 'Community patrimony', the *acquis communautaire*. Such provisions of the Community Treaties, of Community legislation and of international agreements as are not amended or replaced by the Union Treaty itself remain in force until such time as they are modified under the procedures laid down in the Treaty. While the form is new, much of the substance is retained.[48]

---

[47] Laeken declaration on the future of the European Union, point II (SN 273/01): 'Should a distinction be made between a basic treaty and the other treaty provisions? Should this distinction involve separating the texts? Could this lead to a distinction between the amendment and ratification procedures for the basic treaty and for the other treaty provisions? Thought would also have to be given to whether the Charter of Fundamental Rights should be included in the basic treaty and to whether the European Community should accede to the European Convention on Human Rights. The question ultimately arises as to whether this simplification and reorganisation might not lead in the long run to the adoption of a constitutional text in the Union. What might the basic features of such a constitution be? The values which the Union cherishes, the fundamental rights and obligations of its citizens, the relationship between Member States in the Union?'

[48] F Capotorti *et al The European Union Treaty* (Clarendon Press, Oxford, 1986), 17 (including the text of the draft Treaty).

But the form, the structure of a normative group, has a very important influence on the substance as well. The Spinelli project may have retained the *acquis* materially, but it introduced a new hierarchical ordering of Community primary law that would not have been without consequence for the interpretation and application of certain provisions, even if their wording remained untouched.

Article 7(2) of the draft European Union Treaty established that,

[t]he provisions of the treaties establishing the European Communities and of the conventions and protocols relating thereto which concern their objectives and scope and which are not explicitly or implicitly amended by this Treaty, shall constitute part of the law of the Union. They may only be amended in accordance with the procedure for revision laid down in Article 84 of this Treaty.

According to Article 7(3),

[t]he other provisions of the treaties, conventions and protocols referred to above shall also constitute part of the law of the Union, in so far as they are not incompatible with this Treaty. They may only be amended by the procedure for organic laws laid down in Article 38 of this Treaty.

As regards the distinction between paragraphs 2 and 3, the commentators recognised at the time that it may 'not always [. . .] be readily apparent which provisions of the Community treaties fall into each category.'[49] It seems to me clear, however, that both the free movement and the competition rules would not have been among the constitutional norms. Hence they would have been subject to their compatibility with higher norms and to a simpler amendment procedure.

This transformation, which modifies the Community economic model (even if 'the substance is retained'), is completed in the field of competence. The only reference to free movement and competition was to be found in provisions that vested powers in the Community institutions but were not directly applicable. According to Article 47,

1. The Union shall have exclusive competence to complete, safeguard and develop the free movement of persons, services, goods and capital within its territory; it shall have exclusive competence for trade between the Member States.

As regards competition, Article 48 provided that 'The Union shall have competence to complete and develop competition policy at the level of the union [. . .].'

Similar proposals were made by the Herman report that led to the Parliament's project for a European Constitution (1994),[50] the report about the institutional implications of enlargement,[51] and a report of the Robert Schuman Centre at the European University Institute of Florence.[52]

---

[49]   F Capotorti *et al The European Union Treaty* (Clarendon Press, Oxford, 1986), 53.

[50]   OJ 1994 C 61/155, Articles 8 and 44.

[51]   R Von Weizsäcker *et alii*, *The Institutional Implications of Enlargement*, Report presented to the European Commission on 18 October 1999, published in *Europe*, 20 October 1999, Documents No 2159, 3.2.

[52]   European Parliament, *Quelle charte constitutionnelle pour l'Union européenne?*, POLI 105 FR, 05–1999, 56–59.

These proposals would 'deconstitutionalise' both the competition and the free movement rules (the heart of the economic constitutional law of the Community), probably entailing a change in the way in which they would be interpreted and applied. Such provisions would be subject to a simpler amendment procedure.

This could be the desired effect of the proposed rearrangement of the legal sources, but it may also be a 'collateral' effect whose consequences have not been sufficiently pondered. It is true that 'not all the provisions included in primary law deserve the qualification of "constitutional law".'[53] The desirable reorganisation of the Treaty, with a view to achieving a simple, comprehensive and understandable constitutional text, will have to select which provisions are to be constitutional. Some would take—and indeed are taking—the quite radical route of expelling from the constitutional level all of Part Three of the Treaty on Community Policies.[54]

In contrast with these views, it seems that the economic freedoms and the basic competition rules, are an original contribution of Community law to contemporary economic constitutionalism and one of the keys of the Community's success in carrying out its central objectives. This is due to the fact that such provisions bind the States and the Community also in the 'weak' moments of the Community political process, thus constituting a stable framework for this process. From this perspective, it may perhaps be important to maintain these rules at the highest level of the hierarchy of Community legal sources. It is this position that has given them their importance for Community law. Their 'deconstitutionalisation' could bring forth a fragmentation of the single market which may be brought about by national or even Community policies, justified by higher principles. This economic fragmentation may in turn bring a degree of political fragmentation: some sort of reverse spill-over.

In any case, no one seems to seriously argue for a revision or downgrading of such rules, which have remained untouched for decades, and constitute the most solid and time-resistant part of the Treaty. As Moravcsik and Nicolaïdis have pointed out, '[t]he one point of agreement at Amsterdam, from the most Eurosceptical government to the most federalist, was the sanctity of provisions guaranteeing free trade in goods and services.'[55] The same could be said of the competition rules. The Nice Treaty does not change this view, but one will have to wait to see the results of the process of constitutional reform launched in Nice to know the fate of the competition and free movement rules. So far, the existing consensus around competition and free movement is also found in the Community requirements to establish closer cooperation between some

---

[53] J Gerkrath, *L'émergence d'un droit constitutionnel pour l'Europe*, (Éditions de l'Université de Bruxelles, Brussels, 1997) 302: 'l'ensemble des articles appartenant au droit originaire ne mérite pas la qualification de "droit constitutionnel".'

[54] *Ibid*, 319.

[55] A Moravcsik and K Nicolaïdis, 'Keynote Article: Federal Ideals and Constitutional Realities in the Treaty of Amsterdam', (1998) 36 *Journal of Common Market Studies*, Annual Review, 13, 36.

Member States. One of the five conditions to do so is that the cooperation proposed 'does not constitute a discrimination or a restriction of trade between Member States and does not distort the conditions of competition between the latter' (Article 11(1)(e) EC).

Finally, a declaration of preservation of the *acquis communautaire* would not suffice for the purpose of maintaining the constitutional character of the said provisions. The effects of the proposed structural changes in the interpretation of the relevant norms could not be nullified by a simple declaration. The interpreter cannot be blinded to the structure of the law. To blind the interpreter to structural changes with such a declaration would render the interpretation of the norms rather poor, creating more problems than it would solve.

The new Florentine report on the reorganisation of the Treaties, prepared this time for the Prodi Commission, has markedly changed with respect to its previous and other traditional proposals. The clauses 22–26 and 29 of the draft *Basic Treaty of the European Union* include the four freedoms among the highest norms of the legal order and constitutionalise by express reference the existence of the competition rules (clause 29: 'there shall be common rules on competition applying to undertakings and concerning aids granted by states, *in accordance with* Articles 81 to 89 of the Treaty establishing the European Community.')

Nonetheless, a shorter version of the Treaty would not include these provisions. The report does not explain the reasons justifying the change with respect to the previous report. It expresses a vague preference for the long version, while remaining silent about the structural and interpretive differences between both options.[56]

This is, to be sure, not only a legal debate about the constitutional structure of the Community, but also and perhaps mainly a political debate about the future economic shape of the European Union. So far, all the proposals have been focused on formal or institutional changes. The substantive transformations that they may entail are not usually discussed. The debate on other possible direct and desired changes—not as indirect consequence of structural or institutional changes—in the economic orientation of the Community is simply not taking place.

---

[56] See European University Institute, *Basic Treaty of the European Union: Draft; A Basic Treaty for the European Union: A Study of the Reorganisation of the Treaties* (European Communities, Italy, 2000), 6–7.

6

Competition and Free Movement

COMPETITION AND FREE movement constitute, together with economic and monetary union and the common commercial policy, the basic layer of the economic constitutional law of the European Community. This chapter surveys the legal nature, similarities and differences between both normative groups. Chapters 8 and 9 are devoted to the problems at the heart of the relationship among them: the eventual application of the free movement rules in the private sphere and of the competition rules to State action.

In both cases we are faced with a gap in the circle of addressees of the relevant norm. The usual solutions given by the Court have opted for an objective interpretation of the norms, in which the nature of the activity becomes decisive, irrespective of the actor. While this solution has the advantage of enhancing the effectiveness of Community law and bridging the gap in hand, it also blurs the line between the respective personal scopes of free movement and competition. This may be problematic for the legal certainty of both States and undertakings, for they may not know the extent of their responsibilities under both sets of rules. Besides, both have different criteria of application and legal consequences. We shall see, especially in chapter 8, how these risks have been avoided by the Court through a formalistic turn in the case law, which has reduced the reach of the initial extension. In spite of these efforts, free movement and competition appear in the current state of the law as partly overlapping normative groups that may sometimes be used to tackle similar problems.

According to VerLoren van Themaat, the importance of this issue lies in that it 'turns out to be not only a fundamental question about the [EC] Treaty provisions concerning the market economy, but mainly a question about the limits of the integration goals of the [EC] Treaty as principles of interpretation.'[1] Thus, the question of the interaction between competition and free movement is important to set the said constitutional limits and, more generally, to reflect on the limits of teleological interpretation applied to the Community constitutional materials.

In addition to the general comparison between both sets of norms, other issues will be dealt with in this chapter. Section 2 dwells on the complementary

---

[1] P VerLoren van Themaat, 'Zum Verhältnis zwischen Artikel 30 und Artikel 85 EWG-Vertrag', in H Gützlen *et al* (eds) *Wettbewerb im Wandel: Eberhard Günther zum 65. Geburtstag* (Nomos, Baden-Baden, 1976) 373, 387: 'nicht nur eine Grundsatzfrage der marktwirtschaftlichen Grundsätze es EWG-Vertrages, sondern vor allem eine Frage der Grenzen der Integrationsziele im EWG-Vertrag als Auslegungsgrundsatz.'

character of free movement and competition. In the following chapters, the free movement rules will be treated as a unit. As a justification, I shall briefly refer in section 3 to the convergence of economic freedoms of the Treaty towards a common interpretation. Free movement of workers, an economic freedom whose social element has become predominant, receives a special consideration in section 4.

The approach to the competition rules will be constitutional in the hard sense, taking seriously their contribution to the preservation of liberty through the control of private economic power.[2] The so-called 'modernisation' in the implementation of the competition rules will be analysed from a constitutional perspective in section 5. To finish the chapter, certain procedural issues concerning preliminary rulings that stand at the origin of the blurring between free movement and competition will be examined.

6.1. THE COMPLEMENTARY CHARACTER OF COMPETITION AND FREE MOVEMENT

Once it is established that free movement and competition constitute the kernel of the economic constitutional law of the Community, one may wonder about how these two sets of provisions co-exist. Is there any tension between their respective aims? Are they really complementary?

Firstly, they should not be seen as isolated and independent groups of norms, but rather as inextricably linked in a functional sense. This connection is clear in the historical sources. The Spaak report, which paved the way for the Treaty of Rome, makes quite clear that the inclusion of competition rules was aimed at preventing private undertakings from re-erecting the barriers to trade that would fall as a consequence of the free movement rules.[3]

Secondly, both have a constitutional rank in the Community legal order and contribute, in the public and private spheres, to the creation and maintenance of a single competitive market, one of the central objectives of the Community.

The basic differences between them are also obvious. The *de minimis* threshold, according to which the competition rules are only applicable when the economic effects of the relevant corporate behaviour are sufficiently appreciable in quantitative terms, does not operate in the field of free movement. Any effect on Community trade, even if it is insignificant or merely potential, is enough to trigger the application of the free movement rules—this is traditionally justified by the potentially pervasive effect on trade of any public measure.

---

[2] For a constitutional approach to the competition rules, see G Amato, *Antitrust and the Bounds of Power* (Hart, Oxford, 1999) 1–4, 109, 113 (emphasising the intimate connection between political and economic freedom, and arguing against a one-dimensional conception of efficiency).

[3] Spaak Report, 16: 'Des règles de concurrence qui s'imposent aux entreprises sont donc nécessaires pour éviter que des doubles prix aient le même effet que des droits de douane, qu'un dumping mette en danger des productions économiquement saines, que la répartition des marchés se substitue à leur cloisonnement.'

Besides, the competition rules may have extraterritorial effects, whereas the free movement rules are confined to intra-Community trade (its external aspects having a specific normative treatment in the Treaty with the common commercial policy, that establishes some principles and confers powers on the institutions for their application and development).

Another important difference is due to the lack of direct effect of Article 81(3) EC. The provisions on free movement are applicable by national courts as a whole (prohibition and exceptions). Articles 81(1) and (2) and 82 EC are also applicable by national courts (prohibitions). However, Regulation 17/62, on the application of the competition rules, entrusts the Commission with an exclusive power to give exemptions pursuant to Article 81(3) EC. The Commission's proposal on the modernisation of the application of the competition rules, to which we shall come back later in this chapter, could change the situation, allowing national courts and competition authorities to apply Article 81(3) EC. But for the time being the application of this provision is administrative in nature, in contrast with other constitutional provisions which are directly applicable. The same is true of most parts of the rules on State aid, whose application is also entrusted to the Commission.

The most important difference among competition and free movement is to be found in their respective personal scopes of application, to which the following chapters are devoted. While competition concerns undertakings, the free movement rules are addressed to the States. These clear-cut circles of addressees would in principle prevent any conflict or overlapping among them. But the dichotomy can present some gaps, some of which may detract from the effectiveness of the provisions from the perspective of their aim of maintaining an integrated and competitive market.

Such gaps may take the following forms: (i) private conduct hindering free movement; (ii) public behaviour negatively affecting competition; and (iii) behaviour of economic actors which are not clearly public nor private, or mixed situations in which different actors intervene, and which present either a free movement or a competition problem, or both.

To bridge these gaps the Court elaborated the two lines of case law that Michel Waelbroeck termed the 'privatisation' of the free movement rules and the 'publicisation' of the competition rules.[4] The consequences are the following: the free movement rules would not be interpreted as being simply directed to the States; the competition norms addressed to undertakings (Articles 81–82 EC), on the other hand, would not be limited to prohibiting corporate anti-competitive behaviour. The focus thus shifted from the addressees to the concrete conducts caught by each set of rules and the values protected thereby.

In spite of certain problems, the change of focus is wholly justified. Private actors may have an interest in fragmenting markets in order to obtain higher

---

[4] M Waelbroeck, 'Les rapports entre les règles sur la libre circulation des marchandises et les règles de concurrence applicables aux entreprises dans la CEE', in F Capotorti *et al* (eds) *Liber Amicorum Pescatore* (Nomos, Baden-Baden, 1987) 781.

profits, to the detriment of consumers. States may limit competition without justification with a view to protecting certain undertakings, regardless of their
nationality. The economy also presents mixed situations in which the public
and private actors or elements of an actor are not easily distinguishable. An
excessive formalism in the personal scopes of application of both sets of norms
thus becomes difficult, if not totally unworkable, in practice.

Even so, the subjective element should not be forgotten. The public and private spheres should not be assimilated to each other. The public/private divide
has deep roots in the functions and legitimacy of both spheres. Even if the divide
has become blurred, the qualification of the actor as public or private may be an
important criterion in order not to impose excessive obligations on economic
operators with regard to the field of free movement rules. Conversely, the democratic legitimacy of certain anticompetitive measures should be taken into
account.

In filling the gaps between free movement and competition one may take a
maximalist approach, arguing that competition and free movement have an
'eventual unity of purpose [that] must lead to the conclusion that they should be
viewed as parts of a coherent whole.'[5] This sort of reasoning persuaded Pierre
Pescatore to fill the gaps he saw in the Treaty. He argued that States are bound
not to frustrate the purpose of the competition rules and '[p]rivate operators are
[. . .] subject to the rules on free movement which not only confer rights, but also
impose obligations on them.'[6]

An opposed minimalist position is taken by Giuliano Marenco, for whom 'the
asymmetries denounced by Judge Pescatore are deliberate and justified and
[. . .] his gap-closing effort to apply antitrust and free movement provisions
indiscriminately to both states and enterprises is therefore neither necessary nor
warranted.'[7] Also on systematic grounds, René Joliet was no less in favour of
keeping free movement and competition within separate spheres according to
their addressees.[8]

Since all these authors base their views on systemic grounds, they clearly
understand the system of the Treaty and the aims of the relevant provisions in
disparate and conflicting ways. These basic positions find expression, as we will
see, in a range of issues concerning the interaction between competition and free
movement.

However, things are not so simple as to conclude either for the teleological
unity of both sets of norms or for their normative independence. Articles 81–82

---

[5] L W Gormley, *Prohibiting Restrictions on Trade within the EEC* (North Holland, Amsterdam, 1985) 233.

[6] P Pescatore, 'Public and Private Aspects of Community Competition Law', in B Bawk (ed) *US and Common Market Antitrust Policies: 1986 Corporate Law Institute* (1987) 428.

[7] G Marenco, 'Competition Between National Economies and Competition Between Businesses—A Response to Judge Pescatore', (1987) *Fordham International Law Journal*, 420, 424.

[8] See R Joliet with D T Keeling, 'Trade Mark Law and the Free Movement of Goods: The Overruling of the Judgment in *Hag I*', (1991) *International Review of Industrial Property and Copyright Law* (IIC), 303, 313.

do not mainly prohibit agreements hindering intra-Community trade, but only those preventing, restricting or distorting competition. Many of the latter may also hinder intra-Community trade incidentally, but such is not the central element of the prohibition contained in the competition rules. The criterion of 'affectation of trade' was usually construed in a similar way as the concept of measures of equivalent effect to quantitative restrictions, but they should not be confused, for, although they are similar, they perform quite different functions. In the field of free movement, this criterion refers to 'all trading rules enacted by Member States which are capable of hindering, directly or indirectly, actually or potentially, intra-Community trade'.[9] This definition has to be compared with the previous definition in *Consten & Grundig* regarding the concept of affectation of trade in the context of Article 81 EC. In this context, the Court has to determine 'whether the agreement is capable of constituting a threat, either direct or indirect, actual or potential, to freedom of trade between Member States in a manner which might harm the attainment of the objectives of a single market between States.'[10] In the context of Article 81 EC, this definition is meant to establish the jurisdictional limit between the application of the Community competition rules and those of the States.[11] In the field of free movement, the definition is the objective element that triggers the effects of the prohibition in Article 28 EC. Thus, the apparent similarities between both sets of norms can be misleading.

The personal scope of application of the competition rules refers to the concept of 'undertaking'; a broad concept indeed, but narrower than the private sphere (as opposed to a public sphere—composed of States and emanations thereof—whose actions fall under the free movement rules). Thus, certain private entities that are not undertakings may escape both sets of rules altogether. The competition rules do not cover, for instance, trade unions or consumers' organisations. But these organisations have an important presence in economic life and may boycott certain products, provoke private protectionism or distort competition. The asymmetry, which according to Marenco would be due to the drafters of the Treaty, may not be satisfactory from a normative perspective.

On the other hand, binding individuals as such to the free movement rules would perhaps be inefficient in economic terms, implying an excessive restriction of their commercial freedom, and an exaggerated increase of the transaction costs they have to bear for minor economic transactions. Similarly, binding States to the competition rules without any qualification may sometimes overlook the democratic legitimacy of some State organs to pursue policies which may require anticompetitive measures. Any solution to the problem

---

[9] Case 8/74 *Dassonville* [1974] ECR 837, para 5.
[10] Joined Cases 56 & 58/64 *Consten & Grundig* [1966] ECR 299, 341.
[11] *Ibid*: 'the concept of an agreement "which may affect trade between Member States" is intended to define, in the law governing cartels, the boundary between the areas respectively covered by Community law and national law.'

should be found in a principled middle way between the indiscriminate enlargement of the respective personal scopes of application and the formalistic position that maintains a rigid public/private distinction.

Both extreme positions can actually be found in the case-law. In *Van den Haar*, a case in which the national court asked whether the criteria used regarding the free movement rules and the competition rules were similar, the Court held that,

> Article [81] of the Treaty belongs to the rules on competition which are *addressed to undertakings and associations of undertakings* and which are intended to maintain effective competition in the common market. [. . .] Article [28], on the other hand, belongs to the rules which seek to ensure the free movement of goods and, to that end, to eliminate *measures taken by Member States* which might in any way impede such free movement.[12]

The Court went on to say that the *de minimis* rule did not apply in the context of the free movement of goods, eventually concluding that both sets of rules pursue different aims.[13]

A somewhat different statement may be found in *Leclerc*, decided one year later:

> Articles 2 and 3 of the Treaty set out to establish a market characterized by the free movement of goods where the terms of competition are not distorted. That objective is secured *inter alia* by Article [28] *et seq.* prohibiting restrictions on intra-Community trade, to which reference was made during the proceedings before the Court, and by Article [81] *et seq.* on the rules on competition.[14]

Both normative groups are now seen as pursuing the same aim, which simultaneously includes free trade and competition.[15]

Beyond these positions, competition and free movement should be seen neither as convergent nor as divergent sets of norms with regard to their aims. They are rather complementary, and this entails a tension between the rules themselves (scope of application, substantial content, etc.) and between the goals they pursue. The main tension is that between their common objective (an open and competitive market) and those more precise aims which are particular of each normative group.[16] Besides the common objective, both sets of rules have other objectives which are not completely harmonious (for example, economic efficiency writ short, for the competition rules, and the defence of interests not represented in the political processes of particular Member States, in the case of

---

[12] Joined Cases 177 & 178/82 *Van de Haar* [1984] ECR 1797, paras 11–12.

[13] *Ibid*, paras 13–14.

[14] Case 229/83 *Leclerc* [1985] ECR 1, para 9.

[15] See M López Escudero, 'Intervencionismo estatal y Derecho comunitario de la competencia en la jurisprudencia del TJCE', (1989) *Revista de instituciones europeas*, 725, 727.

[16] B E Hawk, 'The American (Anti-trust) Revolution: Lessons for the EEC?', (1988) *European Competition Law Review*, 33, 56, refers to 'the tension between the market integration goal and the more traditional "competition" goals many of which the EEC and United States share' as 'one of the most, if not the most, important issues facing the EEC'

the free movement rules). In practice, the creation of a single market may negatively affect national competition which may not be automatically replaced by Community competition and thus lead to a temporary decrease in competition in certain markets. Finding the appropriate size of the firm in the new competitive conditions of the single market may take time and competition may be distorted until the structure of the economy adapts to the new framework.

Sometimes the objectives of free movement conflict with those of competition. Thus, the overruling of *Hag I* in *Hag II* can be seen as a change in the relative weight given to free movement and the protection of trade mark rights as an essential element of competition. In the first case, free movement was deemed more important than trade mark rights and competition. The Court held that:

> one cannot allow the holder of a trade mark to rely upon the exclusiveness of a trade mark right—which may be the consequence of the territorial limitation of national legislations—with a view to prohibiting the marketing in a Member State of goods legally produced in another Member State under an identical trade mark having the same origin; such a prohibition which would legitimize the isolation of national markets, would collide with one of the essential objects of the treaty, which is to unite national markets in a single market.[17]

In the second case, following the proposal of overruling made by Advocate General Jacobs, who had highlighted that trade marks constitute the basis of much competition in the market,[18] the Court gave more weight to the protection of the trade mark as an 'an essential element in the system of undistorted competition which the Treaty seeks to establish and maintain'. The Court concluded that Articles 28–30 EC,

> do not preclude national legislation from allowing an undertaking which is the proprietor of a trade mark in a Member State to oppose the importation from another Member State of similar goods lawfully bearing in the latter State an identical trade mark or one which is liable to be confused with the protected mark [. . .].[19]

This shows again that the relationship between competition and free movement, despite their complementary character, is not always harmonious.

6.2. A COMMON APPROACH TO THE FREE MOVEMENT RULES

The free movement provisions are treated throughout this enquiry as a coherent whole, instead of as separate legal rules, in the wake of the convergence in their interpretation by the Court. In this section, I shall be discussing this convergence, and some of the limits thereof.

---

[17] Case 192/73 *Hag I* [1974] ECR 731, paras 12–13.
[18] Case C–10/89 *Hag II* [1990] ECR I–3711, paras 16–19 of the Opinion.
[19] *Ibid*, paras 13 and 20.

This issue provokes diverse reactions in the literature. In spite of the gradual convergence in the application of the free movement rules, some still find 'considerable differences' among them,[20] arguing that the alleged 'unification' springs from 'a superficial reading of the case-law.'[21]

In contrast to these readings of the case law, it can hardly be denied that the Court has attempted to elaborate a 'uniform interpretation of the free movement rules' reflected in a test 'common to all fundamental freedoms of the EC Treaty.'[22]

This process started in the mid 1970s, with the attribution of direct effect to all the free movement rules—in the case of capital, for reasons related to its specificity, direct effect was not recognised until 1995, after the Maastricht amendments.[23] This recognition of direct effect was not hampered by the different texts presented by the free movement rules.

Direct effect brought more and more cases to the Court, stressing the judicial (constitutional) application of these norms, over their legislative development.

The next step was the generalisation of the *Dassonville* and *Cassis de Dijon*[24] tests. The free movement rules are interpreted as prohibitions of measures restrictive of trade, regardless of their discriminatory character. This development took place even in the presence of an express reference to discrimination in the text of the relevant provision. Mandatory requirements or overriding reasons of public interest were added to open the possibility of justification of such restrictive indistinctly applicable measures.[25] Such requirements were added to those already existing in the Treaty, such as those in Article 30 EC, completing them. This case law enlarges the Court's review of State measures: more and more measures fall under the free movement rules. At the same time, more measures can be justified on public interest grounds.

The *Keck* judgment[26] can be interpreted as a fracture or discontinuity in this process of convergence. This 1993 decision refocused the interpretation of Article 28 EC (free movement of goods). Its relevance for the other freedoms and even its own health in the field of goods are contentious matters.

---

[20] V Hatzopoulos, 'Recent Developments of the Case Law of the ECJ in the Field of Services', (2000) *Common Market Law Review*, 43, 65.

[21] D Martin, ' "Discriminations", "entraves" et "raisons impérieuses" dans le Traité CE : trois concepts en quête d'identité', (1998) *Cahiers de droit européen*, 261: 'une lecture superficielle de la jurisprudence.'

[22] M Poiares Maduro, *We the Court* (Hart, Oxford, 1998) 101.

[23] Goods: Article 25 [12]: Case 26/62 *Van Gend en Loos* [1963] ECR 1; Article 28 [30]: Case 74/76 *Iannelli* [1977] ECR 557; Article 29 [34]: Case 53/76 *Bouhelier* [1977] ECR 197; workers: Case 167/73 *Commission v France* [1974] ECR 359; establishment: Case 2/74 *Reyners* [1974] ECR 631; services: Case 33/74 *Van Binsbergen* [1974] ECR 1299; capital and payments: Joined Cases C–163, 165 & 250/94 *Sanz de Lera* [1995] ECR I–4821.

[24] Case 8/74 *Dassonville* [1974] ECR 837; Case 120/78 *Cassis de Dijon* [1979] ECR 649.

[25] Case C–76/90 *Säger* [1991] ECR I–4221 (services); Case C–55/94 *Gebhard* [1995] ECR I–4165 (establishment); Cases C–415/93 *Bosman* [1995] ECR I–4921 and C–190/98 *Graf* [2000] ECR I–493, para 18 (workers); regarding capital, see the Opinion of Advocate General Léger in Case C–439/97 *Sandoz* [1999] ECR I–7041, paras 38 *et seq.*

[26] Joined Cases C–267 & C–268/91 *Keck and Mithouard* [1993] ECR I–6097.

This precedent has usually been avoided by the Court in the context of the other freedoms, even when the parties have invoked it. The substantial extension of *Keck* to the other economic freedoms has been avoided in fact through the flexible application of the alternative 'market access' criterion—which, curiously, is also present in *Keck*. Formally, nonetheless, the door has been left open for its possible future application in the context of the other freedoms.

This is clear in the textual analysis of judgments such as *Bosman* and *Alpine Investments*. In both the Court does not apply *Keck* to the case in hand, but it does not do so by holding that *Keck* is not pertinent. In both cases, the *Keck* jurisprudence is put forward and then the Court explains why the fact that access to market is directly impaired means that the conditions for the application of *Keck* are not met, so that the measures in hand could not be considered as 'selling arrangements'.[27] This could mean that the Court implicitly accepts the relevance of *Keck* to the other freedoms, but focuses instead on the previous requirement that State measures do not affect access to market (the clearest form of restriction), something which is also the wording of *Keck*, as has been pointed out.[28] The interesting development in the field is that the criterion of market access appeared in *Keck* as a consequence of the conditions established in paragraph 16.[29] Now the market access criterion is used as an independent condition that is applied before or to the exclusion of the test in paragraph 16 of *Keck*. The autonomy of this criterion appears with clarity in *Gourmet International*:

> according to paragraph 17 of its judgment in Keck and Mithouard, if national provisions restricting or prohibiting certain selling arrangements are to avoid being caught by Article [28] of the Treaty, they must not be of such a kind as to prevent access to the market by products from another Member State or to impede access any more than they impede the access of domestic products.[30]

In this context, there seems to be no major impediment to extending *Keck* to the other freedoms. To be sure, the distinction in *Keck* between certain selling arrangements and product characteristics, which is hardly applicable beyond

---

[27] See Cases C–415/93 *Bosman* [1995] ECR I–4921, para 103: 'the rules in issue in the main proceedings [. . .] directly affect players' access to the employment market in other Member States and are thus capable of impeding freedom of movement for workers. They cannot, thus, be deemed comparable to the rules on selling arrangements for goods which in Keck and Mithouard were held to fall outside the ambit of Article [28] of the Treaty'; see also Case C–384/93 *Alpine Investments* [1995] ECR I–1141, paras 36–38.

[28] Joined Cases C–267 & C–268/91 *Keck and Mithouard* [1993] ECR I–6097, para 17: 'Provided that those conditions are fulfilled, the application of such rules to the sale of products from another Member State meeting the requirements laid down by that State *is not by nature such as to prevent their access to the market or to impede access any more than it impedes the access of domestic products*. Such rules therefore fall outside the scope of Article 30 of the Treaty' (emphasis added).

[29] *Ibid*, para 16: certain selling arrangements escape Article 28 if they 'apply to all relevant traders operating within the national territory and so long as they affect in the same manner, in law and in fact, the marketing of domestic products and of those from other Member States.'

[30] Case C–405/98 *Gourmet International* [2001] ECR I–1795, para 18 (compare with para 17 of *Keck*).

the field of goods, would have to be transposed to the context of the other freedoms as a distinction between 'conditions of *access to* and conditions of *exercise of* the relevant economic activity.'[31]

Nevertheless, *Keck*'s vitality has been seriously eroded through a series of judgments that reveal a weakening and fragmentation of this line of case law. In some of these cases, the category of 'selling arrangements' is quite narrowly defined.[32] In others, the stress is put on the 'too uncertain and indirect' ('trop aléatoires et trop indirectes') or 'merely hypothetical' effects on trade tests, and in the very 'market access' test, which has also been used in the field of goods. These minor tests have sometimes been applied while ignoring *Keck* altogether.[33] This is no appropriate place for reconsidering the *Keck* case-law in all its complexity, an exercise that would require another volume. The only conclusion to be drawn from the previous analysis for the rest of the chapter is that *Keck* is not a major barrier for the convergence of the free movement rules.

Beyond the case law, Article 14 EC, introduced by the Single European Act, declares that '[t]he internal market shall comprise an area without internal frontiers in which the free movement of goods, persons, services and capital is ensured in accordance with the provisions of this Treaty.' This norm also reflects the convergence among the various economic freedoms from the perspective of the objectives of the Treaty. We have seen that this provision enshrines a political objective that merely translates a constitutional principle that was previously recognised by the Court.

Besides, with the exception of the free movement of workers, to which we shall come back in the following section, there are no overriding arguments not to apply a single standard to all the economic freedoms. The Treaty aims at the integration of the markets and includes a series of directly effective norms that prohibit State measures which go against this objective. There is no reason to allow different degrees of protectionism with regard to the various economic factors.

Everything points to the possibility of establishing a single test, and even a single norm. Certainly, the facts of the cases will distinguish different situations. A more stringent approach regarding mandatory requirements in the field of establishment—where a stronger control may be justified on the part of the Member States—would, for instance, differentiate it with respect to services. Certain nuances or a different norm would also differentiate free movement of workers to prevent their commodification. But legal certainty would be assured through a simple rule of predictable application common to the economic freedoms. This provision could read as follows:

---

[31] V Hatzopoulos, 'Recent Developments of the Case Law of the ECJ in the Field of Services', above n 20, 68.

[32] See, for example, Case C–254/98 *TK-Heimdienst* [2000] ECR I–151.

[33] See, for example, Case C–44/98 *BASF* [1999] ECR I–6269; Case C–266/96 *Corsica Ferries France* [1998] ECR I–3949, paras 29–32 and 55–61; Case 379/92 *Peralta* [1994] ECR I–3453.

1. All restrictions on the free movement of economic factors shall be prohibited between the Member States.
2. This prohibition shall not preclude restrictions on free movement justified on grounds of public interest, such as public morality, public policy or public security; the protection of health and life of humans, animals or plants; the protection of national treasures possessing artistic, historic or archaeological value; the protection of industrial, consumer, environmental policy, or commercial property.
3. No restriction shall be justified if it constitutes a disguised restriction of trade between the Member States, or if the levels of protection attained by the relevant Member States with different means are equivalent.

One could argue that a similar norm is already being applied by the Court beyond the straitjacket of the various texts. In any case, and from the point of view of the interaction of competition and free movement, it is clear that a single legal approach to the free movement rules is warranted—always with the exception of workers—at least regarding their personal scope, and increasingly regarding the substance of the norms as well.

The comparison between the decisions in *Decker* and *Kohll* may help to substantiate this contention.[34] Both cases concerned cross-border access to medical care: the latter goods (spectacles); the former services (orthodontic treatment). The Court used very much the same reasoning and reached similar conclusions in considering the measures in question to be unjustified restrictions to free movement. Some differences may be seen regarding the arguments put forward by the parties for justification. While both failed to be justified in the end, the Court's approach in the case of services was somewhat more lenient, since it 'based the [possible] right of Member States to restrict the freedom to provide and receive medical services on Article 56 of the Treaty', implying 'that also discriminatory measures which make a distinction between medical care provided in other Member States and care provided in the national territory can possibly be justified',[35] while in the case of goods it was only a mandatory requirement (the financial balance of the social security system) that could in theory justify only State indistinctly-applicable—that is, not discriminatory but restrictive—measures. Certainly, *Decker* and other more recent judgments such as *PreussenElektra* could also be interpreted to mean that, although the Court has not completely settled this question, it may sometimes use mandatory requirements to justify distinctly applicable measures.[36]

---

[34] Cases C–120/95 *Decker* [1998] ECR I–1831; C–158/96 *Kohll* [1998] ECR I–1931.

[35] A P van der Mei, 'Cross-Border Access to Medical Care within the European Union—Some Reflections on the Judgments in *Decker* and *Kohll*', (1998) *Maastricht Journal of European and Comparative Law*, 277, 295.

[36] See Cases C–379/98 *PreussenElektra* [2001] ECR I–2099; C–389/96 *Aher-Waggon* [1998] ECR I–4473; C–2/90 *Commission v Belgium* [1992] ECR I–4431. For a more detailed analysis, see J Baquero Cruz and F Castillo de la Torre, 'A Note on *PreussenElektra*', (2001) *European Law Review*, 489, 497–500.

The fact of classifying an activity or situation under goods, capital, services or establishment is therefore increasingly irrelevant, as the legal consequences are almost identical. Certain nuances, needed for the sake of the different nature of the economic factors involved, may perhaps be introduced at the level of justification rather than at the level of transgression.[37] This approach could provide certainty and uniformity in the field of free movement—as the sort of measures subject to review will not vary depending on the economic factor— and yet a degree of flexibility to enable the Court to render fair rulings, made possible by this fine-tuning through the application to different factual situations of the exceptions to free movement.

6.3. THE SPECIAL CASE OF THE FREE MOVEMENT OF WORKERS

The position of workers among the other economic factors demands more reflection. To avoid their commodification, a different rule or a different interpretation of the same rule may be needed. This interpretation would put the emphasis on the social dimension and the rights of workers rather than on the economic dimension related to the protectionism of measures related to the labour market and 'social dumping'.

Such is, to a certain extent, the current situation in the case law, which has developed the social aspects of the free movement of workers over and beyond its economic aspects. A parallel could be drawn with the evolution in the interpretation of Article 141 EC, a provision clearly related to free movement of workers which also has an economic origin and has been 'socialised' through the case law.

In *Defrenne* (1976), the Court interpreted Article 141 (then 119) EC in the light of its two objectives: the economic objective ('to avoid a situation in which undertakings established in states which have actually implemented the principle of equal pay suffer a competitive disadvantage in intra-community competition as compared with undertakings established in States which have not yet eliminated discrimination against women workers as regards pay') and the social objective ('to ensure social progress and seek the constant improvement of the living and working conditions').[38] This was a step forward at the time, allowing the Court to extract many consequences from this provision.

Twenty-five years later, in *Deutsche Post*, the Court (sixth chamber) has held that 'the economic aim pursued by Article [141] of the Treaty, namely the elimination of distortions of competition between undertakings established in different Member States, is secondary to the social aim pursued by the same provision, which constitutes the expression of a fundamental human right.'[39] It

---

[37] *Contra* V Hatzopoulos, 'Recent Developments of the Case Law of the ECJ in the Field of Services', above n 20, 72 (proposing a single justification but different transgression theories for each freedom).

[38] Case 43/75 *Defrenne* [1976] ECR 173, paras 8–12.

[39] Joined Cases C–270/97 and C–271/97 *Deutsche Post* [2000] ECR I–929, para 57.

could be doubted that the characterisation of Article 141 as a fundamental human right is shared by the free movement of workers, which is a 'constitutional' right but cannot be conceptualised as a 'fundamental human right'. Even so, the case law on free movement of workers also shows that the economic dimension is now secondary to its social dimension.

Even if the free movement of workers has a very important social dimension, Article 39 has a limited scope of application: it protects the rights of workers only inasmuch as they are workers moving within the Community. In this sense, the reference to 'persons' in the heading of Title III, Part Three of the Treaty, may be misleading, and does not have an autonomous normative meaning. It is indeed entitled 'Free Movement of *Persons*, Services and Capital' just in order to cover 'workers' (chapter 1) and legal persons or companies (chapter 2, on the right of establishment). The reference to persons in this context, or in that of Article 14(2) EC, does not extend beyond these two realities.

This limitation of the free movement rules should entail, in my view, the autonomous application of Article 18(1) EC to secure the free movement and residence rights of citizens regardless of their qualification as workers. This provision establishes that every citizen of the Union 'shall have the right to move and reside freely within the territory of the Member States, *subject to the limitations and conditions laid down in this Treaty and by the measures adopted to give it effect.*' The words in emphasis cannot be ignored, but they should not be read to prevent the provision from conferring constitutional rights. And the provision clearly confers a right of a constitutional, probably fundamental, nature.

It should be noted that the Court has recently declared, in *Grzelczyk*, that,

> Union citizenship is destined to be the fundamental status of nationals of the Member States, enabling those who find themselves in the same situation to enjoy the same treatment in law irrespective of their nationality, subject to such exceptions as are expressly provided for.[40]

The Court has not yet recognised a direct effect to this provision, but it may do so in the near future, in view of Opinions in this sense of several Advocates General.[41] In any event, the Court has already extracted many important consequences from this notion of Union citizenship, that some deemed empty and purely rhetoric, when it was inserted in the Treaty in the Maastricht reform.[42]

This is not the place to examine the ever richer and more complex jurisprudence of the Court on citizenship of the Union. In the context of the aim of this section (the analysis of the free movement of workers as a predominantly social

---

[40] Case C–184/99 *Grzelczyk* [2001] ECR I–6193, para 31.

[41] Advocate General Geelhoed, in Case C–413/99 *Baumbast* [2001] ECR (pending), paras 101 *et seq.*, particularly para 110 (arguing that the limitations and conditions referred to in Article 18(1) EC 'may not be arbitrary and may not deprive the right of residence of its substantive content'; see also Advocate General Cosmas in Case C–378/97 *Wijsenbeek* [1999] ECR I–6207; and Advocate General La Pergola in Case C–85/96 *Martínez Sala* [1998] ECR I–2691.

[42] See J H H Weiler, *The Constitution of Europe* (Cambridge University Press, Cambridge, 1999) 325–326.

freedom), it should be noted that insofar as limitations and conditions referred to in Article 18(1) EC are not expressly laid down in primary or secondary law, Union citizens, as citizens and not as workers, have a constitutional right to move freely and establish their residence in the Member States. This provision, not Article 39 EC, is the non-economic provision through which a general free movement right may be recognised for persons, not just workers. Such conditions and limitations should not touch upon the essential content of this right.

Finally, perhaps the convergence among the free movement rules should not lead us to think that they are instances of a general freedom of trade implicit in the system of the Treaty, as proposed by Pierre Pescatore.[43] The free movement rules are perhaps best seen as instances of a general prohibition on all kinds of State protectionism imposed by the Treaty, the positive facet of which prohibition are the rights recognised for individuals. These individual rights springing from the freedoms are not, however, the main intent of the Treaty with such freedoms, but rather an instrumental effect resulting from the need for an effective supervision of the observance of these rules by the States.[44] Thus, they are *constitutional rights* but not *fundamental constitutional rights*—which are not instrumental but enjoyed by their holders for their own sake. The German category of 'subjective public rights' (*subjektiv-öffentlichen Rechte*) perhaps suits the freedoms movement rules perfectly if we only add the transnational and constitutional elements and recognise that private entities may sometimes be bound by them, as we will see in the next chapter.[45] Freedom of trade may nonetheless be found, as a distinct legal reality, among the fundamental rights that the Court recognises and protects as general principles of Community law.[46] In the latter, the emphasis is on individual freedom. In the free movement rules, the most important aim is ensuring the unity of the market. Their interpretation as individual rights is secondary to their anti-protectionist aim.

6.4. SHIFTING ATTITUDES TOWARDS THE COMPETITION RULES

The interaction between the particular aims of competition and free movement may change over time. Thus, it has been argued that after the completion of the single market 'the emphasis on competition law as a tool of integration needs

---

[43] See P Pescatore, 'Les objectifs de la Communauté européenne comme principes d'interprétation dans la jurisprudence de la Cour de Justice', in *Miscellanea W J Ganshof van der Meersch* (vol 2, Bruylant, Brussels, 1972) 325, 339.

[44] Cf Case 26/62 *Van Gend & Loos* [1963] ECR 1, 13: 'The vigilance of individuals concerned to protect their rights amounts to an effective supervision in addition to the supervision entrusted by Articles 169 and 170 to the diligence of the Commission and of the Member States.'

[45] See T Kingreen, *Die Struktur der Grundfreiheiten des Europäischen Gemeinschaftsrechts* (Duncker & Humblot, Berlin, 1999) 15: 'Die Grundfreiheiten sind die bedeutsamen subjectiv-öffentlichen Rechte des primären Gemeinschaftsrechts.'

[46] See, for example, Case 44/79 *Hauer* [1979] ECR, 3727 (on the freedom to pursue a trade or profession).

re-evaluation',[47] meaning that the competition rules should become autonomous from the goal of market integration, pursuing only economic efficiency.

This interpretation would depart from an originalist interpretation of the Treaty. As we have seen, the *Spaak Report* explains that competition rules were introduced in the Treaty 'to prevent double pricing having the same effect as customs duties, dumping putting in danger healthy economic productions, and an allocation of the markets taking the place of their compartmentalisation.'[48] Their complementary character and subservience to the goals of market integration are therefore obvious in an originalist interpretation of the Treaty (the meaning given to it by its authors). Nonetheless, it is well known that originalist interpretation is not determinant in Community law.

For Hawk, this was one of the main differences between Community competition law and US antitrust law:

> The primary goal of EEC competition policy is that of the EEC Treaty itself—the promotion of integration of the separate economies of the Member States into a unified 'common market'. Elimination of private practices that interfere with market integration is the first principle of EEC competition law. There is no analogue in US anti-trust law.[49]

In recent years, this approach may have changed, both in the competition policy of the Commission and in the case law of the Court of First Instance.

In the 1966 *Consten & Grundig* case, the Court noted that the Treaty, 'whose preamble and content aim at abolishing the barriers between the States, and which in several provisions gives evidence of a stern attitude with regard to their reappearance, could not allow undertakings to reconstruct such barriers.'[50] The competition rules appear to be subservient of market integration.

The same principles are more clearly expressed in *Italy v Council and Commission*. In this case, the Italian government sought on various grounds the annulment of Regulation 19/65, adopted by virtue of Article 87 of the Treaty, through which the Council conferred on the Commission the power to enact block exemptions. The Court noted that,

> Article [81] as a whole should be read in the context of the provisions of the preamble to the Treaty which clarify it and reference should be particularly be made to those relating to the 'elimination of barriers' and to 'fair competition' both of which are necessary for bringing about a single market.
>
> An agreement between producer and distributor intended to restore national partitioning in trade between Member States could be such as to run counter to the most

---

[47] I Maher, 'Competition Law and Intellectual Property Rights: Evolving Formalism' in P Craig and G de Búrca (eds) *The Evolution of EU Law* (OUP, Oxford, 1999) 597, 619.

[48] Spaak Report, 16: 'Des règles de concurrence qui s'imposent aux entreprises sont donc nécessaires pour éviter que des doubles prix aient le même effet que des droits de douane, qu'un dumping mette en danger des productions économiquement saines, que la répartition des marchés se substitue à leur cloisonnement.'

[49] B E Hawk, 'The American (Anti-trust) Revolution: Lessons for the EEC?', above n 16, 54.

[50] Cases 56 and 58/64 *Consten & Grundig* [1966] 299, 340.

fundamental objectives of the Community. The preamble to and the body of the Treaty are aimed at removing barriers between States and in many provisions the Treaty firmly opposes their re-appearances. It could not allow undertakings to recreate such barriers.[51]

A generation of Community scholars shared this interpretation of the competition rules. Pierre Pescatore, for example, thought 'that the first objective of the competition rules is to contribute to establishing and maintaining a single market in the Community and to preventing the re-erection of economic barriers by private agreements.'[52] This opinion was indeed predominant, but in the 1990s there was a change of focus. For some at least, the competition rules have gained autonomy from the free movement rules, mainly aiming at preserving competition and efficiency, which are to be distinguished from the objective of market integration.

This may be interpreted as a consequence of the realisation of the single market programme. The argument would go as follows: once we have a single market, the competition rules would become independent and exclusively oriented towards efficiency. This argument is questionable.

For one thing, the single market is still not completely achieved. It is not a definitive reality no longer in need of some supervision and maintenance. Besides, other factors may have had a stronger influence on these developments, leading to the 'majority' of the competition rules.

One among these factors may have been the creation of the Court of First Instance, whose most important head of jurisdiction pertains to competition cases brought by undertakings against decisions of the Commission. When the Nice Treaty enters into force, Article 225 EC will be amended and the jurisdiction of the Court of First Instance may be expanded—if Article 51 of the Statute of the Court of Justice is amended—but competition cases will still be an important part of its docket. At the same time, the European Court of Justice decides fewer competition cases than before, and most of the time on appeal (where the grounds are severely limited). Preliminary rulings are sparse in the field. The Court of First Instance, for its part, tends to sit as a specialised court, and sometimes interprets and applies the competition rules in a highly technical fashion which may neglect their character as provisions belonging to the constitutional law of the Community. It may also neglect their non-economic functions—such as preserving individual economic liberty or market integration—and forget their close relationship with the free movement rules.

For example, in *Bayer* the Court of First Instance interpreted Article 81 EC in a somewhat restrictive manner as regards vertical restraints of competition. It required the existence of a formal agreement in a situation in which the different bargaining power of the parties to a distribution relationship means that one the producer may impose certain restraints on the distributor in the framework

---

[51] Case 32/65 *Italy v Council and Commission* [1966] ECR 389, 405 and 408.
[52] P Pescatore, 'Public and Private Aspects of Community Competition Law', above n 6, 392.

of a series of continuing commercial relationships.[53] This case may have received a different solution if individual economic freedom and market integration had been considered as important functions and interpretive elements of the competition rules. Almost simultaneously, a different chamber of the Court of First Instance said something quite different in *Volkswagen*, assuming that an agreement existed in the context of a series of continuous commercial relationships without express consent of the distributors to the restraint of competition—and in spite of the fact that the restraint was imposed by the producer.[54] The Court of Justice may be called upon to settle these diverse approaches found in different chambers of the Court of First Instance.

From this perspective, the current separation between the free movement rules—mainly applied by the Court of Justice and national courts—and the competition rules—mainly applied by the Commission under the supervision of the Court of First Instance—may create systemic problems for which the existing jurisdictional setting allows no apparent solution.

This evolution towards a liberation of the competition rules from the goal of market integration may also be found in the more lenient attitude of the Commission vis-à-vis vertical restraints. Vertical restraints are problematic for the single market—although they may be neutral and sometimes efficient from an economic perspective. In this context, this change of policy appears to be more efficiency-oriented and less and less linked to the goal of market integration.[55] Perhaps the Commission no longer deems it wise to 'sacrifice distribution efficiencies to advance market integration, that is, accept possible short-term efficiency losses to achieve perceived long-term gains from a single market.'[56]

This liberation may be only partial. The decision to limit the exemption on vertical agreements to undertakings whose market share does not exceed 30 per cent of the relevant product market limits the higher tolerance to vertical restraints (Article 3 of the block exemption). The fact is also significant that the Commission may withdraw the benefit of the exemption,

> where it finds in any particular case that vertical agreements to which this Regulation applies nevertheless have effects which are incompatible with the conditions laid down in Article 81(3) of the Treaty, and in particular *where access to the relevant market or competition therein is significantly restricted by the cumulative effect of parallel networks of similar vertical restraints implemented by competing suppliers or buyers* [Article 6]

Article 7 empowers the State competition authorities to grant the exemption when a State or a part thereof constitutes a separate geographic market). These

---

[53] Case T–41/96 *Bayer* [2000] ECR II–3383.

[54] Joined Cases T–123/96 and T–143/96 *Volkswagen* [1999] ECR II–3663.

[55] See Commission Regulation (EC) No 2790 of 22 December 1999 on the application of Article 81(3) of the Treaty to categories of vertical agreements and concerted practices (OJ 1999 L 336/21–25).

[56] B E Hawk, 'The American (Anti-trust) Revolution: Lessons for the EEC?', above n 16, 55.

limitations may be seen as standing for the remnants of the market integration element in the competition rules.

Finally, in the *White Paper on Modernisation of the Rules Implementing Articles 81 and 82* the Commission expresses with clarity the idea that the competition policy should be autonomous from market integration:

> *At the beginning* the focus of its activity *was* on establishing rules on restrictive practices interfering directly with *the goal of market integration*. [. . .] The Commission has *now* come to concentrate more on *ensuring effective competition* by detecting and stopping cross-border cartels and maintaining competitive market structures.[57]

There is a change of focus, from integration to economic efficiency. There is also a pragmatic reason behind the proposal. The Commission, overwhelmed by competition files, seeks the active cooperation of national competition authorities and courts, and a degree of decentralisation in the application of the competition rules. It does not attach any relevance to the fact that such authorities, and competition law in most Member States, is administrative or statutory, not constitutional law as in the Community legal order.

On the other hand, the proposal to make Article 81 directly applicable in its entirety, including its paragraph 3 (exemptions to anti-competitive agreements, currently only applicable by the Commission) would give greater emphasis to competition *law*, as opposed to competition *policy*, and greater role to courts, rather than administration, in the application of this branch of the law. Thus, the Commission proposal for a new implementing regulation of the competition rules makes clear in its Articles 1 and 4 to 6 that Article 81 would become directly applicable in its entirety, and that it is to be applied by the Commission, the competition authorities of the States and national courts.[58]

On the whole, these shifting attitudes towards the competition rules not only show a tendency to move away from the single market approach towards a more autonomous approach, but also show two tensions: that between the administrative and the constitutional approaches and that between their consideration as law and as policy.

Depending on how it is carried out in practice, the audacious reform proposed by the Commission may actually bring an enhanced constitutional approach to Community competition law. Making Article 81 EC directly applicable as a whole would probably force the Court to receive more preliminary references concerning that provision. This could lead the Court to overruling the case law on the principle of limited judicial review in the field of competition law. According to this principle, judicial review of Commission decisions in this field is limited to manifest errors of assessment, because complex economic facts are involved and the Commission has a degree of

---

[57] European Commission, *White Paper on Modernisation of the Rules Implementing Articles [81] and [82] of the EC Treaty*, executive summary, point 8 (my emphasis).

[58] See the Commission's proposal for a Council Regulation on the implementation of Articles 81 and 82 of the Treaty, COM (2000) 582 final, 2000/0243 (CNS) (OJ 2000 C 365/284).

administrative discretion.[59] According to Emil Paulis, the reform will make Article 81(3) justiciable, replacing the current degree of judicial review with a stricter review.[60] In the new framework, the Court and national courts will have a greater role in the development of Community competition law. The Commission will continue to develop competition policy, to be sure, but within the stricter constitutional constraints established by the Court.

6.5. PROCEDURAL REASONS FOR THE BLURRING BETWEEN THE SCOPES OF COMPETITION AND FREE MOVEMENT

The blurring between the personal scopes of application of the competition and the free movement rules makes them concurrent routes for a number of problems. Part of the blurring is due to the fact that, in most cases, the route chosen by the Court for the resolution of a case (free movement or competition or both) is highly dependent on the questions posed by the national court. If the national court, for example, raised the question of the compatibility of national measures with the competition State action doctrine, the Court generally will be bound to this perspective. If the national court does not mention it, the Court will probably analyse the issue from the perspective of the free movement rules. The Court may also reformulate the question, disregard some points of law or introduce other points. However, there are no criteria defining when the Court may reformulate the questions posed.

On the other hand, it is interesting to note that in this context the Court has adopted a preference for the free movement route, couched in terms of the requirement for more factual and legal information in the case of preliminary rulings on competition. In a series of cases starting with *Telemarsicabruzzo*, the Court has dismissed several references or parts of references related to competition when the national court did not provide detailed, sometimes too detailed, information concerning economic facts and the legal context, generally choosing to address the case from the angle of the free movement rules when this was possible. This preference may be due to judicial self-restraint, as will be explained in chapter 7, when the *Bosman* case is analysed. The Court perceives competition as requiring sophisticated economic analysis which is impossible without detailed factual information.[61] This preference may have to do not only

---

[59] See Cases 42/84 *Remia* [1985] ECR 2545, para 34; T–17/93 *Matra* [1994] ECR II–595, para 104; C–7/95 P *John Deere* [1998] ECR I–3111, para 34.

[60] E Paulis, 'Coherent Application of EC Competition Law in a System of Parallel Competences', in C D Ehlermann and I Atanasiu (eds) *European Competition Law Annual 2000: The Modernisation of EC Antitrust Policy* (Hart, Oxford, 2001).

[61] See Joined Cases C–320 to 322/90 *Telemarsicabruzzo* [1993] ECR I–393, paras 6–7; Case 67/96 *Albany* [1999] ECR I–5751, paras 39–40 (sufficient information in a reference confined to the competition rules); Joined Cases C–51/96 and C–191/97 *Deliège* [2000] ECR I–2549, paras 29–37 (insufficient information for the application of the competition rules, but sufficient for the free movement rules).

with the need for detailed information, but also with the fact that national courts cannot apply Article 81(3). The reform of the competition system proposed by the Commission may probably make it easier for a national court to refer a question on the interpretation of the competition rules, for it would not create the risk of annulling agreements that have not been notified but would deserve an exemption.

As to the reformulation of questions in the overlapping areas, sometimes the Court will raise the State action doctrine of its own motion. In other cases it will do the opposite, as in *Deutsche Grammophon*, in which the question posed by the national court related to Articles 10, 81 and 82. The Court started with the analysis of the competition rules but introduced as well the free movement provisions, according to which it finally decided the case.[62]

The general rule would be that 'Article [234] of the Treaty does not confer on the Court jurisdiction to rule on questions that have not been referred to it.'[63] But the Court of Justice has sometimes expressed a different position: '[t]he question referred [. . .] must be resolved in the light of all the provisions of the Treaty and of secondary legislation which may be relevant to the problem.'[64] The case-law provides no clear guidance on this issue.[65]

It does not seem an easy task to put forward criteria as to how and why the Court may raise new points of law or reformulate the questions referred by the national court. But there can be no doubt that part of the confusion in the relationship between competition and free movement is due to this sort of procedural difficulty.

---

[62] Case 78/70 *Deutsche Grammophon* [1971] ECR 487, para 7.
[63] Case 22/79 *Greenwich* [1979] ECR 3275, 3288; Opinion Warner, 3295–3296.
[64] Case 137/84 *Mutsch* [1985] ECR 2681, para 10.
[65] See Cases 83/78 *Pigs Marketing Board* [1978] ECR 2366; C–315/92 *Clinique* [1994] ECR I–317, para 7; 209 to 213/84 *Asjes* [1986] ECR 1425, para 15.

7

Free Movement and the Private Sphere[1]

7.1. STATEMENT OF THE PROBLEM

THE TOPIC ADDRESSED in this chapter seems quite simple at first sight: are actors in the private sphere (individuals, corporations, private associations . . .) bound by the free movement rules? The question is actually rather thorny. Its complexity springs from a possible gap in the constitutional law of the Community, a lacuna between competition and free movement, which is affected by the interpretive tensions between both normative groups.

The alleged gap appears to lie in the fact that some private conduct may run counter to the purpose of the free movement rules: the guarantee of the unity of the market through the constitutional control of protectionism. Such rules, mandatory for the States, would not be so for private actors. This situation would prevent a more perfect integration of the markets. A solution could be to apply the free movement rules to private actors insofar as their purpose would be defeated by private action not falling foul of the competition rules. This argument, based on the need to ensure the effectiveness of Community law (*effet utile*), will be rejected by those who propose a restrictive interpretation of the Treaty.

The question has a constitutional importance. If the free movement rules were also obligatory in the private sphere, their effectiveness would be enhanced. Besides, they would not only create the conditions for a single market to emerge spontaneously, but actually oblige individuals and traders to realise it. At the same time, their liberty would be limited beyond measure. The problem then also involves the issue of the limits of Community law vis-à-vis individual autonomy.

Some may be prompted to think that this is a *faux problème*: the creation of a lunatic lawyer tilting at windmills. But take the example of an advertising campaign launched by a private consumers' organisation against foreign products. This action does not come under the competition rules nor can it be reviewed under the free movement rules, but it still greatly endangers the unity of the market.[2] This is no windmill, but a gigantic conundrum to which Community law has no clear response. The problem may actually become

[1] This chapter is based on my article 'Free Movement and Private Autonomy' (1999) *European Law Review*, 603.

[2] For further examples see P Oliver, *Free Movement of Goods in the European Community* (3rd edn, Sweet & Maxwell, London, 1996), 56.

graver as public participation in the economy shrinks and privatisation proceeds. Private conduct will then be more crucial for the organisation and operation of the market. This new economy will bring before the Court new cases of 'private protectionism', which are already an important part of its case law. Such jurisprudence is assessed here and some ideas are proposed for its better understanding and development.

7.2. HORIZONTAL DIRECT EFFECT?

Many refer to our topic as the problem of the 'horizontal direct effect' of the free movement rules.[3] This terminology will be avoided here, because it describes the issue imperfectly: the abstract determination of the personal scope of the free movement provisions, rather than the kind of proceedings in which they may be invoked. This misunderstanding can be seen, for instance, in one book which gives Article 28 both as an instance of a provision having horizontal direct effect, creating obligations between individuals, and of a provision only having vertical effect, binding the States.[4]

The seminal cases on direct effect insist that Community law 'not only imposes obligations on individuals but is also intended to confer upon them rights which become part of their legal heritage',[5] being 'a body of law which binds both their nationals and [the States]',[6] and composed of provisions which constitute 'a direct source of rights and duties for all those affected thereby, whether Member States or individuals, who are parties to legal relationships under Community law.'[7] This case law makes clear that the Treaty *may* impose obligations on both the States and individuals. In its ECSC order in *San Michele* (1965), the Court had already stated that 'the participation of the Italian Republic in the common institutions and in the rights and obligations arising from the Treaty in fact precludes its nationals from avoiding the complete and uniform application of the Treaty and from thus obtaining different treatment from that of other nationals in the Community.'[8] However, these general statements of principle are not conclusive in respect of our problem, since they refer to the potential characteristics of Community law as a whole, not to the actual effects of particular provisions thereof.

The distinction between vertical and horizontal effect belongs to the context of the effects of Directives in the event of deficient or no transposition. In such

---

[3] P Oliver, *Free Movement of Goods in the European Community*, above n 2, 56–57; D Schaefer, *Die unmittelbare Wirkung des Verbots der nichttarifären Handelshemmnisse (Art 30 EWGV) in den Rechtsbeziehungen zwischen Privaten: Probleme der horizontalen unmittelbaren Wirkung des Gemeinschaftsrechts, gezeigt am Beispiel des Art 30 EWGV* (Lang, Frankfurt a-M, 1987).

[4] D Simon, *Le système juridique communautaire* (PUF, Paris, 1997) 247.

[5] Case 26/62 *Van Gend en Loos* [1963] ECR 1, 12.

[6] Case 6/64 *Costa v ENEL* [1964] ECR 585, 593.

[7] Case 106/77 *Simmenthal* [1978] ECR 629, 643 para 15.

[8] Case 9/65 *San Michele* [1965] ECR 29, at 30.

cases, a Directive is given (vertical) direct effect when applied in a legal dispute involving a private party who claims a Community right against the State or an emanation thereof. Such Directive is denied (horizontal) direct effect in conflicts involving two private parties.[9] In my view, the distinction creates confusion when used in other fields.

The free movement provisions have been constantly applied in disputes between private parties when there was a link to State legislation that could be contrary to the Treaty. This was the case of intellectual property cases, which sometimes are mentioned as an example of situations in which individuals are bound by the free movement rules.[10] This is probably incorrect. In these cases, individual behaviour is not subject, as such, to the free movement rules. Thus, individuals have fulfilled their role as indirect supervisors of the compatibility of national law with Community law.

The question posed by this chapter is a different one: may private conduct violate in itself the free movement provisions, in the absence of State legislation in breach of the Treaty?[11] The situation in the field of Directives is different, if only because the estoppel rationale for their direct effect (the State cannot profit from its defective transposition) does not apply to Treaty provisions, which have to be applied by national courts when the conditions for direct effect are fulfilled. Our problem is whether the private sphere is bound by the free movement rules in contractual situations or in private unilateral actions (individual or collective). In other words, whether private action that restricts trade, and that is not effective *erga omnes* by virtue of national legislation—as in the intellectual property cases—nor falls under the competition rules may breach the free movement rules.

A clearer consideration of the nature of direct effect may be of use. For Eleftheriadis, a Community provision which has fulfilled the criteria to be suited to produce direct effect is 'capable of judicial adjudication',[12] but one has yet to determine whether it is applicable to the case in hand: '[l]egal effects do not just follow inherent qualities of Community or other rules but are the result of the interpretation and application of a rule to a concrete situation'.[13]

Here two questions are crucial: the material content of the norm and its addressees (*who* is obliged to do or not to do *what* to *whom*). The question relevant for us is the latter: the addressees of the free movement rules. Once established that they are suited to produce direct effect, one should determine their scope, a different question from that of the potential direct effect of a provision.

---

[9] See Cases 152/84 *Marshall* [1986] ECR 723 and C–91/92 *Faccini Dori* [1994] I–3325.

[10] See, for example, M Waelbroeck, 'Droit des marques et règles du Traité de Rome: au terme d'une évolution?', (1977) *Revue critique de jurisprudence belge*, 219, 227.

[11] In this sense, E Steindorff, *EG-Vertrag und Privatrecht* (Nomos, Baden-Baden, 1996) 279.

[12] P Pescatore, 'The Doctrine of Direct Effect: An Infant Disease of Community Law', (1983) *European Law Review*, 155, 176.

[13] P Eleftheriadis, 'The Direct Effect of Community Law: Conceptual Issues', (1996) *Yearbook of European Law*, 205, 212.

The question of the field of application of a provision should not be confused with the question of the kind of proceedings in which it may be invoked. In theory, at least four sorts of proceedings are conceivable. Two of them are horizontal: (i) the Commission or a State against a State claiming that it has violated the free movement rules through Articles 226 and 227 of the Treaty; (ii) an individual against another individual claiming that the latter has violated the free movement rules before a national court. The other two are vertical: (iii) a State against an individual before a national court; (iv) an individual against a State before a national court.

These procedural situations, which in the case of Directives matter so much, are not so important in the case of the free movement rules. If we decide the abstract question of the addressees of the free movement rules in the sense that only the States are bound to respect the free movement rules, they would be so in vertical proceedings (an individual against the State) and horizontal proceedings (a State or the Commission against another State; an individual against another individual when the former is indirectly challenging a piece of State legislation). If, on the contrary, we decide the question in the affirmative we will give horizontal effect to such rules in pure conflicts between individuals (in the sphere of their private autonomy) but also vertical direct effect in hypothetical conflicts of States against individuals. It is in this sense that the horizontal/vertical terminology may be misleading, giving a false image of our problem, which is more properly formulated as that of whether private parties, in their realm of private autonomy, are included among the addressees of the free movement rules.[14]

7.3. LEADING CASES

Against the clear position of the Commission, which since the mid–1970's has constantly maintained that private parties are not bound by the free movement rules,[15] the Court, in a series of cases, has taken them to be so bound under certain circumstances.[16]

---

[14] The German expression *unmittelbare Drittwirkung* tersely captures this notion. See M Jaensch, *Die unmittelbare Drittwirkung der Grundfreiheiten* (Nomos, Baden-Baden, 1997) 28–30. The expression *Privatwirkung* (private effect) is equally apt. See S Wernicke, *Die Privatwirkung im Europäischen Gemeinschaftsrecht* (Nomos, Baden-Baden, 2002).

[15] See, for instance, Responses to Written Questions to the Commission: 909/79 by Mr Moreland (OJ 1980 C 156/10–11); 835/82 by Mr Schwartzenberg (OJ 1983 C 93/1–2). For the Commission, free movement of workers would be an exception, since Article 7(4) of Council Regulation 1612/18/EEC, on the free movement of workers within the Community, makes null and void any clause of collective or individual labour agreements discriminating against nationals of other Member States (OJ 1968 L 257/2). Secondary law on the other free movement provisions merely refers to legislative or administrative rules or practice.

[16] See also Cases 43/75 *Defrenne* [1976] ECR 455 (about Article 141 EC); 251/83 *Haug-Adrion* [1984] ECR 4277; C–16/94 *Dubois* [1995] ECR I–2421.

A. *Walrave* (1974)

In *Walrave*, decided in 1974 and confirmed by *Donà* in 1976,[17] the question was posed to the Court whether Articles 12, 39 and 49 precluded the application of a rule of the Union Cycliste Internationale, a private organisation, relating to world cycling championships behind motorcycles, according to which the pace-maker had to be the same nationality as the cyclist.

The Court ruled that the provisions do 'not only apply to the action of public authorities but extend likewise to rules of any other nature aimed at regulating in a collective manner gainful employment and the provision of services.'[18] The reason was that

> the abolition [. . .] of obstacles to freedom of movement for persons and to freedom to provide services, which are fundamental objectives of the Community contained in Article 3 (c) of the Treaty, would be compromised if the abolition of barriers of national origin could be neutralized by obstacles resulting from the exercise of their legal autonomy by associations or organizations which do not come under public law.[19]

The rationale used to fill the gap in the Treaty is parallel to the one used in the Spaak report to justify the introduction of competition rules in the Treaty (State barriers could be replaced by private barriers to trade), also present in the case law of the Court.

The Commission argued that only free movement of workers would apply to private situations, whereas the free provision of services could just create obligations for the States. The Court clarified the point that both may impose obligations on individuals, because 'the fact that [services] are performed outside the ties of a contract of employment [. . .] cannot justify a more restrictive interpretation of the scope of the freedom to be ensured.'[20] This reasoning may no longer be sound, since free movement of workers has a social aspect which is perhaps more important than its economic dimension.

Delannay, writing at the time of the decision, gave an optimistic account of this judgment, describing it as 'a step towards a system which is more constitutional than international.'[21] According to him, *Walrave* is not limited to rules of a collective nature, but applies with equal force to individual contracts, because the objectives of the Treaty would be equally endangered by both.[22] This view seems a bit exaggerated, since collective private rules pose a greater threat to free movement than a single contract.

---

[17] Case 13/76 *Donà* [1976] ECR 1333. On establishment see Case 90/76 *van Ameyde* [1977] ECR 1091.

[18] Case 36/74 *Walrave* [1974] ECR 1405, para 17.

[19] *Ibid*, para 18.

[20] *Ibid*, paras 23–24.

[21] P Delannay, Annotation on *Walrave*, (1976) *Cahiers de droit européen*, 209, 223: 'un pas de plus vers un système plus constitutionnel qu'international.'

[22] *Ibid*, 220.

B. *Dansk Supermarked* (1981)

In *Dansk Supermarked* (1981), Imerco, a Danish group of merchants, commissioned in the United Kingdom a china service bearing the words 'Imerco fiftieth anniversary', the sale of which was reserved to its members. Imerco and the manufacturer agreed that some substandard pieces could be marketed by the manufacturer in the United Kingdom. The latter undertook not to export them to Denmark. However, Dansk Supermarked obtained a number of services in the United Kingdom and offered them in Denmark at lower prices than those charged for perfect pieces in Denmark. A Danish court prohibited such sale as a breach of the Danish law on unfair competition. On appeal, the Danish Supreme Court asked the Court whether the provisions of the Treaty precluded the application of the Danish laws on copyright, trademarks and marketing.

In the second part of the judgment, on whether unfair competition may be used to prevent the imports at stake, the Court held that

> *it is impossible in any circumstances for agreements between individuals to derogate from the mandatory provisions of the Treaty on the free movement of goods.* It follows that *an agreement involving a prohibition on the importation into a Member State of goods lawfully marketed in another Member State may not be relied upon or taken into consideration in order to classify the marketing of such goods as an improper or unfair commercial practice.*[23]

This passage (mandatory rules bind individuals) goes well beyond *Walrave* (private conduct caught if amounting to collective rules). The implication is that individuals cannot derogate from free movement in their contractual relations, thereby restricting their private autonomy even without any connection to the State.[24]

This judgment may no longer be good law. It is a chamber judgment, and a statement of this sort has not been repeated—with the exception of *Angonese*, a recent judgment to which we shall return.

The solution proposed by René Joliet to this kind of cases is more convincing: a State provision on unfair competition that precludes the commercialisation of a product coming from another Member State in breach of a contractual clause is incompatible with Article 28 when such contractual clause is itself in breach of Article 81.[25]

In the case in hand the agreement between Imerco and the producer was enforceable *erga omnes* through the application of State legislation; it would give Imerco absolute territorial protection, a *per se* violation of Article 81 and

---

[23] Case 58/80 *Dansk Supermarked* [1981] ECR 181, para 17 (my emphasis). In similar terms, Case 102/81 *Nordsee* [1982] ECR 1095, para 14.

[24] E Steindorff, *EG-Vertrag und Privatrecht* (Nomos, Baden-Baden, 1996) 282.

[25] R Joliet, 'Derecho de la competencia desleal y libre circulación de mercancías', (1995) *Revista General de Derecho* 493, 520.

anathema under Community competition law, possibly even if its effects on competition were not appreciable.[26] Such an agreement, void under Community law, could not be taken into account in order to forbid the sale under State legislation on unfair competition.

C. *Bosman* (1995)

In *Bosman* (1995), the Court was asked to give a preliminary ruling on the compatibility with Articles 39, 81 and 82 of the FIFA rules governing transfers of football players and the nationality clauses limiting the number of foreigners per team. The question arose of whether such rules could be challenged through Article 39, since FIFA and its affiliated national federations are private associations. The Court repeated the principle established in *Walrave*: 'Article [39] not only applies to the action of public authorities but extends also to *rules of any other nature aimed at regulating gainful employment in a collective manner*.'[27]

As to the objection advanced by UEFA 'that such an interpretation makes Article [39] of the Treaty more restrictive in relation to individuals than in relation to Member States, which are alone in being able to rely on limitations justified on grounds of public policy, public security or public health', the Court held that '[t]here is nothing to preclude individuals from relying on justifications on grounds of public policy, public security or public health. *Neither the scope nor the content of those grounds of justification is in any way affected by the public or private nature of the rules in question.*'[28]

This latter part is new: private parties may also justify restrictive rules of their own under the very grounds of justification applying to State measures.[29] The argument according to which the private nature of the rules does not change the content of the available justifications seems correct. However, the part concerning its scope may be questioned. The proportionality review of measures taken by private actors should be more stringent, because private actors may have a natural impulse to act in their own interest and they lack the legitimacy of public authorities.

Another important aspect of this judgment has to do with the relationship between free movement and competition. The case may have also been seen from two other perspectives: (i) that of competition, involving agreements between undertakings aimed at restraining competition in the labour market; (ii) as a failure of the States to fulfil their obligations under Article 39 EC in conjunction with Article 10 EC, for allowing such systems of transfer and nationality clauses to exist.

---

[26] See, for example, Case 258/78 *Nungesser* [1982] ECR 2015, paras 53–61.

[27] Case C–415/93 *Bosman* [1995] ECR I–4921, para 82 (my emphasis).

[28] *Ibid*, paras 85–86 (my emphasis).

[29] This refutes Roth's argument that individuals are not bound by the free movement rules because the exceptions are addressed to the States ('Drittwirkung der Grundfreiheiten?', in O Due *et al* (eds) *Festschrift für Ulrich Everling* (Nomos, Baden-Baden, 1995) 1241, 1241–1242).

The referring court actually asked for guidance regarding Articles 81 and 82. One may wonder why the Court limited itself to holding that '[s]ince both types of rule to which the national court's question refer are contrary to Article [39], it is not necessary to rule on the interpretation of Articles [81] and [82] of the Treaty.'[30] One author has argued that the Court thus evaded 'the full implications of an approach based on Article [81]', which Article 'may be used to sweep away the last vestige of the transfer system in the EC, filling the jurisdictional gap caused by the Court's unwillingness to extend Article [39] to purely internal situations.'[31] In this sense, Advocate General Lenz saw no reason 'why the rules at issue in this case should not be subject to both Article [39] and to EC competition law [. . .]. [B]oth sets of rules may be applicable to a single factual situation.'[32] The 'judicial self-restraint'[33] of the Court in *Bosman* is to be found in its refusal to apply the competition rules alongside the free movement rules, thus reducing the impact of its judgment, for this approach allows for the application of the transfer rules in purely internal situations.

D. *Commission v France* (1997)

In this judgment, concerning the French Republic's failure to take effective action regarding continued violent acts by French farmers against Spanish agricultural products, the Court held that,

> by failing to adopt all necessary and proportionate measures in order to prevent the free movement of fruit and vegetables from being obstructed by actions by private individuals, the French Government has failed to fulfil its obligations under Article [28], in conjunction with Article [10], of the Treaty.[34]

This judgment confirms the old theory that Article 28, and probably the remaining free movement provisions, in conjunction with Article 10, create not only a negative obligation on the part of States but also a positive obligation to prevent individuals from impairing free movement. This idea was already implicit in *de Peijper*,[35] but the Court has so far not had the chance to apply it in a concrete case.

The Court, following the Opinion of Advocate General Lenz, held that

> [t]he fact that a Member State abstains from taking action or [. . .] fails to adopt adequate measures to prevent obstacles to the free movement of goods that are created

---

[30] Case C–415/93 *Bosman* [1995] ECR I–4921, para 138.
[31] S Weatherill, Annotation on *Bosman*, (1996) *Common Market Law Review*, 991, 1024 and 1026.
[32] Case C–415/93 *Bosman* [1995] ECR I–4921, Opinion of Advocate General Lenz, para 253.
[33] C Joerges, 'The Impact of European Integration on Private Law: Reductionist Perceptions, True Conflicts and a New Constitutional Perspective', (1997) *European Law Journal*, 378, 406.
[34] Case C–265/95 *Commission v France* [1997] ECR I–6959, para 66.
[35] Case 104/75 *de Peijper* [1976] ECR 635.

[. . .] by actions by private individuals on its territory aimed at products originating in other Member States is just as likely to obstruct intra-Community trade as is a positive act.

Therefore, Article 28

requires the Member States not merely themselves to abstain from adopting measures or engaging in conduct liable to constitute an obstacle to trade but also, when read with Article [10] of the Treaty, to take all necessary and appropriate measures to ensure that that fundamental freedom is respected on their territory.[36]

In spite of the margin of discretion of the States as regards public order and internal security 'it falls to the Court [. . .], to verify, in cases brought before it, whether the Member State concerned has adopted appropriate measures for ensuring the free movement of goods.'[37]

This judgment retains a wide significance for the future, even though the conditions set by the Court may be quite difficult to fulfil, probably leading to a marginal use of this route. Only some rather obvious and persistent cases of private barriers to trade which are not caught by the competition rules may give rise to a judgment against the State for a failure to fulfil the obligations stemming from the free movement rules.

With a view to developing the principles contained in this judgment, the Council adopted Regulation No 2679/98,[38] which establishes a simplified procedure for the Commission to prosecute obstacles to the free movement of goods caused by action or inaction on the part of Member States (in particular, according to Article 1(2) of the Regulation, 'when the competent authorities of a Member State, in the presence of an obstacle caused by private individuals, fails to take all necessary and proportionate measures within their powers with a view to removing the obstacles and ensuring the free movement of goods in their territory').

It seems that the situations covered by the Regulation will be but a few. To begin with, it only extends to free movement of goods, to the exclusion of the other freedoms. The possibility of holding a State responsible for its failure to prevent individuals from impairing free movement is quite restricted by the margin of appreciation left to the States. Thus, it is not a perfect solution to our problem, and it may still be sensible to apply directly the free movement rules to other private situations. It is finally submitted that the recognition by the Court of such a possibility does not rule out nor resolve the question of the applicability of the free movement rules in the private sphere, which was not addressed in this judgment.

However, some commentators have argued that *Commission v France* made 'clear that Art. 28 relates only to acts attributable to public authorities—and,

---

[36] Case C–265/95 *Commission v France* [1997] ECR I–6959, paras 31–32.
[37] *Ibid*, para 35.
[38] Council Regulation (EC) No 2679/98 of 7 December 1998 on the functioning of the internal market in relation to the free movement of goods among the Member States (OJ 1998 L 337/8).

when read with Art. 10 (ex 5), to omissions attributable to them.'[39] But this judgment cannot support such a conclusion, for it does not address, much less resolve, the question. It seems that both lines of case law (direct application of the free movement rules to private actors in limited cases / application of the free movement rules with Article 10 to the omissions of the States) are meant by the Court to be complementary, so that the line of case law inaugurated by *Walrave* has not been undermined by *Commision v France*, which stands for a different principle to be applied in limited factual situations.

E. Recent Cases

Subsequent cases such as *Deliège* and *Lehtonen* have reaffirmed the principles stated in *Walrave* and *Bosman*.[40]

The judgments in *Angonese* and *Ferlini* present important novelties.

Mr Angonese, an Italian national whose mother tongue was German and who was resident in Bolzano (Italy), had pursued studies in Austria and then applied for a post at a private undertaking in Bolzano. Among the requirements to apply for the post was the production of a certificate of bilingualism that was only issued by the public authorities of Bolzano, after an examination which was only held there. There was no other way to prove Italian/German bilingualism. Mr Angonese was not admitted to the competition because he did not produce the relevant certificate. He challenged the requirement as incompatible with Article 39 EC and Articles 3(1) and 7(1) and (4) of Regulation 1612/68, on freedom of movement of workers within the Community.[41]

The Court declared that the Regulation was not applicable to the case, and moved to Article 39. After repeating the traditional case law on collective regulations, the Court evoked *Defrenne*,[42] which in 1976 had extended the application of Article 141 to individual contracts. This conclusion applies *a fortiori* to Article 39 EC, according to the Court, so that 'the prohibition of discrimination on grounds of nationality laid down in Article [39] of the Treaty must be regarded as applying to private persons as well.'[43]

This judgment extends the applicability of Article 39 EC beyond collective private regulations (to which *Bosman* was restricted), covering not only private

---

[39] P Oliver, 'Some Further Reflections on the Scope of Articles 28–30 (ex 30–36) EC', (1999) *Common Market Law Review*, 783, 791; J Stuyck, 'Libre circulation et concurrence: les deux pilliers du marché commun', in M Dony (ed) *Mélanges en hommage à Michel Waelbroeck* (vol II Bruylant, Brussels, 1999) 1477, 1489–1492 (preferring the solution in *Commission v France* to that in *Walrave* and *Bosman*).

[40] Case C–176/96 *Lehtonen* [2000] ECR I–2681, para 35; Joined Cases C–51/96 and C–191/97 *Deliège* [2000] ECR I–2549, para 47.

[41] OJ, English Special Edition 1968 II, 475.

[42] Cases 43/75 *Defrenne* [1976] ECR 455.

[43] Case C–281/98 *Angonese* [2000] ECR I–4139, para 36.

contracts (as *Defrenne*), but even unilateral behaviour such as the conditions established by a private undertaking for an employment competition.

The decision, however, is limited (i) to the rule of non-discrimination—not being, unlike *Bosman*, relevant for non-discriminatory restrictions—and (ii) to the field of workers—not being relevant, in principle, for the other free movement rules.

Angonese proves that free movement of workers is different. The Treaty does not consider them as economic factors: it protects them as such. The Court sees discriminating against workers as graver than discriminating against goods or services, which seems reasonable. Private discrimination against other economic factors should be compatible with the Treaty, inasmuch as its effects on competition are not appreciable (if it is an agreement) or the undertaking does not have a dominant position (if it is unilateral behaviour).

It would have been possible to achieve the same practical result through an interpretation of Regulation 1612/86. This solution would have preserved a single scope for all the economic freedoms as a matter of Community constitutional law. The special scope for the workers provision would have been considered a matter of secondary or statutory law. The Court preferred to follow the constitutional route, not that of secondary law, including any private conduct within the purview of Article 39 EC. Thus, workers are given an enhanced protection, because it does not rest on a decision of the legislator, but on an interpretation of the Treaty itself.

In *Ferlini*, a Community official working in Luxembourg for the Commission, realised that the scales of hospital fees applicable to persons and bodies not affiliated to the national social security scheme were fixed unilaterally by all the Luxembourg hospitals within the 'Entente des Hôpitaux Luxembourgeois'. These scales were agreed as part of the national legislation on social security, which permitted price-fixing, and were blatantly discriminatory. When his wife gave birth, Mr Ferlini had to pay 71.43 per cent more than a person subject to Luxembourg social security.

The Tribunal d'Arrondissement referred to the Court of Justice a question about whether the Grand Ducal Regulation and the agreement between the 'Entente des Hôpitaux' were compatible with Articles 12, 39 and 81(1) of the Treaty, and with Regulations 1612/68 and 1408/71.

The case is peculiar because of its facts, but the decision has a wider significance, beyond the law of the officials of the Community.

Community officials are not workers within the meaning of Regulation 1408/71, on social security, because they are not subject to national legislation on social security. They are migrant workers, certainly, but the application of fees for hospital maternity services cannot be regarded as a condition of work within the meaning of Article 39 nor as a social advantage under Regulation 1612/68.

The Court was thus left with Article 12, a keystone of the Treaty prohibiting, within its scope of application, and without prejudice to any special provision contained therein, any discrimination on grounds of nationality.

The problem for the Court was the personal scope of application of Article 12. Before this case, it was not clear whether it covered private action such as the unilateral fixing of the scales by the 'Entente des Hôpitaux'. In paragraph 50, the Court held that

> according to the case-law of the Court, the first paragraph of Article 12 of the Treaty also applies in cases when a group or organisation such as the [entente] exercises a certain power over individuals and is in a position to impose on them conditions which adversely affect the exercise of the fundamental freedoms guaranteed by the Treaty.[44]

The Court referred to *Walrave*, *Defrenne* and *Bosman* as precedents. Only *Walrave* refers to Article 12, and quite laterally indeed, as more 'special' provisions were applicable in that case. What the Court seems to be suggesting is that, since the prohibition of discrimination is also part of the rules on free movement, the personal scope of application of Article 12 should not be dissimilar from that of the free movement rules.

This judgment shows how a development in the economic constitutional law of the Community is exported into its general constitutional law (Article 12). Another positive feature lies in the fact that the Court no longer refers to the enigmatic concept of collective private rules, but explains that these are rules enacted by a group with a certain power over individuals. The difference in treatment was held to be discriminatory, disproportionate and unjustified. As in *Bosman*, the Court added that it was 'not necessary to examine the question in the light of Article 81 of the Treaty.'[45] This shows that the Court prefers to dispose of cases under the free movement rules, perhaps once again for reasons of self-restraint.

The case law in the field is not completely coherent. Some judgments, like *Dansk Supermarked* or *Angonese*, seem to stand for the interpretation that all contracts—even individual—are subject to the free movement rules. In *Vlaamse Reisbureaus* there is an *obiter dictum* to the effect that 'Articles [28] and [29] of the Treaty concern only public measures and not the conduct of undertakings.'[46] Besides, a series of judgments assess under the free movement provisions private rules of a collective nature, whatever that may mean. It seems that a single solution as to the proper personal scope of the free movement rules is needed for all free movement provisions—with the exception of workers. Such a solution is to be based on convincing argumentation, and will lie beyond certain dogmatic positions (complete inclusion/exclusion).

---

[44] Case C–411/98 *Ferlini* [2000] ECR I–8081, para 50.
[45] *Ibid*, para 61.
[46] Case 311/85 *Vlaamse Reisbureaus* [1987] ECR 3801, para 30.

7.4. AN ANALYSIS OF CERTAIN PROPOSALS

Certain authors have proposed solutions and routes, based on various legal constructions, to tackle this issue. Before proposing my own views on the issue, it may be useful to outline the proposals of some of these authors and comment upon them.

A. Detlef Shaefer and Fundamental Rights

Detlef Schaefer argued that the free movement rules would bind individuals, with the limit of fundamental rights. This construction seems to put the free movement rules at the same level as fundamental rights, because they would bind individuals (they would have *Drittwirkung*) and they would be pitted and balanced against fundamental rights.

Schaefer gives a series of examples of situations and how he would solve them through balancing (private 'buy national' campaigns, which could not be justified on commercial speech grounds; strikes boycotting imports, which would not normally be justified through the right to strike, etc.).[47]

This solution would involve a formidable extension of the reach of those provisions, and in turn of the Court's and national courts' jurisdiction. Placing the free movement rules and fundamental rights on an equal footing is also dubious, as I shall argue below. The Court would no doubt get enmeshed in cases involving difficult balancing exercises and mild restrictions to trade.

The indiscriminate inclusion of private conduct does not seem to be compatible with the rationale of *Keck*. This judgment showed the willingness of the Court to limit the review of measures under the free movement provisions—at least under Article 28 EC—following Advocate General Tesauro's opinion in *Hünermund*. For Tesauro,

> the purpose of Article [28] is to ensure the free movement of goods in order to establish a single integrated market, eliminating therefore those national measures which in any way create an obstacle to or even mere difficulties for the movement of goods; its purpose is not to strike down the most widely differing measures in order, essentially, to ensure the greatest possible expansion of trade.[48]

If this is the philosophy behind *Keck*, an extension of the field of application of the free movement rules to all private measures seems unlikely.

Note, however, that Schaefer was writing before *Keck*, in years in which the interpretation of the free movement rules as individual rights seemed to prevail over their interpretation as anti-protectionist rules.

---

[47] D Schaefer, *Die unmittelbare Wirkung des Verbots der nichttarifären Handelshemmnisse (Art 30 EWGV) in den Rechtsbeziehungen zwischen Privaten* (Lang, Frankfurt a-M, 1987) 232–244.
[48] C–292/92 *Hünermund* [1993] ECR I–6787, para 28 of the Opinion.

With US economic constitutional law in mind, the understanding of the free movement of rules seems closer to some sort of dormant commerce clause (US Constitution: Article I, § 8) aimed at preventing protectionism, than it is to an economic right to free trade similar to the guarantee of substantive due process (14th Amendment). Thus, the arguments on the effects of fundamental rights in relations between individuals—a classic but still controversial debate in many constitutional systems and in public international law—would only be partially pertinent for us if the free movement rules are seen mainly as an anti-protectionist device.

Miguel Poiares Maduro has written that the Court has a 'conception of the free movement provisions as fundamental rights' and argues that 'the borderline between securing access to the market for further market integration and securing access to the market to enhance economic freedom is thin and often non-existent'.[49] This view does not take into account that these constitutional rights may be *fundamental for economic integration* (hence fundamental Community rights but not fundamental human rights), but they are not *fundamental rights* in the sense that the constitutional rights to life or equality may be. The line dividing both interpretations of the Community free movement provisions may be thin, but never non-existent. This line is actually quite important, for it distinguishes between warranted interpretations of such provisions (as prohibiting unjustified restrictions of trade: ie an antiprotectionist construction) and unwarranted interpretations thereof (as prohibiting all hindrance of individual commercial freedom, i.e. an economic rights construction).[50]

This line, based on the distinction between fundamental rights as ends in themselves and free movement rights as instrumental rights for the realisation of the internal market, is clearly drawn in the case law.[51]

A different theme is whether private action could be checked under the fundamental rights doctrine of the Court of Justice (freedom of trade). This fundamental right, taking the form of a general principle of Community law, should be distinguished from the free movement rules. The Court itself has drawn such distinction in *Huiles usagées*, where it held that 'the principles of free movement of goods and freedom of competition, *together with freedom of trade as a fundamental right*, are general principles of Community law of which the Court ensures observance.'[52]

---

[49] M Poiares Maduro, 'Striking the Elusive Balance Between Economic Freedoms and Social Rights in the EU', in P Alston (ed) *The EU and Human Rights* (OUP, Oxford, 1999) 449, 450 and 451.

[50] N Bernard, 'La libre circulation des marchandises, des personnes et des services dans le Traité CE sous l'angle de la compétence', (1998) *Cahiers de droit européen*, 11, 31: 'la Cour considère que la question-clef pour le droit de la libre circulation est celle du compartimentage du marché et non celle de la liberté commerciale.'

[51] Case C–265/95 *Commission v France* [1997] ECR I–6959, para 30; Opinion 1/91 [1991] ECR I–6079, paras 17–18.

[52] Case 240/83 *Huiles usagées* [1985] ECR 531, para 9 (my emphasis). The point is also made by N Bernard, 'La libre circulation des marchandises, des personnes et des services dans le Traité CE sous l'angle de la compétence', above n 50, 29.

B. Wulf-Henning Roth and Article 12

Roth strongly argued against the application of the free movement rules to individuals. His conclusion is the following: the prohibition of discrimination on the grounds of nationality enshrined in Article 12 would bind individuals, with two provisos. Firstly, Article 12 would not apply in those cases in which the free movement rules exceptionally apply to private conduct. Such cases include the activity of private institutions in which public authority is vested and the phenomenon of private legislation (*Rechtsetzung durch Private*) by associations which enact rules which application cannot be evaded by individuals (except when there are several associations effectively competing with each other). Secondly, Article 12 would not apply in the field of competition, in order to maintain the *de minimis* rule.[53]

The problem with this proposal is that Article 12 only applies '[w]ithin the scope of application of [the] Treaty, and without prejudice to any special provisions contained therein [. . .].' In the presence of a more concrete provision Article 12 steps back, or more precisely, its normative substance is applied through the more concrete provision.[54] As Advocate General Lenz argued in his Opinion in *Cowan*, '[a]s a specific prohibition of discrimination, Article [49] constitutes a particular manifestation of the general prohibition of discrimination under Article [12]; it applies the latter in a concrete form but does not supersede it.'[55] The prohibition of discrimination is thus implicit in the free movement rules, although the latter also cover non-discriminatory restrictions of trade.[56] It can be said that every discrimination is usually a restriction—although not every restriction is discriminatory. The concept of restriction thus includes and is broader than the concept of discrimination.

Until quite recently, moreover, it was not clear whether Article 12 would bind individuals. *Ferlini*, to which we have just referred, makes clear that this provision extends to collective measures, just like the free movement rules. It cannot be otherwise: a dissociation between their scopes of application would give rise to problems: how could Article 12 extend beyond the scope of the free movement provisions if it applies within the scope of the Treaty and without prejudice to other special provisions thereof? How could it apply in the fields of goods and capital, irrespective of the nationality of the trader?

These questions and problems show that the application of Article 12 to private conduct is no panacea. The basis for a possible application of the free movement rules in the private sphere is to be found in those rules themselves rather than in the residuary non-discrimination clause of Article 12.

---

[53] W-H Roth, 'Drittwirkung der Grundfreiheiten?', above n 29, 1245–1247.
[54] See Case 186/87 *Cowan* [1989] ECR 195, para 14.
[55] *Ibid*, Opinion of the Advocate General, para 40.
[56] See Case 33/88 *Allué* [1989] ECR 1591.

C. Milner-Moore, Steindorff and the Last Sentence of Article 30

In the field of free movement of goods, Milner-Moore concluded that

> Community law should be interpreted to impose obligations upon private parties under the free movement of goods principle. Article [30](2) [*sic*] should be regarded as prohibiting private parties from exercising arbitrary discrimination and from erecting restrictions upon trade between Member States.[57]

Ernst Steindorff also advances this view and seems not to limit this construction to the free movement of goods.[58] Although the prohibition of arbitrary discrimination and disguised restrictions is only stated in the provisions on goods and capital, this rationale could be extended to the remaining free movement provisions through the application of the proportionality principle.[59]

However, this proposal is not logical. The scope of the exception to the public interest justifications included in Article 30 EC and equivalent provisions (arbitrary discrimination and disguised restrictions) cannot be wider than the scope of the exceptions, let alone of the prohibition itself. In other words, if the prohibition of restrictions to free movement only binds the States, the conditions for an exception to such a prohibition are also applicable to the States, and cannot be held to bind individuals. Giving an independent normative status to the tail of Article 30 EC involves a daring exercise in interpretation, since it is inextricably linked to the first sentence of the provision, and the provision is itself nothing but an exception to Articles 28 and 29, actually referring back to them. Admittedly, the law is not limited to logical discourse, but it is based on it. The fact that a legal solution is logical does not make it automatically just, but the illogical construction of a provision is generally unwarranted.

D. Binding Individuals Through National Courts?

Since national courts are bound to apply Community law, it has been proposed that they are also bound not to enforce contractual clauses restrictive of trade.[60] This proposition may find some support in *Dansk Supermarked*—which may no longer be good law—where the Court held that,

> judicial authorities of a Member State may not prohibit, on the basis of a copyright or of a trade mark, the marketing on the territory of that state of a product to which one

---

[57] G R Milner-Moore, *The Private Accountability of Private Parties under the Free Movement of Goods Principle* (Harvard Jean Monnet Working Paper 9/95), see the conclusion and section D.

[58] E Steindorff, *EG-Vertrag und Privatrecht*, above n 24, 299.

[59] See Cases 115/81 *Adoui* [1982] ECR 1665 (workers) and 41/74 *Van Duyn* [1974] ECR 1337 (services).

[60] See Advocate General Van Gerven, in Case C–339/89 *Alsthom Atlantique* [1991] ECR 117, para 6.

of those rights applies if that product has been lawfully marketed on the territory of another Member State by the proprietor of such rights or with his consent.[61]

However, the qualifying element of the restriction was not the national judgment, but the copyright or trademark based on State legislation.

The contention seems mistaken. National courts, even if they are taken to be organs of the State, operate as Community courts when they apply Community law. They have to apply such law inasmuch as they have to apply State law, but they are not bound by Community law as the States or individuals may be. Courts are not subjects of Community—or State—law, but part of the machinery of its application. Lower national courts may not apply Community law well, but this does not make their judgments measures of equivalent effect. Higher courts are different to the extent that they sometimes perform a law-creating activity, not unlike a legislator. There seems to be however no need to include them among the addressees of the free movement provisions in order to prevent judicially-driven protectionism, since they are obliged to refer questions on Community law to the Court. There may be extreme cases where a higher court refuses to refer. In those cases, the State itself—not the national court—may be held responsible for the breach of the Treaty by the higher national court, a breach of an obligation under Article 234, not under the economic freedoms. But the fact that national courts are obliged to apply Community law cannot of itself alter the substantive content nor the proper scope of the provisions that they are bound to apply.

7.5. REFINING THE CONCEPT OF COLLECTIVE PRIVATE MEASURES

The wording of the provisions that we are to apply is not conclusive.[62] The solution should be based on a structural interpretation of the norms in the framework of the Treaty.

The point of departure could be the non-textual postulate, springing from the structure of the Treaty, to the effect that free movement rules normally bind the States, while competition rules normally bind enterprises. Thus, in principle the free movement rules should not limit private behaviour and autonomy.

This postulate is implicit in the case law in which the Court tried to qualify a measure as a public measure.[63] Such an effort would only be warranted if the Court did not see private actors as bound by the free movement rules. In *Apple and Pear Development Council* the Court stated that,

> a body [. . .] which is set up by the government of a Member State and is financed by a charge imposed on growers, cannot under Community law enjoy the same freedom

---

[61] Case 58/80 *Dansk Supermarked* [1981] ECR 181, para 12.

[62] In this sense, E Steindorff, *EG-Vertrag und Privatrecht*, above n 24, 285.

[63] Case 249/81 *Commission v Ireland* (Buy Irish) [1982] ECR 4005; Joined Cases 266 & 267/87 *Royal Pharmaceutical Society* [1989] ECR 1295.

as regards the methods of advertising used as that enjoyed by producers themselves or producers' associations of a voluntary character.[64]

This paragraph may show the willingness of the Court to apply the free movement rules to private associations of an obligatory character, even if they do not receive financial support and are not vested with special powers from the State, since they truly have the means to enforce measures amounting to private protectionism.

Kluth has argued that the application of the free movement rules to private conduct would raise questions about the boundary between the power of the State and private autonomy,[65] involving an important degree of socialisation of private law, and causing the end of the private law society and the departure from the liberal concept of the single market as a fundamental pillar of the Community.[66]

These ideas are obviously of some import, together with what Roth argued about private regulation. The principle of a uniform application of Community law is to be preserved as much as possible if its aims are to be secured. Free movement rules should not be applied differently in the States depending on the degree of privatisation or nationalisation of their societies. However, since the limits between State and society, between legislation and private governance, vary in the Member States, they would inescapably produce a breach in the uniform application of Community law. Thus, not only should State and private associations which exercise powers delegated by the State be bound by the free movement rules (as 'emanations' of the State). Also purely private conduct should be caught when it amounts to what Roth calls private legislation (*Rechtsetzung durch Private*)[67] and others self-regulation.[68] This inclusion may be vital for the proper functioning of the single market if one acknowledges that EC economic freedoms strengthen the autonomy of economic actors and that the process of privatisation 'widens the private realm'[69] and correspondingly narrows the public sphere and, accordingly, the importance of the traditional scope of operation of the free movement rules. The effectiveness of the free movement rules would be hampered if their scope of application did not adapt to this process of privatisation of the economy.

Here one may recall something that was stressed in the introduction to this chapter: the single market is to result spontaneously, mainly from the dismantling of State barriers to trade, and individuals should not be forced to realise it. The

---

[64] Case 222/82 *Apple and Pear Development Council* [1983] ECR 4083, para 17.

[65] W Kluth, 'Die Bindung privater Wirtschaftsteilnehmer an die Grundfreiheiten des EG-Vertrages', (1997) *Archiv des öffentliches Rechts*, 567, 561.

[66] *Ibid*, 581.

[67] W-H Roth, 'Drittwirkung der Grundfreiheiten?', above n 29, 1247.

[68] G Majone, *Regulating Europe* (Routledge, London, 1996) 23, defines self-regulation as the delegation of 'responsibilities to private or semi-private bodies', a technique which had 'a long tradition among the craft and the professions, but in recent times it has extended into other areas such as technical standardization, industrial safety and financial services.'

[69] C Joerges, 'The Impact of European Integration on Private Law: Reductionist Perceptions, True Conflicts and a New Constitutional Perspective', above n 33, 388.

free movement provisions are designed to create the conditions of possibility for a single market to emerge spontaneously and flourish through trade, but cannot have this effect without the free behaviour of individuals.

The formula that private measures which are 'collective in nature' or regulate some area in a collective manner may be caught by the free movement rules seems therefore to be correct, although one should try to explain its rationale and reach.

The clarification of the concept of collective private measures entails a discussion about the public/private divide. Such divide depends on various factors: the degree of privatisation in each State, the kind of activities into which the State intervenes and the intensity of such intervention, and the corresponding capacity of civil society to organise itself independently. The Community should not draw the scope of the free movement rules along the lines of the public/private divide, because there is not one single and constant divide for all the Member States. Moreover, an increasing number of legal realities embody an inextricably linked mixture of private and public that resists any classification.

Thus, the public or private nature of the actor will not determine for the scope of application of the free movement rules. This scope will be rather determined by the nature of the action—hence the personal scope of application will vary depending on the material scope of application.

What is relevant for Community law should then be to determine whether private or mixed (public/private) action qualifies as a restriction of free movement. Such action is still mainly or partly private and the nature of the actor is not changed. Review under the free movement rules does not assimilate it to public action, nor does it mean that the relevant body qualifies as public. In this context, it seems that merely individual action is not and should not be caught by those provisions. As regards collective action, it seems reasonable that not all collective measures should be caught. For example, the bylaws of a private corporation, even if they are collective, should not be caught in principle by the free movement provisions.

Thus, private action may be caught by the Treaty rules on free movement only when it has the capacity to restrict free movement with a protectionist intent or effect. Other private action will be caught by the competition rules or by the fundamental rights jurisprudence of the Court of Justice.

The monopolistic character of the association is not to be regarded as decisive. The test is whether the private association has power over that individual, and whether this power is used with a protectionist intent or effect. Let us give an example in the field of free movement of capital. In this field, consumers are usually forced to accept the general contractual conditions imposed by banks (a sort of private collective regulation). Thus, the relevant norm of the Treaty would be applicable, if such general conditions amount to an obstacle to the movement of capital under Article 56 EC.[70]

---

[70] Ph-E Partsch, comment on Article 56 EC, in Ph Léger (ed) *Commentaire article par article des traités EU et CE* (Helbing and Lichtenhahn, Basle, 2000) 478, 492.

Note that not only collective rules, but also collective action (by a trade union, for example), could be covered by the economic freedoms of the Treaty. The substantial content of the free movement rules vis-à-vis private rules and action would furthermore be the same where public measures are concerned. Thus this would include indistinctly applicable measures, and the grounds of justification—as *Bosman* makes clear—although the proportionality test applied to private actors should be stricter. In contrast, private behaviour that lacks this dimension of 'power over individuals'—for example, the refusal of an undertaking to provide a service to a foreigner and other such behaviour— would not be caught by the free movement rules, because they have nothing to do with protectionism.

The free movement of workers is and should be interpreted differently. The whole field of free movement of workers is mostly outside the purview of the competition rules. Collective agreements do not fall under the competition rules when they fulfil the conditions established by the Court in *Albany*.[71] Labour contracts do not fall under Article 81. Workers do not have the same contractual power as employers, which gives the rule on free movement of workers its social dimension. This is why secondary legislation on the free movement of workers has extended the prohibition to collective agreements and individual contracts.[72] The Court, as it has already been seen, has extended, in *Angonese*, the prohibition of discrimination enshrined in Article 39 EC to all sorts of private action, contractual or even unilateral.

From the point of view of the convergence of the free movement rules, this solution is not problematic for the interaction between competition and free movement. Thus State action will be covered by the competition rules if the State acts as a market participant (through public undertakings, for example). Private action with a public purpose could be justified in the framework of the competition rules, if it is proportionate. Private regulation would be covered by the free movement rules, and by the competition rules inasmuch as it has anticompetitive aspects.

Concerning secondary law, harmonisation measures pursuant to Article 95 EC may impose obligations on individuals and reach the spheres of private law, insofar as it proves necessary in order to smoothen the barriers to trade beyond the reach of directly applicable Treaty provisions. In my view, it seems beyond doubt that, if we are to harmonise effectively, the potential personal scope of Article 95 must be wider than that of the free movement rules. In this context, however, the limitations imposed by the Community on private autonomy should be as limited as possible and in any case proportionate to the ends pursued by harmonisation.[73]

---

[71] Case C–67/96 *Albany* [1999] ECR I–5751; see below, chapter 8.
[72] See Article 7 of Council Regulation 1612/68 (OJ 1968 L 257/2).
[73] See Case C–200/96 *Metronome* [1998] ECR I–1953.

In sum, from the perspective of the free movement of economic factors, private barriers to trade are no windmills, but not giants either if the competition rules are correctly applied, fundamental rights (such as freedom of trade) are protected and, by way of exception, certain cases of private action fall under the free movement rules—save in the case of workers, where a broader application would be justified.

8

State Action Doctrine and Community Competition Law

THE ISSUES PRESENTED by anticompetitive State action in Community law mirror those of the effect of the free movement rules in the private sphere. The jurist faces here another constitutional gap and its potential filling through the application of general principles. There are some differences, for in the present context it is the States and the competition rules, not individuals or private associations and the free movement rules, which are concerned by the gap-filling exercise.

The relevant questions are the following: May the competition rules or their underlying principles be applied to the States? Under what conditions? If they are so applied, what substantial content should they be given? Is such an extension legitimate as a matter of constitutional interpretation? Are there any limits to this extension related to the political structure of the Community and the respect for the States' democratic processes? Should we devise one standard for all public measures or rather establish different degrees of review depending on the author of the measure?

The analysis begins with a consideration of the relevant texts and the structural context. The other available routes to approach our problem will also be examined. Then the most important judgments will be reported, concluding with a personal assessment of the issue.

The examination will give a prominent place to constitutional considerations, for they should be, and perhaps already are, decisive in this field. The perplexity of the competition lawyer faced with the State action doctrine is understandable insofar as the case law is exclusively analysed through the prism of economic efficiency. In the context of the State action doctrine, however, economic efficiency has not been the only nor the main concern of the Court, and perhaps rightly so. This doctrine may be best justified as the expression of certain constitutional principles related to the political structure of the Community. The analysis is difficult, because these principles have never been explicitly stated in the case law.

Our analysis finds inspiration at some points in the 'State action doctrine' in US antitrust law. This doctrine establishes an immunity for the States regarding the antitrust laws, whereas the Community case law has the opposite aim: to determine under what conditions the competition rules may be applied to public action. It is however useful to compare the respective conditions for the extension or the immunity in each legal system. The US doctrine of antitrust federalism is particularly useful because it is explicitly based on constitutional grounds.

8.2. RELEVANT TEXTS, STRUCTURE AND OTHER AVAILABLE ROUTES

As we have seen in chapter 7, the free movement rules are silent about their application to private entities. The non-textual structural assumption is that they only apply to the States, which leaves the gap to be filled by the Community judiciary in exceptional cases.

The textual point of departure is quite different in the case of the competition rules, included in Part Three, Title VI, Chapter 1 of the Treaty. As is well known, this chapter is divided in two sections: Section 1 includes the rules applying to undertakings; section 2 is devoted to the aids granted by States. The private/public divide is therefore part of the structure of this chapter of the Treaty, and there can be no doubt that, in and of themselves, Articles 81 and 82 EC only apply to undertakings.

The concept of 'undertaking' has been constantly defined by the Court as encompassing 'every entity engaged in an economic activity, regardless of the legal status of the entity and the way in which it is financed'[1]—'economic activity' covering any offering of goods or services on a given market.[2] Wide enough a concept, to be sure, but insufficient to attract to the competition rules applicable to undertakings all sorts of State action that may negatively affect the effectiveness of the competition rules.

What about other provisions of the Treaty? Are there other routes to deal with this problem that make the State action doctrine redundant and superfluous?

A. The Enforcement Mechanism

Articles 83–85 EC are devoted to the implementation of Articles 81–82 EC, including for such purposes a deferment to secondary law and some transitional rules. Incidentally, the regulations and directives of Article 83 are intended to give effect to the principles of Articles 81 and 82, not 86, which has its own enforcement mechanism. It is debatable whether Article 83 could provide a legal basis to create an enforcement mechanism for the State action doctrine, if indeed

---

[1] Case C–41/90 *Höfner* [1991] ECR I–1979, para 21.
[2] See Cases 118/85 *Commission v Italy* [1987] ECR 2599, para 7; C–35/96 *Commission v Italy* [1998] ECR I–3851, para 36.

there is need for it. Arguably, Articles 96–97 EC—and perhaps Article 85—may allow the Commission to take some action against anticompetitive State behaviour not falling under a concrete Treaty rule.

At first sight, it could be thought that the State action doctrine lacks an enforcement mechanism because Regulation 17/62 only applies to undertakings. Nonetheless, inasmuch as it is a State that breaches the Treaty, the procedures of Articles 226 and 227 are open for the Commission or other Member States to bring an action against the infringing State. And an undertaking may always invoke the breach of this case law before a national court. A different theme is that perhaps the Commission does not pursue this kind of violation of the Treaty with sufficient vigour, but this does not mean that it will not be able to do it more systematically in the future. A first example is the 1998 case *Commission v Italy*,[3] on the tariffs fixed by Italian customs agents in a public context, which will be discussed below.

In mixed situations, a simultaneous action under Article 226—against the State—and Regulation 17/62—against the undertaking or undertakings involved—would be the appropriate procedural route. This double action has already been used by the Commission.[4]

Another potential problem with the State action doctrine is the fact that, for the time being, the Commission has sole power to give exemptions to anticompetitive agreements pursuant to Article 81(3) under Article 9(1) of Regulation 17/62, so that States would be condemned under Article 81(1) without the possibility of an exemption. Independently of the fate of the modernisation programme launched by the Commission and referred to in chapter 7, which could end with this sole power of the Commission to exempt agreements, in fact the State action doctrine is not based on the application of Article 81 alone, but on the combined application of Articles 3(1)(g), 10 and 81–82. Any limitation of the State action doctrine on grounds of general interest would be internal to the doctrine itself, and therefore open to its assessment and application also by national courts, with the guidance of the Court of Justice under the preliminary rulings procedure.

B. Article 86 EC

Article 86 refers to three special categories of undertakings: 'public undertakings', 'undertakings to which Member States grant special or exclusive rights' and undertakings 'entrusted with the operation of services of general economic interest or having the character of a revenue-producing monopoly'. When interpreting

---

[3] Case C–35/96 *Commission v Italy* [1998] ECR I–3851.

[4] Prior to *Commission v Italy*, cited in the previous note, the Commission had adopted in the same factual context Decision 93/438/EEC, relating to proceedings pursuant to the then Article 85 of the EEC Treaty (IV/33.407—CNSD, OJ 1993 L 203/27).

this provision, one should not forget that it is included in section 1 of the Treaty chapter on competition, entitled 'rules applying to *undertakings*.' With regard to the first two categories, the provision simply states that the States 'shall neither enact nor maintain into force any measure contrary to the rules contained in this Treaty, in particular to those rules provided for in Article 12 and Articles 81 to 89.' With regard to the third, Article 86(2) establishes that they are subject to the Treaty only insofar as its application 'does not obstruct the performance, in law or in fact, of the particular tasks assigned to them.'

This provision does not take us far in terms of the shortcomings of the scope of the competition rules and tackling the present problem of anticompetitive State action. The concept of undertaking in Article 86 is identical to that in Articles 81–82. The limited effect of this provision is to confirm and at most to reinforce the application of the Treaty to some kinds of undertakings, to slightly extend the application of the competition rules to the States in their special relations with such kinds of undertakings, and to establish a restriction in the case of undertakings entrusted with services of public economic interest. This provision has little normative content of its own, and fails to cover all sorts of State action that may interfere with the application of the competition rules.

There is some confusion regarding the interaction between this provision and the State action doctrine. It is beyond doubt that there is a close relationship between Article 86 and the State action doctrine, but perhaps it is slightly different from that of *lex specialis/lex generalis*, which is normally attributed to them.[5] There could be a relationship of this sort between Article 10, paragraph 2, and Article 86, if only the former had direct effect. But if one sees Article 86 as *lex specialis* with respect to the State action doctrine, there is the risk of using the latter in favour of competition and economic efficiency, disregarding the constitutional elements of the State action doctrine and the important differences that distinguish it from the limited ratio and purpose of Article 86.

The main difference between the State action doctrine and Article 86 comes precisely from the fact that the focus of Article 86 is mainly competition. The measures it refers to are measures affecting concrete undertakings. Its aim is that the public economic sector, and State action directly related to this sector, be also subject to the competition rules.

In contrast, the measures falling under the State action doctrine are usually general regulatory policies and/or implementing measures thereof that may affect public and private undertakings alike. The State action doctrine is about controlling public action itself—inasmuch as it interferes with the behaviour of undertakings—not simply about what public officials may do through or with public undertakings or undertakings holding special or exclusive rights.

This difference in focus may explain the divergence between the case law concerning the general doctrine and that on Article 86. This is fully justified in view of the diverse rationales and functions of the State action doctrine and Article 86.

---

[5] Case C–67/96 *Albany* [1999] ECR I–5751, Opinion of Advocate General Jacobs, para 372.

Thus, an extension of the approach under Article 86 to the State action doctrine could produce undesirable results. Such an extension has been proposed with a view to ensuring an efficient allocation of market resources.[6] This extension would entail a review that would either be (i) too intrusive, submitting policy problems to rigid rules of economic efficiency or (ii) too deferential, in which case too many situations would be reviewed that should not really be reviewed in the light of the principles of competition.

C. State Aids

In the chapter on competition one also finds provisions specifically addressed to the States (section 2, aids granted by States, Articles 87–89 EC). This could be a systemic argument against the extension of the competition rules beyond undertakings, since the rules directly addressed to the States are confined to the field of aids. Against this argument, one could say that the State action doctrine does not only aim at reviewing State action as such, but in those situations in which it is closely mixed with corporate behaviour which—alone or together with the public action—breaches the competition rules.

Besides, despite their importance the State aid rules have a rather limited field of application. They are subject to a political mechanism of enforcement and for the most part they do not have direct effect, that is, with some exceptions, the parties concerned cannot invoke them before national courts without having previously followed the procedure before the Commission.[7] National courts cannot determine whether aid is compatible or not with the Common Market, a decision which is the monopoly of the Commission (much as Article 81(3) EC). The application of the State aid provisions is thus administrative in nature. In this system, national courts must ensure that the Member States comply with their procedural obligations (notification of aid to the Commission, etc.) and the consequences of their breach for individuals.

In its 1990 survey on State aids, the Commission defined the scope of Article 87 EC as covering aids 'granted through State resources which by favouring *certain undertakings* or the production of *certain goods* distorts or threatens to distort competition and affects trade between Member States.' In contrast, general measures 'comprise any state interventions that apply uniformly across the economy and which do not favour certain enterprises or sectors.' General measures fall 'within the scope of Articles [96/97].'[8] The Commission considers that general measures are not so disruptive of competition as aids. Such measures,

---

⁶ See C Chung, 'The Relationship Between State Regulation and EC Competition Law', (1995) *European Competition Law Review*, 87.

⁷ Case 74/76 *Iannelli* [1977] ECR 557, para 12.

⁸ European Commission, *Second Survey on State Aids in the European Community in the Manufacture and Certain Other Sectors*, 4–5.

and other concrete measures not qualifying as aids, would be the specific object of the State action doctrine.

D. Free Movement

The free movement rules would be the preferred—but not the only—route to tackle our problem, and this for various reasons.

To begin with, State courts are probably better suited to apply the free move-ment rules than the competition rules. Besides, in the free movement context there is no *de minimis* limit, so that more situations will be caught under these rules. As a procedural matter, it is also easier to get a useful preliminary ruling on the free movement rules, as there is no need to provide as much information with the reference as in competition cases. As was shown in chapter 6, the Court has demonstrated a marked procedural preference for free movement over competition.

Miguel Poiares Maduro has argued that the structural rationale for constitu-tional review under the free movement rules can be found in the protection of Union citizens who are not represented in State political processes. Under his proposal, 'the Court of Justice will only review national regulatory policies where there is a suspicion of representative malfunction in the national political process with regard to nationals of other Member States.'[9]

This opinion is interesting, even if the conclusions that the free movement rules 'increase the representation of nationals of other Member States' or can be interpreted as a 'fundamental political right'[10] seem somewhat exaggerated, since they are based on the concept of virtual representation, which is highly questionable in democratic terms.

The free movement rules remain provisions aimed mainly at guaranteeing the unity of the market through the judicial review of protectionism, only indirectly vesting economic not political rights. National political processes may have a protectionist bias that justifies the Court's intervention. But the political process rationale for the Court's intervention is a general rationale for judicial review, not just for review under the free movement rules. This process-based theory of judicial review, a product of US scholarship,[11] is only one among several reasons for review under the negative commerce clause. Among the more specific grounds related to the dormant commerce clause are the fundamental value of economic unity, arguments of economic efficiency and the protection of citizens against restrictions of free trade.

---

[9] M Poiares Maduro, *We the Court* (Hart, Oxford, 1998) 174.

[10] *Ibid*, 171 and 166.

[11] See J H Ely, *Democracy and Distrust* (Harvard University Press, Cambridge, Mass, 1980); J Eule has applied a similar approach to the dormant commerce clause in 'Laying the Dormant Commerce Clause to Rest', (1982) *Yale Law Journal*, 425.

The same sort of arguments may justify the review of national measures under the free movement rules of the Treaty. In Community law, besides, the explicit language of the relevant provisions provides for a stronger basis for such review (in the United States it is just a jurisprudential creation in view of the silence of the Constitution).

The foregoing idea points to the preference for the free movement route if the State action at issue comes from a democratically elected legislator. Deference should be paid to State legislatures insofar as all those affected by their measures are represented in the State democratic process and its outcome is not a violation of fundamental rights or concrete Treaty rules such as the free movement rules. If a State measure has a protectionist dimension, the rationale for review and its base in the Treaty are clear: Union citizens from other States were not represented and deserve protection through the free movement rules. If the relevant piece of legislation simply affects competition irrespective of State borders, all the interests affected would have been represented when it was enacted, and the rationale for deference to democratic processes has more force, that is, review should tend to be minimal, regarding only the 'reasonableness' of the measure. The restraint of competition would appear in this case as a natural outcome of democratic processes, not as a defective result thereof, unless representative malfunction or 'capture' by private interests were proven. Most defects of the political process should be corrected by the political process itself, unless they were too obvious or specially grave—this is yet another reason to carry out a minimal review in this field in the absence of a free movement problem. Otherwise one would review through the backdoor most of the questions that were avoided with the *Keck* shift in the free movement field.

The case law itself has only condemned a State for a violation of the State action doctrine on a few occasions,[12] which shows the ECJ's prudence in the application of the doctrine. Nonetheless, the reasons for this soft application of the doctrine are never explained in the judgments themselves. Such implicit reasons have produced an unsatisfactory and partly unprincipled formalism that will become apparent through the analysis of the case law.

For all their advantages, the free movement rules are not without certain drawbacks. They are not applicable to purely internal situations and, in principle, they do not prevent reverse discrimination (that is, the discrimination that a State inflicts on its own nationals). Such limitation of the free movement rules has been criticised. The opening in the *Pistre* and *Lancry* judgments[13]—which seemed to imply that certain purely internal situations would fall under the free movement rules in view of the impossibility of distinguishing what is internal

---

[12] Cases 311/85 *Vlaamse Reisbureaus* [1987] ECR 3801; 209 to 213/84 *Asjes* [1986] ECR 1425; 66/86 *Ahmed Saaed* [1989] ECR 803; C–35/96 *Commission v Italy* [1998] ECR I–3851.

[13] See Joined Cases C–363/93 and C–407 to 411/93 *Lancry* [1994] ECR I–3957; C–321 to 324/94 *Pistre* [1997] ECR I–2343. For a restrictive interpretation of these cases, see P Oliver, 'Some Further Reflections on the Scope of Articles 28–30 (ex 30–36) EC', (1999) *Common Market Law Review*, 783, 784–788. His views seem to be confirmed by the *Guimont* judgment.

and what affects Community trade in a market without borders—may have been aborted by *Guimont*, which insists again on the limits of the free movement rules.[14] Their application to State action is quite selective: only the inter-State dimension of the State measure is subject to scrutiny, while the purely internal dimensions of the measure at issue are not subject to review.

Besides, the *Keck* line of case law has softened the prohibition enshrined in the free movement rules regarding selling arrangements to a rule of non-discrimination, limiting their availability as an alternative route. *Keck* was intended to redirect the focus of the free movement rules to problems of protectionism, that is, to State measures which restrain trade and competition across State borders. Other situations that restrain trade in general and affect competition between private economic operators irrespective of State borders escape the free movement rules altogether. A regulation of tobacco prices, such as the one examined in *GB-INNO-BM*, would not fall under Article 28, being considered a selling arrangement (the regulation at issue in *Keck* itself was an indistinctly applicable price regulation prohibiting sales below cost).[15]

E. Other Provisions

Articles 31 and 96–97 EC are other available routes to reach State restrictions of competition not falling under other provisions of the Treaty, but their field of application is rather narrow. Article 31 only applies to 'State monopolies of a commercial character'. Articles 96–97 do not impose obligations on the States;[16] they are just procedural rules allowing the Community institutions to act when the disparities between States' legislation produces anticompetitive effects. Some of the cases covered by the State action doctrine could give rise to Commission intervention under Article 96, but that would not mean that this line of case law is redundant, for there are various routes to approach the issue.

Indeed, competition in the single market is generally distorted by this disparity between regulatory systems in the different States, even when mutual recognition reduces its protectionist effects and negative spill-over across State borders. When all States have the same legislation, that is, identical mixes of competition and regulation, or when the Community itself enacts legislation, there are no anticompetitive effects. Competition is then levelled in terms of the regulated elements.

---

[14] Case C–448/98 *Guimont* [2000] ECR I–10663, paras 12–21.

[15] See Joined Cases C–267 and C–268/91 *Keck and Mithouard* [1993] ECR I–6097. See also Case C–63/94 *Belgapom v ITM Belgium* [1995] ECR I–2467, in which a price control was classified as a selling arrangement.

[16] A Bach, *Wettbewerbsrechtliche Schranken für staatliche Maßnahmen nach europäischem Gemeinschaftsrecht* (Mohr, Tübingen, 1992) 18.

A problem would only arise when regulations are different and actually *distort* competition along State borders. This is normally seen as a free movement problem, which may explain the sparse use of the special procedure established in Articles 96–97, since this is precisely the case covered by these provisions but the free movement rules and harmonisation measures under Article 95 are far more effective. Besides, legislative disparities are not reproachable in themselves, only insofar as they hide a protectionist effect or intent.

A competition problem would arise when regulations drastically reduce the parameters of competition. This is a problem distinct from that affecting free movement, which is merely an interstate problem. In particular, some of the trade creation benefits expected from the internal market may be cancelled with trade diversion if State measures do not strike a reasonable mix of competition and regulation. Something must be done in such cases. The free movement rules are of no avail, since it is a competition problem, having nothing to do with State borders or protectionism. The issue is whether something must be done by the judiciary or by the legislator. And, if the judiciary is to act, one will have to decide the intensity of its review.

Articles 96–97 have not been much used so far. Their activation by the Commission could provide political solutions to some of these problems—the sort of regulation in a given field—for which judicial decision-making may not always be so well-suited.

This complex array of provisions clearly fails to cover the whole range of situations in which the States can endanger competition through their normal activity (that is, when they do not act as or through public undertakings; when they do so, Article 86 is applicable). On the whole they give a confusing and disparate impression, all the more so when one reads Article 3(1)(g) of the Treaty, according to which the activities of the Community are supposed to include '*a system ensuring that competition in the internal market is not distorted.*' The keyword here is 'system'. The Treaty wants a comprehensive structure ensuring that competition is not distorted.

To some, it is obvious that there is no comprehensive system insofar as State anticompetitive behaviour is concerned. There is hence a gap between the objectives of the Community and the concrete provisions giving effect to them. Such a gap, they will contend, should be filled with a view to preventing the single competitive market from being distorted by State action not contemplated by any specific Treaty provision. The case law of the Court would be fully justified. Perhaps it needs to be completed.

Others argue that the gap was a choice of the drafters of the Treaty. A solution to these problems should be political, not judicial.

These two basic positions are well represented in the Pescatore/Marenco polemic. Pescatore, using a constitutional interpretation, would fill many of the gaps between competition and free movement in order to reduce the asymmetries between the provisions addressed to States and those addressed to undertakings.[17] Marenco, in contrast, would be more cautious. Pescatore's opinion, in his view, would limit too much the powers of the States in the economic field. Thus, concludes Marenco, the *GB-INNO-BM* line of case law should be limited to exceptional cases.[18]

8.3. LEADING CASES

This section presents and analyses the most important judgments in the field. The case law is quite voluminous, and grows each year in spite of the restrictions imposed by the Court on the test and the few occasions on which the party invoking it has prevailed.[19] The sheer number of judgments may be taken as a sign of the vitality of the line of case law and also of the fact that its contours are not perfectly defined. Particular attention will be paid to the subtle but significant shifts in the formula created by the Court.

A. *GB-INNO-BM* (1977)

This was the first case in which the Court addressed the question of the anti-competitive effects of State measures. It was a preliminary ruling rendered in the context of a legal dispute between a Belgian chain of supermarkets (GB-INNO-BM) and an association of tobacco retailers (ATAB). The supermarkets were selling cigarettes at a price lower than the price stated on the tax label in contravention of Belgian VAT law, which obliged retailers to respect the prices freely fixed in tax labels by manufacturers or importers.

ATAB brought proceedings against GB-INNO-BM, which was ordered to discontinue the selling of cigarettes at such prices. On appeal, GB-INNO-BM raised the issue of whether the Belgian legislation was compatible with the Treaty. The Belgian Court of Cassation decided to refer to the Court several questions on the interpretation of Article 3(1)(g), the second paragraph of Article 10, Articles 28, 82 and 86 of the Treaty.

The facts involved a typical private/public situation: prices fixed by manufacturers and importers were imposed through State law on retailers who may have wanted to undercut such prices. The economic effects of the legislation were equivalent to those of a web of resale price maintenance agreements between all manufacturers and importers and their retailers. This piece of legislation destroyed intra-brand competition and artificially kept prices up. Its apparent

---

[17] P Pescatore, 'Public and Private Aspects of Community Competition Law', in B Hawk (ed) *US and Common Market Antitrust Policies: 1986 Corporate Law Institute* (1987) 381, 382.

[18] G Marenco, 'Competition Between National Economies and Competition Between Business—A Response to Judge Pescatore', (1987) *Fordham International Law Journal*, 420, 422.

[19] For an exhaustive analysis of this case law, see U B Neergaard, *Competition & Competences* (DJØF Publishing, Copenhagen, 1988).

public purpose was to protect small retailers from the competition of chain supermarkets.

After describing the facts and the Belgian legislation at issue, the Court stated that,

> [t]he single market system which the Treaty seeks to create excludes any national system of regulation hindering directly or indirectly, actually or potentially, trade within the Community.
>
> Secondly, the general objective set out in Article 3 [(1)(g)] is made specific in several Treaty provisions concerning the rules on competition, including Article [82], which states that any abuse by one or more undertakings of a dominant position shall be prohibited as incompatible with the common market in so far as it may affect trade between Member States.[20]

This judgment was drafted at a time when competition and free movement were still perceived as parts of a normative unit aimed at a single objective. This is how one should read the implicit quotation of *Dassonville*,[21] which in 1974 had taken the formula of *Consten & Grundig* from competition to the free movement of goods.[22]

In paragraph 31, the Court referred to Article 10 of the Treaty, in view of which, 'while it is true that Article [82] is directed at undertakings, nonetheless *it is also true that the Treaty imposes a duty on Member States not to adopt or maintain in force any measure which could deprive that provision of its effectiveness*';[23] that is, a wide but rather vague obligation to abstain from depriving Article 82 of its effectiveness. 'Likewise,' continued the Court in paragraph 33, 'Member States may not enact measures enabling private undertakings to escape from the constraints imposed by Articles [81] to [89] of the Treaty.'[24]

The fact that the Court followed the curious route of the joint application of Articles 10 and 82 is not only attributable to its excessive creativity, but to the questions posed by the Belgian court, which by asking about the consequences of such a legal construction paved the way to the erection of the State action doctrine precisely in that form.

The Court then recognised the overlap of this doctrine with the free movement rules, but it did not express any procedural or substantial preference for any of them:

> a national measure which has the effect of facilitating the abuse of a dominant position capable of affecting trade between Member States will generally be incompatible with Articles [28] and [29], which prohibit quantitative restrictions on imports and exports and all measures having equivalent effect.[25]

---

[20] Case 13/77 *GB-Inno-BM v ATAB* [1977] ECR 2115, paras 28–29.
[21] Case 8/74 *Dassonville* [1974] ECR 837, 852.
[22] Joined Cases 56 & 58/64 *Consten & Grundig* [1966] ECR 299.
[23] Case 13/77 *GB-Inno-BM v ATAB* [1977] ECR 2115, para 31 (my emphasis).
[24] *Ibid*, para 33.
[25] *Ibid*, para 35.

In the end, the Court left a very large leeway to the national court, which had to consider several criteria in order to appraise the consequences of the doctrine. The Court limited itself to announcing the State action doctrine, largely leaving not only its application but the very interpretation of the doctrine to the discretion of the Belgian court.

The issue also arose of whether the manufacturers and importers could be considered to fall under Article 86, since they may have been granted special or exclusive rights through the right to fix the selling price. The Court deemed it 'questionable whether those undertakings can properly be described as having been granted "special", and at all events "exclusive", rights, since that possibility is open to an indefinite class of undertakings.'[26] Unfortunately, the Court did not drive the argument to its logical conclusion and left the question open, considering Article 86 as 'only a particular application of certain general principles which bind the Member States.'[27] In the opinion of the Court, Article 86 would be a reflection of such principles in the Treaty.

The Court made clear that Articles 82 and 28–30 remain operative, even in the presence of the State action doctrine. In assessing compatibility with the Treaty of the Belgian system, 'a national court must take into account all the conditions for the application of the provisions of Community law which have been referred to.'[28] The provisions were Articles 3(1)(g), 10, 82, 86, 81–89 and 28–30. The Court seems to consider jointly all of these norms, a method which has the virtues of comprehensiveness and the problems inherent to overlapping fields of application. The State action doctrine thus appears less as a device to fill a gap in the scope of the competition rules than as a last resort to fill systemic gaps *between competition and free movement*.

According to René Joliet, paragraphs 31 and 33 of *GB-Inno-BM*, in which the Court put forward its State action doctrine, 'were capable of being interpreted in different ways and left the door open to fresh developments.'[29] It is indeed in these central paragraphs that one finds both the force and the weakness of *GB-Inno-BM*, and the tensions of the doctrine itself.

The style of interpretation is usual for the time: teleological and structural arguments are given more force than textual, historical or prudential considerations. The general rule announced in paragraph 31 is rather vague: Article 10, when read with Articles 81 and 82, imposes a concrete and enforceable duty on the States not to detract from the effectiveness of the latter. This duty is constitutional, and it gives rise to individual rights that courts must protect.

In contrast, the dictum in paragraph 33, to the effect that 'Member States may not enact measures enabling private undertakings to escape from the constraints

---

[26] Case13/77 *GB-Inno-BM v ATAB* [1977] ECR 2115, para 41.
[27] *Ibid*, para 42.
[28] Case13/77 *GB-Inno-BM v ATAB* [1977] ECR 2115, para 36 (my emphasis).
[29] R Joliet, 'National Anti-Competitive Legislation and Community Law', in B Hawk (ed) *1987 Fordham Corporate Law Institute* (1988) 16–5.

imposed by Articles [81] to [89] of the Treaty', seems to be more limited than the general rule of paragraph 31.

The general rule could be interpreted to mean that the States may be responsible for anticompetitive conduct in and of themselves. It could have the effect, for example, of declaring incompatible with the Treaty a regulation that had an effect equivalent to that of a web of anticompetitive agreements, regardless of the fact that it is the will of a legislator. No regard would be given to the fact that the reasons that have led public authorities to adopt such a measure could be different from those behind corporate conduct in breach of the competition rules. No explicit regard is given, in other words, to the legitimacy of the public sphere.

The dictum, in contrast, limits itself to stating that States should not enact measures that could shield anticompetitive corporate behaviour. This additional requirement could mean that genuine anticompetitive behaviour is needed on the part of undertakings for the State action doctrine to be applicable. The evolution of the case law has been dictated by this second element.

The problem with this jurisprudential norm is its vagueness. The Court does not explain what kind of State action impairs the effectiveness of the competition rules. This will be done in later judgments. The whole line of case law can be read as a gradual clarification of the principles enunciated by the Court in *GB-Inno-BM*.

B. The 1985 Judgments: *Leclerc* and *Cullet*

The doctrine was to remain dormant until 1985. Meanwhile, two judgments interpreted it in a minimalist fashion and approached the problems from the angle of free movement: *Buys* and *Van de Haar*.[30]

In January 1985, two important decisions (*Leclerc* and *Cullet*) were taken by the Court on grounds of the State action doctrine. A third decision in which the Court could have applied the doctrine was *BNIC*. The Court nevertheless resolved the latter exclusively on competition grounds, by focusing on the existing agreements between undertakings.[31] *BNIC* stands for the principle that undertakings still infringe Article 81 when they do so in the context of a semi-public organisation. It does not say anything as such about State action.

In *Leclerc*, a French distributor challenged the Lang Law on book prices, which obliged all publishers or importers of books to fix retail prices for all books. Retailers could only grant up to a 5 per cent discount off that price. The Court of Appeal from Poitiers submitted questions to the Court on the compatibility of the law with the State action doctrine. In a rare move, the Court introduced Article 28 EC, even when it had been ignored by the referring court.

---

[30] Case 5/79 *Buys* [1979] ECR 3203, para 30; Joined Cases 177–178/82 *van de Haar* [1984] ECR 1797, para 24.
[31] See Case 123/83 *BNIC* [1985] ECR 391.

The Commission presented a quite restrictive argument concerning the State action doctrine. It argued that it was only applicable as an 'exceptional case— where a Member State required or facilitated the conclusion of prohibited agreements, heightened their impact by extending them to third parties or pursued the specific aim of enabling undertakings to circumvent the competition rules.'[32] Both the Commission and France considered that Article 28 was the only relevant provision for the case in hand.

Note that in the interpretive tension between paragraphs 31 and 33 of *GB-Inno-BM* the Commission clearly sides with the second, no doubt influenced by the views of Giuliano Marenco, the Commission's legal advisor who had submitted observations in *Cullet*. The Court will, in a future case, adopt a test which comes close to the formulation proposed by the Commission.

Quoting *Walt Wilhelm* and *GB-Inno-BM*, the Court held that:

> [w]hilst it is true that the rules of competition are concerned with the conduct of undertakings and not with national legislation, Member States are none the less obliged under the second paragraph of Article [10] of the Treaty not to detract, by means of national legislation, from the full and uniform application of Community law or from the effectiveness of its implementing measures; nor may they introduce or maintain in force measures, even of a legislative nature, which may render ineffective the competition rules applicable to undertakings.[33]

'However,' continued the Court:

> legislation of the type at issue does not require agreements to be concluded between publishers or other behaviour of the sort contemplated by Article [81] (1) of the Treaty; it imposes on publishers and importers a statutory obligation to fix retail prices unilaterally. Accordingly, the question arises as to whether national legislation which renders corporate behaviour of the kind prohibited by Article [85](1) *superfluous [rend inutiles]* by making the book publisher or importer responsible for freely fixing binding retail prices, detracts from the effectiveness of Article [81] and is therefore contrary to the second paragraph of Article [10] of the Treaty.[34]

Having stated these principles, the Court rendered its decision on practical grounds related to the specificity of the book sector and the absence of a Community policy regarding this sector:

> the purely national systems and practices in the book trade have not yet been subject to a Community competition policy with which the Member States would be required to comply by virtue of their duty to abstain from any measure which might jeopardize the attainment of the objectives of the Treaty. It follows that, *as Community law now stands*, Member States' obligations under Article [10] [. . .], in conjunction with Articles 3[(g)] and [81], are not specific enough to preclude them from enacting legislation of the type at issue on competition in the retail prices of books, provided that

---

[32]   Case 229/83 *Leclerc* [1985] ECR 1, para 12.
[33]   *Ibid*, para 14.
[34]   *Ibid*, para 15 (my emphasis).

such legislation is consonant with the other specific Treaty provisions, in particular those concerning the free movement of goods.[35]

This part of the decision could be criticised, for the effect of directly applicable Treaty provisions does not depend on action on the part of the Community. However, the Court has sometimes shown some flexibility by exceptionally softening the rigour of a provision in light of practical considerations.[36] René Joliet took the view that the conclusion of the Court 'as Community law stands' means that it was guided by considerations of legal certainty.[37]

This sort of pronouncement can be interpreted from the perspective of the separation of powers in the Community. The reference of the Court to the absence of a specific policy in the sector means that the Community Court considers that this sort of decision corresponds to the political institutions. In view of their inaction, the Member States may act—respecting, to be sure, the free movement rules. But the institutional competence of the Court is limited when it has to assess decisions affecting the kind of regulation and the field left to competition. The Court is aware of the limits imposed on its function as guarantor that the law is applied and its position in the institutional setting.

Analysing the issue from the angle of the free movement rules allowed the Court to limit its judgment to imports and re-imports, to the exclusion of books published and sold in France. The provisions related to imports and re-imports were declared to be measures of equivalent effect under Article 28, since they established different rules for French and imported books or discouraged parallel imports and thus hindered intra-Community trade. The French legislation could not be justified by reference to consumer protection.[38] Only in the case of exportation 'for the sole purpose of re-importation in order to circumvent legislation of the type at issue'[39] does the obligation to respect fixed prices remain applicable.

Pierre Pescatore criticised the judgment for its use of prudential grounds and the introduction of the free movement issue, which had not been raised by the referring court.[40] Marenco was also critical, but for different reasons: 'If it were accepted that such a "rendering superfluous" was illegal, Member States could no longer enact anticompetitive legislation and would therefore no longer be able to regulate their economies.'[41]

In sum, nobody seemed to be happy with *Leclerc*: the ruling was at once too narrow (in the concrete result) and too wide (in the order of principles, with the

---

[35] *Ibid*, para 20 (my emphasis).

[36] Some such considerations have guided the Court in the recent judgment in Case C–379/98 *PreussenElektra* [2001] ECR I–2099. See J Baquero Cruz and F Castillo de la Torre, 'A Note on *PreussenElektra*' (2001) *European Law Review*, 489.

[37] R Joliet, 'National Anti-Competitive Legislation and Community Law', above n 29, 16–11.

[38] Case 229/83 *Leclerc* [1985] ECR 1 paras 28–30.

[39] *Ibid*, para 27.

[40] P Pescatore, 'Public and Private Aspects of Community Competition Law', above n 17, 423.

[41] G Marenco, 'Competition Between National Economies and Competition Between Business— A Response to Judge Pescatore', above n 18, 439.

'render superfluous' criterion). With hindsight, *Leclerc* can also be read as a step ahead. It is clearer than *GB-INNO-BM*, for it contains the seeds of the future formula scattered among its paragraphs—although the 'render superfluous' part will not appear again. The preference for the free movement route is now explicit. Such a preference can be explained in terms of judicial self-restraint, since in the field of free movement the legislation is not declared incompatible with the Treaty as a whole, only insofar as imports and re-imports are concerned. The consequences of a competition ruling would have been far more dramatic, as the whole regulation could have been declared incompatible with the Treaty.

France complied with the free movement rules simply by adding a clause to the Lang Law that excluded the obligation to respect the prices fixed by the publisher in the case of books imported from another Member State, unless they were abusively imported in order to avoid the application of the law.

Recently, a French court referred a preliminary question to the Court on the *Leclerc* judgment. The Court held that the interpretation given in the judgment could not be called into question because of certain changes in the Treaty (in particular, the insertion of Articles 4 and 14).[42]

In *Cullet*, a judgment that was rendered some weeks after *Leclerc*, the Court was to consider French rules on fuel prices. The facts were quite similar to those in *Leclerc*, but there were some significant differences. A French regulation established that the French authorities would fix the minimum price for the sale of fuel to the consumer through a complicated system. Leclerc, the same group of firms as in the previous case, was selling fuel below the minimum price. Henry Cullet, a competitor, brought proceedings against Leclerc.

The Court repeated verbatim the *Leclerc* formula, arguing that,

> rules such as those concerned in this case are not intended to compel suppliers and retailers to conclude agreements or to take any other action of the kind referred to in Article [81] (1) of the Treaty. On the contrary, they entrust responsibility for fixing prices to the public authorities, which for that purpose consider various factors of a different kind.[43]

The French regime was declared to be compatible with the State action doctrine, and had to be analysed under the free movement rules, which the Court again raised of its own motion.

This part of the judgment attracted the criticism of Luc Gyselen, who argued that the distinction between the cases where prices are fixed by a public authority and those in which prices are fixed by private operators was 'rather artificial [. . .]. The nature of the product concerned in one sector (for instance, gasoline) may give the public authorities an option (*e.g.*, to set the price themselves) which they do not have with regard to other products (*i.e.*, books).'[44]

---

[42] Case C–9/99 *Échirolles* [2000] ECR I–8207, paras 22–25.

[43] Case 231/83 *Cullet* [1985] ECR 305, para 17.

[44] L Gyselen, 'State Action and the Effectiveness of the EEC Treaty's Competition Provisions', (1989) *Common Market Law Review*, 33, 44.

The French rules were considered a measure of equivalent effect because the ceiling price, which was calculated 'on the basis solely of the cost prices of the national refineries where the European rates for fuel differ[ed] from those prices by more than 8 per cent, plac[ed] imported products at a disadvantage by depriving them of the opportunity of enjoying, as a result of a lower cost price, competitive advantages in sales to the consumer.'[45] This distinctly applicable rule could not be justified on the grounds of Article 30. It seems that once again France easily complied with the judgment by taking into account European refinery cost prices even when they differed by more than 8 per cent from the French prices.[46]

C. The Test Refined: *Asjes, Vlaamse Reisbureaus, Van Eycke* (1986–1988)

Asjes was a preliminary ruling in the course of criminal proceedings against the executives of various airlines and travel agencies who had infringed certain provisions of the French civil aviation code by selling air tickets at tariffs that had not been submitted to the competent Minister for approval or differed from approved tariffs. The national court decided to ask the Court for a ruling as to whether such provisions were in conformity with Community law.

This decision contains interesting developments concerning the transitional provisions for the implementation of the competition rules, but I shall limit my analysis to the part on the State action doctrine. The Court repeated the principle stated in *GB-INNO-BM* to the effect that 'the Treaty imposes a duty on Member States not to adopt or maintain in force any measure which could deprive those provisions of their effectiveness.'[47] 'Such would be the case, in particular, if a Member State were to require or favour the adoption of agreements, decisions or concerted practices contrary to Article [81] or to reinforce the effects thereof.'[48] In its reply the Court held the measure to be in breach of the State action doctrine, even if it was probably going to be upheld by the national court for procedural reasons connected to the air transport sector.

What should be retained from this judgment is that the Court announced for the first time some examples of State conducts that would be in breach of the doctrine ('Such would be the case, *in particular* . . .'). This list of examples appears to be non-exhaustive. Nonetheless, the part of *Leclerc* on national measures that renders superfluous anticompetitive behaviour on the part of undertakings is not among the examples.

In *Vlaamse Reisbureaus* the Court was asked to rule on the compatibility with Articles 81 and 28 of the Treaty of a Belgian statute according to which travel agents had to observe the prices and fares agreed upon or required by law, and

---

[45] Case 231/83 *Cullet* [1985] ECR 305, para 29.

[46] In this sense, Y Galmot and J Biancarelli, 'Les réglementations nationales en matière de prix au regard du droit communautaire', (1985) *Revue trimestrielle de droit communautaire*, 269, 308.

[47] Joined Cases 209–213/84 *Asjes* [1986] ECR, 1425, para 71.

[48] *Ibid*, para 72.

could not share commissions with clients, grant rebates or offer any kind of benefits contrary to commercial practices.

The Court repeated the *Asjes* formula: general principle plus open list of examples. Note that among the examples are only the requirement or favouring of agreements contrary to Article 81 and the reinforcement of their effects. The 'rendering superfluous' part (*Leclerc*) is again absent.

The Court's approach was quite formalistic: it looked for an agreement and then tried to determine whether the Belgian provisions tended to reinforce its effects. Since both elements were present—the existence of an agreement and the State regulation giving it a permanent character and a reinforcement. The Belgian regulation was declared in breach of Articles 3, 10 and 81 EC.[49]

Articles 28–30 EC were held to be inapplicable, since travel agents are involved in provisions of services, not movement of goods. In any event, there was no need to examine the national legislation in the light of the free movement rules, for the State action doctrine already made all the relevant provisions incompatible with Community law.

The formalism of the Court regarding the doctrine raised some problems. In *Vlaamse Reisbureaus*, the Belgian provisions would have stood scrutiny had there been no proof of previous anticompetitive agreements, as later happened in *Meng*. Their effect on competition seems to be the same, but they would have escaped analysis under the general doctrine.

Van Eycke, decided in 1988, is not simply 'a convenient restatement of the current case law' (Gyselen) or a mere change in terminology (López Escudero).[50] It is an important judgment for various reasons. It introduces a new case of a situation covered by the doctrine: the delegation of economic decision-making power to undertakings. A new example and a new theme, for the delegation in itself does not mean much: everything depends on what is done with the delegated power. The behaviour of the delegatee could also be reviewed under the free movement rules, inasmuch as private actors use it to enact private rules of a collective nature which fall under such rules. It may also be reviewed under the competition rules, or both. The act of delegation in itself may also be in breach of the State action doctrine if it contains a 'blank cheque' to the private sphere. The State is obliged to supervise effectively the way in the delegated powers are used.

The case concerned the compatibility with Community law of national legislation restricting the benefit of a tax exemption on interest income to a certain category of savings deposits. The Court held that

> Articles [81] and [82] of the Treaty *per se* are concerned only with the conduct of undertakings and not with national legislation. The Court has consistently held, however, that Articles [81] and [82] of the Treaty, in conjunction with Article [10], require

---

[49] Case 311/85 *Vlaamse Reisbureaus* [1987] ECR 3801, para 23.

[50] L Gyselen, 'Anti-Competitive Measures under the EC Treaty: Towards a Substantive Legality Standard', (1993) *European Law Review*, CC55, 57; M López Escudero, 'Intervencionismo estatal y Derecho comunitario de la competencia en la jurisprudencia del TJCE', (1989) *Revista de instituciones europeas*, 725, 752.

the Member States not to introduce or maintain in force measures, even of a legislative nature, which may render ineffective the competition rules applicable to undertakings. Such would be the case, the Court has held, if a Member State were to require or favour the adoption of agreements, decisions or concerted practices contrary to Article [81] or to reinforce their effects, *or to deprive its own legislation of its official character by delegating to private traders responsibility for taking decisions affecting the economic sphere.*[51]

Note that the Court introduced the 'delegation test' without acknowledging its novelty. It could be thought that it rescues the 'rendering superfluous' test in *Leclerc*, but the new branch of the test seems to be different. Besides, the absence of the expression 'in particular' shows that the list is closed and exhaustive: the *GB-INNO-BM* line of case law reaches its final form in *Van Eycke*. It has not changed so far.

In a less noticed part of the judgment, the Court held that 'legislation may be regarded as intended to reinforce the effects of pre-existing agreements [. . .] only if it incorporates either wholly or in part the terms of agreements concluded between undertakings and requires or encourages compliance on the part of those undertakings.'[52]

This was another novelty hidden in *Van Eycke*. The rule which is enunciated could to be too restrictive, for it makes the State liable only if it makes agreements or part of them subject to an statutory obligation for *those* undertakings that were party to the pre-existing agreements (not, for instance, for other undertakings that were not obliged by the said agreements). The statutory extension or reinforcement of the effects of agreements to those that did not enter into them seems to be even graver than the incorporation into legislation of agreements affecting only those that were party to them.

D. The 1993 Cases: 'November Revolution'?

Meng, Reiff and *OHRA*, decided in 1993 by a full Court, constitute for Norbert Reich—together with *Keck*[53] and *Audi*[54]—either a 'revolution' or an 'evolution' of the Community 'economic constitution'.[55] This view is somewhat exaggerated. Inasmuch as *Meng, Reiff* and *OHRA* are concerned, the Court simply followed *Van Eycke*.

Meng and *OHRA* concerned 'two pieces of national legislation, one German and the other Dutch, prohibiting insurance undertakings and intermediaries

---

[51] Case 267/86 *Van Eycke* [1988] ECR 4769, para 16 (my emphasis).
[52] *Ibid*, para 18.
[53] Joined Cases C–267 and C–268/91 *Keck and Mithouard* [1993] ECR I–6097.
[54] Case C–317/91 *Audi* [1993] ECR I–6227.
[55] N Reich, 'The "November Revolution" of the European Court of Justice: *Keck, Meng* and *Audi* Revisited', (1994) *Common Market Law Review*, 459, 492.

from granting their clients special advantages of any kind.'[56] The facts were very similar to those in *Vlaamse Reisbureaus*. *Reiff* concerned the mandatory approval procedure laid down by German law for road transport tariffs.

Advocate General Tesauro's Opinion in *Meng* and *OHRA* proposes a particularly restrictive and formalistic interpretation of the case law—that the Court did not follow in its entirety. For Tesauro, inasmuch as State measures are concerned, the Treaty cannot prevent their indirect effect on competition 'when that effect has no link with the conduct of undertakings or in fact with Article [81], that is to say when it does not in any way cloak, directly or indirectly, conduct—actual, nor merely ostensible conduct, let it be repeated—on the part of undertakings.'[57]

The opposite solution, 'although attractive', was said to remain, 'in the absence of any legal basis, purely academic.'[58] Tesauro then argued that 'the only State measures that must be considered incompatible with Community law are those which the authors of the Treaty themselves specifically identified in Articles [86], [87] and [88], *and no others.*' He considered,

> however, that the effort made in the case law to treat as being similarly unlawful those measures which facilitate, encourage or render inevitable the infringement of the provisions addressed to undertakings must be correctly appraised and that *the seemingly less rigorous approach adopted merely reflects recourse to systematic interpretation*, by virtue of which provisions are construed in conjunction with and by reference to each other—although, needless to say, *the process should not be taken too far* and the progressive development of the case law should not lose sight of *the ever necessary normative aspect, which underlies and shapes the strict interpretative approach which must be adopted in reading the Treaty.*[59]

The Advocate General proposed a literal interpretation of the Treaty, which is not in tune with the constitutional methods of interpretation usually employed by the Court when interpreting the Treaty. With such premises, his conclusion comes as no surprise:

> the second paragraph of Article [10], in conjunction with Articles 3([g]) and [81](1), may not be used as a basis for reviewing the legality of a State measure in the absence of any link with anti-competitive conduct by individuals, even though, objectively, that measure has an effect equivalent to that of an agreement prohibited by Article [81].[60]

The Court did not follow Advocate General Tesauro, and limited itself to repeating *Van Eycke*.[61] In all three judgments the State action doctrine was not

---

[56] Case C–2/91 *Meng* [1993] ECR I–5751, I–5773 (Opinion of Advocate General Tesauro).
[57] Case C–2/91 *Meng* [1993] ECR I–5786.
[58] *Ibid*, I–5787.
[59] *Ibid*, I–5788 (my emphases).
[60] *Ibid*, I–5790.
[61] *Ibid*, para 14; Case C–245/91 *Ohra* [1993] ECR I–5851, para 10; Case C–185/91 *Reiff* [1993] ECR I–5801, para 14.

applicable, because a link with an agreement or the unsupervised delegation of public functions to private actors were absent. The 'reinforcement' criterion received again a narrow application in *Meng*, in the line of *Vlaamse Reisbureaus*. The Commission had argued that some undertakings had concluded similar agreements in the life assurance sector, that were statutorily extended to other sectors of the insurance market. Since the life assurance sector was not covered by the facts of the case, the Court concluded that the rules did not reinforce the effects of pre-existing agreements in the specific context of life insurance.[62] This was criticised as an artificial distinction.[63] Another convincing critique was based on the merely formal differences between *Vlaamse Reisbureaus* and *Meng*, which did not justify different results.[64]

In *Reiff*, a case concerning the delegation of private powers in the field of economic decision-making, the members of the German commission that fixed tariffs for road transport under the supervision of the competent ministry were not considered by the Court to be representatives of undertakings. Albrecht Bach remarked that this practically overruled *BNIC* with an approach that lacked realism: 'Why should a simple change of hat provide independence and why should the manager of a company pursue interests different from those defined by the company once he is—following a proposal of that very company— appointed to any commission with regulatory power?'[65] Recently, *Reiff* itself may have been weakened by *Commission v Italy* (the customs agents case), which will be analysed in the next section.

E. Recent Judgments

Recent cases are mainly chamber cases. The Court sees the law in the field as settled, and does not show any intention of changing it.[66] Most of the judgments apply mechanically the test established in *Van Eycke*.

In *Spediporto*, a transport company sought payment of the price of road transport services rendered to another, which in turn refused to pay because it deemed the prices, governed by an Italian law establishing a system of bracket tariffs, to be excessive. The Tribunale di Genova referred a question on the interpretation of Articles 3(1)(g), 10, 28, 81, 82 and 86 of the Treaty.

---

[62] *Ibid (Meng)*, para 19.

[63] B van der Esch, 'Loyauté fédérale et subsidiarité: à propos des arrêts du 17 novembre 1993 dans les affaires C–2/91 (Meng), C–245/91 (Ohra) et C–185/91 (Reiff)', (1994) *Cahiers de droit européen*, 523, 538: 'il suffit dorénavant à un État membre de modifier de façon marginale les paramètres de l'entente anti-concurrentielle pour faire échapper la mesure à une incompatibilité avec les obligations de l'article 5, CE.'

[64] N Reich, 'The 'November Revolution' of the European Court of Justice: *Keck*, *Meng* and *Audi* Revisited', above n 55, 475 (emphasis added).

[65] A Bach, 'Annotation on *Reiff*, *Meng* and *OHRA*', (1994) *Common Market Law Review*, 1357, 1367.

[66] Case C–266/96 *Corsica Ferries* [1998] ECR I–3949, para 35; Case C–96/94 *Spediporto* [1995] ECR I–2883, para 20 (both referring to the State action doctrine as 'settled law').

The Court repeated the standard formula and decided that the case did not fall under the State action doctrine, as there was no proof of agreements between undertakings being required, favoured or reinforced. Neither could the Italian system be seen as delegating responsibility for taking economic decisions to private enterprises, since the minister had 'the power to approve [the tariffs], to reject them or to amend them before bringing them into force.'[67]

As regards Articles 3(1)(g), 5 and 86 of the Treaty, the Court elaborated a distinct test: these provisions,

> could only apply to legislation of the kind contained in the Italian Law if it were proved that the legislation concerned placed an undertaking in a position of economic strength enabling it to prevent effective competition from being maintained on the relevant market by placing it in a position to behave to an appreciable extent independently of its competitors, of its customers and ultimately of the consumers.[68]

Since there was no collective dominant position, the legislation was declared compatible with Community law.

For Ulla Neergaard *Spediporto* 'must be seen as one of the milestones in the case law concerning anti-competitive state measures because the Court now clearly divides the doctrine into two, one concerning Articles 3(1)(g), [10](2) and [81] EC and one concerning Articles 3(1)(g), [10](2) and [82] EC.'[69] This dichotomy would have been confirmed in *DIP*.[70] This may be incorrect, since *GB-INNO-BM* was already about Article 82.

Commission v Italy (the customs agents case) is an important judgment which facts closely resemble those in *BNIC* and *Reiff*. The solution comes actually closer to *BNIC* than to *Reiff*. It is also important because *for the first time* the Commission brought an Article 266 action against a State for failure to fulfil its obligations under the State action doctrine—all previous cases had been preliminary rulings. The Court clearly established an infringement of the State action doctrine.

The important task for the Court was to determine whether the CNSD, the public law body through which representatives of customs agents fixed compulsory tariffs for their services, was acting as an association of undertakings when fixing those tariffs. The Commission had already decided that the tariff fixing through the CNSD was an infringement of Article 81.[71] Repeating *BNIC*, the Court held the public law character of the CNSD to be 'irrelevant as far as the applicability of the Community rules on competition [. . .] are concerned.'[72]

---

[67] Case C–96/94 *Spediporto* [1995] ECR I–2883, (*Spediporto*), para 27.

[68] *Ibid*, para 31.

[69] U B Neergaard, *Competition & Competences*, above n 19, 99.

[70] Joined Cases C–140 to 142/94 *DIP* [1995] ECR I–3257.

[71] 93/438/EEC, Commission Decision of 30 June 1993 relating to a proceeding under Article 85 of the EEC Treaty (IV/33.407—CNSD), OJ L 203/27. This Decision has recently been confirmed by the Court of First Instance in Case T–513/93 *CNSD v Commission* [2000] ECR II–1807.

[72] Case C–35/96 *Commission v Italy* [1998] ECR I–3851, para 40; Case 123/83 *BNIC* [1985] ECR 391, para 17.

Unlike the German legislation in *Reiff*, 'nothing in the national legislation concerned prevents the CNSD from acting in the exclusive interest of the profession.'[73]

Note that the analysis remains quite formalistic, as the fact that the text of the legislation directs representatives of undertakings to act as independent experts in the general interest does not mean that they do so in practice—and, in any case, the underlying conflict of interests remains. In sum, a host of elements drive the Court to the conclusion that the public supervision of the regulatory body is not sufficient, so that its actions fall under Article 81 EC, which is infringed by the fixing of tariffs. Also the Italian Republic, in addition to the CNSD, is responsible for the infringement, because it 'not only *required the conclusion of an agreement* contrary to Article [81] of the Treaty and *declined to influence its terms,* but *also assists in ensuring compliance with the agreement*'[74] by providing for sanctions and the official publication of the tariffs in the Italian official journal.

In her note on this case, Ulla Neergaard criticises the Court for not taking into account constitutional considerations. She proposes an alternative test that would immunise any State measure from the application of the competition rules. She considers that the consent given by the ministry would be enough to declare the compatibility of the measure with the Treaty, in view of its democratic legitimacy.[75]

One may agree with the constitutional criticism. The test proposed, however, is not really a test, but an almost complete demise of the State action doctrine. In contrast, it seems that this case was correctly decided, even though the reasoning of the Court could have been clearer. It is true that democratic decisions deserve deference from the judiciary. It is difficult, nonetheless, to see the fixing of tariffs within the CNSD as a democratic decision or the safeguard of a public interest that should be protected in spite of the damage done to competition. Its only apparent objective is to favour the customs agents themselves by creating a price cartel. There is a major difference, from the point of view of democratic legitimacy, between measures adopted by a minister and measures adopted by the legislator. Finally, it is not the same to decide democratically to limit competition in a given field for reasons of general interest, with a delegation of certain powers to the private sphere with an adequate public supervision, and to decide democratically to empower a certain category of economic actors to freely fix obligatory and official tariffs to the detriment of other economic actors and consumers. The second situation is an indication that regulatory capture of the political process may have happened. The representative malfunction reflected in a democratic decision that clearly favours and empowers customs agents as a group vis-à-vis other groups justifies judicial intervention to correct such malfunction.

---

[73] *Ibid* (*Commission v Italy*), para 41.

[74] *Ibid*, para 55 (my emphasis).

[75] U B Neergaard, 'State Action and European Competition Rules: A New Path?', (1999) *Maastricht Journal of European and Comparative Law*, 380, 396.

Albany is important because it excludes from the application of the competition rules, by reason of its nature and purpose, collective agreements reached after collective bargaining between employers and employees in pursuit of social objectives.[76] Concerning the State action doctrine, the Court repeated verbatim its usual formula.[77] Since the agreement in hand was not in breach of the competition rules, for it benefited from the exception created by the Court—as its purpose was to guarantee a certain level of pension for all workers in the relevant sector and its nature was that of a collective agreement—the decision of the public authorities to make it compulsory did not fall within the scope of the State action doctrine, for there was no agreement in breach of the competition rules.

In *Pavlov*, a similar case to *Albany*, the Court had to determine whether the Netherlands rules on compulsory affiliation for medical specialists to professional supplementary pension schemes infringed the State action doctrine. The argument of the medical specialists—who had refused to pay their contributions to the fund—is not wholly unconvincing:

> Medical specialists are undertakings for the purpose of the competition rules. The setting up of the [fund] must be analysed as a decision of an association of undertakings within the meaning of Article [81(1)]. That decision restricts competition between medical specialists and competition on the pension insurance market and also affects trade between Member States. Article [81(1)] is thus infringed. By making affiliation to that pension scheme compulsory the Netherlands favours the adoption of a decision contrary to Article [81(1)] and/or reinforces its effects. Under the Court's case law the decree is therefore contrary to Articles [10] and [81].[78]

. Advocate General Jacobs proposed to the Court something new:

> I must confess that I do not find that case law with its automatic link between the legality of a private and a Member State's measure very satisfactory in cases such as the present one: the [undertaking's] decision is not caught by Article [81](1) because any restrictive effects are the result of subsequent State intervention; that State intervention is in turn not caught by Article [10] because the [undertaking's] decision as such is not restrictive enough [. . .].

To overcome this problem, Jacobs proposes to,

> accept a *prima facie* infringement justifiable on public interest grounds. In [his] view, measures taken by the Member States comply with Article [10](2) when, although they reinforce the restrictive effects of a concertation between undertakings, they are taken in pursuit of a legitimate and clearly defined public interest objective and where Member States actively supervise that concertation.[79]

---

[76] Case C–67/96 *Albany* [1999] ECR I–5751, para 64.
[77] *Ibid*, para 46.
[78] Joined Cases C–180 to C–184/98 *Pavlov* [2000] ECR I–6451, para 68 (Opinion Jacobs).
[79] *Ibid*, 161 and 163 (Opinion Jacobs).

Jacobs also proposed to solve the case on a minor and narrow ground, without prejudging the anticompetitive effects of the contested national measure: by holding that the restriction of competition is *de minimis*, because, as Advocate General Jacobs argues, the harmonisation of just one insignificant cost factor in the profession does not restrain competition to an appreciable extent.[80] This was, eventually, the route followed by the Court:

> the cost of the supplementary pension scheme has only a marginal and indirect influence on the final cost of the services offered by self-employed medical specialists. [. . .] [A] decision by the members of a profession to set up a pension fund entrusted with the management of a supplementary pension scheme does not appreciably restrict competition within the common market.[81]

The resolution of the case on a minor ground may be interpreted as self-restraint on the part of the Court. The problem with this solution is the following: if the case is disposed of by applying the *de minimis* principle, which belongs to the competition rules, does this mean that the competition rules are applicable to the States as such? Certainly not. It may rather mean that the State action doctrine is not applicable in the absence of a breach of the competition rules on the part of undertakings. From a logical point of view, this solution is unsatisfactory, for the issue of the scope of application is previous and distinct from the issue of the application of the substantive content of the competition rules.

Besides, the test proposed by Jacobs would lead the Court to review too much, and mainly measures that would be compatible with the Treaty. Jacobs was also propounding a test seemingly similar to the US test. But there is an important difference. In US antitrust law there is no need to respect the requirement of active supervision when it is the legislature itself that adopts the anti-competitive policy. This requirement is only relevant for private regulatory power openly delegated by the State.[82] In the case in hand the final decision belonged to the minister. Is this final decision equivalent to the necessary supervision by public authorities?

In February 2002, the Court of Justice has rendered two interesting judgments concerning the application of the competition rules to the legal profession. Both have to do with the topic of this chapter.

In *Wouters*,[84] the Court had to rule on whether a regulation enacted by the Bar of the Netherlands that prohibited partnerships between members of the Bar and accountants violated the Community rules on competition or free movement.

---

[80] *Ibid*, paras 134–143 (Opinion Jacobs).

[81] *Ibid*, paras 95 and 97 of the judgment.

[82] See *Hoover*, 466 US 558 (1984). See also T M Jorde, 'Antitrust and the New State Action Doctrine: A Return to Deferential Economic Federalism', (1987) *California Law Review*, 227, 240–242.

[84] Case C–309/99 *Wouters* [2002] ECR 0000.

The Court had first to decide whether such a regulation constitutes a decision adopted by an association of undertakings within the meaning of Article 81(1) EC. The Court based its decision on this point on a distinction between two 'approaches':

> The first is that a Member State, when it grants regulatory powers to a professional association, is careful to define the public-interest criteria and the essential principles with which its rules must comply and also retains its power to adopt decisions in the last resort. In that case the rules adopted by the professional association remain State measures and are not covered by the Treaty rules applicable to undertakings.
>
> The second approach is that the rules adopted by the professional association are attributable to it alone. Certainly, in so far as Article [81](1) of the Treaty applies, the association must notify those rules to the Commission. That obligation is not, however, such as unduly to paralyse the regulatory activity of professional associations, as the German Government submits, since it is always open to the Commission inter alia to issue a block exemption regulation pursuant to Article [81](3) of the Treaty.[85]

Since the regulation in hand corresponded to the second 'approach', the Court held that it fell within the meaning of Article 81(1) EC. It is unclear whether this rigid distinction, that follows closely the public/private divide, will also be applicable and indeed useful to cases in which the dividing line is blurred.

In the second part of the judgment in *Wouters*, the Court reached the conclusion that the regulation adopted by the Bar of the Netherlands does not infringe Article 81(1) EC, since that body could reasonably have considered that that regulation, despite the effects restrictive of competition that are inherent in it, is necessary for the proper practice of the legal profession, as organised in the Member State concerned. This is the most interesting part of the judgment, since the Court declared that,

> not every agreement between undertakings or any decision of an association of undertakings which restricts the freedom of action of the parties or of one of them necessarily falls within the prohibition laid down in Article [81](1) of the Treaty. For the purposes of application of that provision to a particular case, account must first of all be taken of the overall context in which the decision of the association of undertakings was taken or produces its effects. More particularly, account must be taken of its objectives, which are here connected with the need to make rules relating to organisation, qualifications, professional ethics, supervision and liability, in order to ensure that the ultimate consumers of legal services and the sound administration of justice are provided with the necessary guarantees in relation to integrity and experience.[86]

The Court then assessed the proportionality of the measure in hand. Before holding that the regulation did not infringe Article 81(1) EC, it was established that the effects restrictive of competition resulting from the regulation did not

---

[85] Case C–309/99 *Wouters* [2002] ECR 0000, paras 68–69.
[86] *Ibid*, para 97.

go beyond what was necessary in order to ensure the proper practice of the legal profession.[87]

In the last part of the judgment, the Court held that the Bar of the Netherlands does not constitute either an undertaking or a group of undertakings for the purposes of Article 82 EC, because it does not carry out an economic activity. Concerning the free movement rules, the Court held that, '[o]n the assumption that the provisions concerning the right of establishment and/or freedom to provide services are applicable to a prohibition of any multi-disciplinary partnerships between members of the Bar and accountants such as that laid down in the 1993 Regulation and that that regulation constitutes a restriction on one or both of those freedoms, that restriction would in any event appear to be justified for the reasons set out in paragraphs 97 to 109 above'.[88] That is, the very reasons that justified the restriction of competition would also justify the restriction of free movement.

Wouters may thus be seen as the pendant of *Cassis de Dijon*[89] (which introduced mandatory requirements in the field of free movement in addition to the justifications contained in the Treaty) and *Bosman*[90] (which established that private actors can also invoke mandatory requirements) for the Community competition rules. *Wouters* may also be read as an example of the opening to non-economic considerations in the interpretation of the competition rules, a line of case law inaugurated by *Albany* in 1999.[91]

The situation in *Arduino*[92] may not be as spectacular as that in *Wouters*, but the judgment is quite important for the State action doctrine. In Italy, compulsory tariffs for fees of members of the Bar are fixed through the approval by the Minister for Justice of a decision taken by the National Council of the Bar. An Italian court wanted to know whether this infringed Articles 10 and 81 EC. The Court held that it did not, basically because the draft tariff is not compulsory without the Minister's approval, who has the power to have the draft amended by the National Council of the Bar. It also took into account the fact that, in certain exceptional circumstances and by duly reasoned decision, a national court fixing the tariffs may depart from the compulsory tariff. Thus, the Italian State could not be said to have delegated to private economic operators responsibility for taking decisions affecting the economic sphere, which would have the effect of depriving the provisions at issue in the main proceedings of the character of legislation.

The previous case law[93] seemed clear in that public/private price- (or tariff-) fixing situations did not violate Article 81(1) EC if a series of requirements were

---

[87] *Ibid*, para 109.
[88] *Ibid*, para 122.
[89] *Case 120/78 Cassis de Dijon* [1979] ECR 649.
[90] Case C–415/93 *Bosman* [1995] ECR I–4921.
[91] Case C–67/96 *Albany* [1999] ECR I–5751.
[92] Case C–35/99 *Arduino* [2002] ECR 0000.
[93] Particularly, Cases C–35/96 *Commission v Italy* [1998] ECR I–3851 and C–185/91 *Reiff* [1993] ECR I–5801.

met. These requirements were quite stringent, which is understandable, as price- or tariff-fixing has grave effects on competition, normally constituting a *per se* violation of the competition rules. The requirements were related, *inter alia*, to the composition and nomination of the members of the private body to which powers were delegated, to the establishment of public interest criteria according to which the private body had to operate and to the possibility that public authorities adopted themselves the final decision. They were meant to make sure that the private body did not use the delegated powers in its own benefit, to the detriment of competition and consumers. The case law was unclear, however, as to whether the requirements were cumulative or one or several of them sufficed. In *Arduino*, only the condition related to a public intervention of last resort appears to be necessary, so that a single and even formal touch of public authorities may sanctify the whole scheme, regardless of its adverse effects on competition. And perhaps public authorities do not need to reserve for themselves the power to adopt a final decision: the power *not to adopt* the tariffs proposed by the private body may save the regulatory scheme.

Seen in this light, the judgment in *Arduino* constitutes an implicit shift (or at least a very significant 'clarification', insofar as it was not clear whether all or some of the requirements were needed) with respect to previous case law, and perhaps one that does not adequately balance the need to preserve competition and the degree of deference due to public authorities.

As it stands, this settled doctrine can be summarised as three rules created by the Court, which are not an open list but a closed set:

(i) Articles 3(1)(g), 10, paragraph 2, and 81 are infringed whenever a State requires or favours the adoption of agreements or concerted practices contrary to Article 85 or reinforces their effects;

(ii) Articles 3(1)(g), 10, paragraph 2, and 81 are also infringed when a State deprives its own rules of the character of legislation by delegating to private economic operators responsibility for taking decisions affecting the economic sphere;

(iii) Articles 3(1)(g), 10, paragraph 2, and 82 of the Treaty are infringed when State action places an undertaking in a position of economic strength enabling it to behave to an appreciable extent independently of its competitors, customers and consumers.

The State action doctrine thus appears to have 'evolved' from a general principle of potentially wide applicability into a 'residuary legal construction, that will be applied in very specific situations.'[94]

---

[94] M López Escudero, 'Las reglamentaciones nacionales anticompetitivas', (1994) *Revista de instituciones europeas*, 917, 933–934: 'una construcción jurídica residual, que se aplicará en situaciones muy específicas.'

8.4. A CONSTITUTIONAL APPROACH

This case law is concerned with the functions and powers of the Member States, and their interaction with private behaviour, but it does not take into account constitutional arguments. This section tries to introduce those arguments in the analysis of anticompetitive State action.

The analysis has two elements. The first tries to identify which of the 'competition' objections to the current formula can be explained on constitutional grounds. The second element outlines the directions of an explicit constitutional analysis.

A. Problems with the State Action Doctrine in its Current Form

The first problem is that the constitutional rationale of the case law is not present in the reasoning adopted by the Court. This rationale is probably 'those other reasons' to which René Joliet referred when he argued that 'the effect on competition is not the criterion adopted by the Court of Justice.'[95]

The implicit grounds that explain the Court's restrictive approach to the doctrine may be found in its deference to State democratic processes.

The radical solution of the unfettered application of the competition rules to the States as if they were undertakings would severely limit the kinds of market regulation that they could undertake in the general interest. The intermediate way of the substantive test with public interest justification proposed by Luc Gyselen[96] or Advocate General Jacobs (in *Pavlov*) would take competition for the ultimate constitutional objective, to which all other constitutional ends and values must bend. There would be no difference according to the degree of democratic legitimacy of the organ that adopted the measure.

To be sure, everything would depend on the kind of proportionality test applied. A very soft analysis could indeed be adopted (a 'reasonableness' test, instead of looking for a 'less anticompetitive option'). This would not excessively impair the margin of decision of public authorities. However, the States would be called upon to justify too many of their actions, and the Court would be reviewing too many measures in this field. Such a decision could be interpreted as an indirect abandonment of *Keck*, inasmuch as many measures that have escaped the free movement field would be examined under this case law.

---

[95] R Joliet, 'National Anti-Competitive Legislation and Community Law', above n 29, 16–12.

[96] L Gyselen, 'Anti-Competitive State Measures under the EC Treaty: Towards a Substantive Legality Standard', above n 50, 66: 'First, does the measure distort competition within the meaning of Article [81]? Secondly, if so, does the measure aim at achieving genuine economic or monetary policy objectives? Thirdly, if it does not, does it serve other legitimate objectives capable of overriding the competition policy concerns?'

As has been argued, in the field of competition the reasons for judicial review of State action are not so strong as they are in the field of free movement. In the field of competition, there are reasons that may justify a marginal review, in certain specific situations in which State action interferes with the application of the competition rules addressed to undertakings.

The constitutional point of departure would be the following: public authorities democratically elected cannot and should not be assimilated to undertakings, and therefore must not be subject, in principle, to the competition rules. Admittedly, States should not be allowed to act in ways that may impair the effectiveness of the competition rules either, and this may justify a marginal judicial control of such action. Areeda and Hovenkamp have pointed out that the object of the antitrust rules 'is the promotion of competition in economic markets, not the correction of defects in political markets.'[97]

One should understand that the States generally pursue policies in the general interest while undertakings normally pursue their own private interests. The competition rules are justified as limits to private economic freedom inasmuch as the unfettered pursuit of private interests by undertakings may negatively affect the public interest in a competitive economic system. Thus it would be absurd to apply the competition rules as such in the public sphere. Even if the public/private divide is not so clear nowadays and, as Waelbroeck and Frignani have argued, the legislator is obviously subject to the pressure of various interest groups, it seems that one shall not conclude, as they do, that there is no longer a justification for subjecting public and private measures to different standards of competition.[98]

On the contrary, Community economic constitutional law itself should trace a difference between the assessment of public and private behaviour. Liberal constitutionalism presupposes and is based precisely on this division between the private and the public sphere.

This approach justifies the application of different standards of competition review according to the degree of democratic legitimacy of the author of the measure, or the absence of such legitimacy. Public bodies democratically elected may pursue anticompetitive measures that would be illegal if they were adopted by undertakings. Such measures should not be impaired by Community law

---

[97] P Areeda and H Hovenkamp, *Antitrust Law* (vol 1A, Aspen Law & Business, New York, 1997) 4.

[98] M Waelbroeck and A Frignani, *Commentaire Mégret* (vol 4, *Concurrence* 2nd edn, Presses de l'Université libre de Bruxelles, Brussels, 1997) 153: 'La conception selon laquelle l'État agit nécessairement dans l'intérêt général, et doit dès lors être soumis à un régime moins contraignant que les opérateurs privés, ignore que dans la vie économique contemporaine la distinction entre l'État et les opérateurs privés tend de plus en plus à s'estomper. D'une part, l'État n'est plus l'arbitre impartial qu'il était jadis entre acteurs en concurrence les uns avec les autres mais devient directement partie prenante au processus concurrentiel par l'entremise de ses entreprises publiques. D'autre part, la formation de la volonté de l'État est influencée dans une mesure croissante par les groupes de pression, lesquels réussissent souvent à imposer l'adoption de mesures visant la protection d'intérêts particuliers. Il est dès lors injustifié d'appliquer deux poids et deux mesures à des phénomènes qui ne sont différents qu'en apparence.'

inasmuch as it is clear that they do not pursue private interests. When such anti-competitive public measures are designed to protect State markets vis-à-vis other Community competitors, the locus of analysis should be that of the free movement rules, which should be the preferred route, for substantive and not merely procedural reasons. Otherwise, the legislators should be allowed, within wide limits, to use regulation in various ways and to strike their preferred mix of competition and regulation through experimentation. Unwise policies in this field preferably ought to be corrected by the political process itself, and only marginally by judicial intervention.

This constitutional argument, to which we will return later, justifies *a* restrictive approach to State anticompetitive regulation, but perhaps not *the* restrictive approach adopted by the Court.

When one looks to the case law, it appears that many of the shortcomings of the current formula cannot be explained under the constitutional principle of judicial deference to the States' political choices, but are due to a formalism whose only ground is the restrictive application of the case law. A new approach should aim at taking into account these constitutional principles, making them explicit. This new approach may lead to a sliding scale test.

To begin with, the Court could render more flexible its case law and allow other situations to be considered. This could be done by opening the list of State actions falling within the case law—a list which has been held to be exhaustive since *Van Eycke*.

In addition, the requirement of a direct link between the State action and the anticompetitive conduct on the part of undertakings is also inconsistent from a constitutional point of view. State conduct completely unconnected to corporate behaviour may restrain competition in benefit of private not public interests. Conversely, State regulatory policies in furtherance of the general interest may require or favour anticompetitive practices on the part of undertakings. Finally, a legislator may incorporate anticompetitive agreements into law in the conviction that they serve the general interest, and in many cases they may indeed do so. Under the present test, the foreseeable solutions to these cases would at least be questionable.

The delegation criterion is also confusing, at least in its current form. The rationale of the State action doctrine is to prevent the States, semi-public or semi-private entities and undertakings acting under a regulatory scheme, from using anticompetitive regulation in pursuance of private interests. They may of course enact anticompetitive regulations in pursuance of public interests. Thus, the fact that a State *deprives its own legislation of its official character by delegating to private traders responsibility for taking economic decisions affecting the economic sphere* (delegation test) does not perforce mean that it is rendering ineffective the competition rules. Everything depends on the actual conduct of the delegatee, and on the framework established by the act of delegation.

This part of the test does not mean much without the additional and joint elements established in *Reiff* and *CNSD* (composition and appointment of the members of the organ, obligation to take into account the general interest, possibility to annul, amend or substitute the private decision taken by the delegatee, additional public measures, etc.). But these latter criteria should be take into account in assessing the delegation in the light of the *GB-INNO-BM* line of case law, whereas the concrete action of the delegatee, inasmuch as it is freely taken, should be examined in the light of the competition rules. Even if the delegation restricts its margin of action, its action may still be corporate behaviour (as in *BNIC*). In deciding whether the competition rules are applicable or not the composition of such organs should be the decisive element, but the other elements should also be met.[99] Inasmuch as those organs aim at a public interest, as legally ordained and defined by the act of delegation, the possibility of justification and a strict proportionality analysis (less onerous option than competition) should be available within the *GB-INNO-BM* case law.

The analysis shows that formalism and the effort to restrict the consequences of the case law are the crucial driving forces behind the test of the Court. Due deference to democratic processes is not explicitly among the reasons for this restrictive approach. In a way, the current case law is deferential, but only because it is restrictive. But deferential review has to be based on constitutional principles, not on deference itself. Formalism has much to commend it, since it realises the goal of legal certainty for the States and undertakings. However, a constitutionally principled formalism would be preferable.

B. A Constitutional Approach

This approach finds inspiration in the *Parker* jurisprudence of the US Supreme Court. In *Parker*, the Supreme Court first enunciated the State action doctrine, which gives immunity to the states from the Sherman Act if certain conditions are met. The basis of the US doctrine was the constitutional principle of federalism: 'We find nothing in the language of the Sherman Act or in its history', held the *Parker* Court, 'which suggests that its purpose was to restrain a state or its officers or agents from activities directed by its legislator. In a dual system of government in which, under the Constitution, the states are sovereign, save only as Congress may constitutionally subtract from their authority, an unexpressed purpose to nullify a states' control over its officers and agents is not lightly to be attributed to Congress.'[100]

After *Parker*, *Midcal* made clear that 'federal antitrust law allows the states to depart from the ordinary market principles underlying the Sherman Act (1) if the state really wants to displace federal antitrust law and manifests that policy choice through an affirmative and clearly articulated expression and (2) if the

---

[99] This is, to be sure, at variance with the approach recently adopted by the Court in Case C–35/99 *Arduino* [2002] ECR 000, examined above pp 153–154.

[100] *Parker v Brown*, 317 US 341, 350–351 (1943).

resulting private power is actively supervised by public officials.'[101] This test rightly puts the stress on a series of requirements that protect constitutional values. If an anticompetitive policy is clearly articulated in legislation, all the interests affected may have had an input in it through their representatives. If the policy was not clearly articulated, its anticompetitive nature may not have been perceived in the decision-making process, which increases the risk of 'capture' of such process by private interests.

The position in US antitrust law may convince the ECJ to enrich its analysis by taking a constitutional perspective, explicitly articulating the hidden reasons behind the State action doctrine. Such reasons also support a restrictive and deferential approach. The following paragraphs aim at providing for such a constitutional analysis.

Competition should be considered as a Community constitutional value among other values. Among the latter also is the supranational structure of the Community, in which decisions are taken at different levels, and other values which may be realised at such levels by decisions that may limit competition but pursue other legitimate aims. The knot between competition, supranationalism as a political structure and all other values protected by the legal order should not be cut for one or the other side. It should rather be softly untied, distinguishing what is distinguishable.

The analysis should ideally lead to clear rules at the core and, if it cannot be avoided, a balancing test of rather limited applicability at the edges. I do not know whether the new test will lead to more or less restrictive review than that under the current one. But the point is not whether to narrow or widen the review, but to refocus it according to constitutional principles.

To begin with, the analysis should not be the same for all State actors. The Community concept of 'the State and its emanations' is too wide to apply the same standard to all public actors. It is common sense that a democratic legislator deserves more deference than a municipality, an administrative body or an agency. In the US context, William Page has highlighted the 'political differences between legislative processes on the one hand and administrative and municipal processes on the other, differences that also affect the degree of deference due to those processes.'[102] These differences are also obscured in the case law of the Court of Justice, which applies the same standard to all sorts of public measures, regardless of the legitimacy enjoyed by their author.

The next element in the analysis would be to disentangle the public from the private. And within the public, to distinguish the legislative from executive action and administrative measures. This is a difficult task, as many of these situations are quite complex, but the analytical effort is necessary. Nonetheless, in

---

[101] P Areeda and H Hovenkamp, *Antitrust Law*, vol I, above n 97, 308 (footnotes omitted). *Midcal*, 445 US 97 (1980). Other interesting judgments are *Fisher v City of Berkeley*, 475 US 260 (1986) and *Liquor v Duffy*, 479 US 335 (1987).

[102] W H Page, 'Interest Groups, Antitrust and State Regulation: *Parker v Brown* in the Economic Theory of Legislation', (1987) *Duke Law Journal*, 618, 629.

order to know whether a mixed public-private situation presents a competition problem, one should assess the common effect of public and private actions, without dividing them in a formalistic fashion. The public/private divide is relevant when assessing the degree of judicial review, and, eventually, the sort of proportionality test to be applied, but not in assessing whether there is a competition problem.

State measures should preferably be examined under the free movement rules, for nationals of other States are not represented in the State political process and regulations may be discriminatory or protectionist. Besides, such negative externalities may have a tendency to remain. Since the nationals of other Member States are not represented in the political process of the author of the measures, they cannot try to change the legislation. In contrast, in issues strictly affecting competition, all the interests concerned are represented in the national political process, and there will be pressure to change the legislation—the political process can correct itself and judicial intervention is not required.

If there is no violation of the free movement rules, it seems that such legislative measures should be subject to a strong presumption of validity under Community law as long as the intention to regulate in the public interest is clear in the measures themselves (*reasonableness test*). The political process has to correct its own imperfections (the Commission may, for example, take action under Articles 96–97 EC). Only if the measures were clearly taken in pursuance of private interests—if they were not 'reasonable' from the point of view of their public interest justification—may the Court intervene (this would be a classic case of representative malfunction or 'capture' of the legislature). Review would be minimal.

Private or public actions *mandated* by clearly articulated legislation, such as the price-fixing of books in *Leclerc*, should in principle benefit from an identical degree of deference, for they pursue the same general interest as the public measure and do not reflect the free anticompetitive will of undertakings. The public interest may sometimes require, of its own nature, a restriction of competition.

The deference due to a democratic legislator is however not to be extended to public or private measures taken by other bodies, in pursuance of such legislation, when they enjoy a large margin of discretion and decision-making power which allows them to act in their own interest (in the case of undertakings) or in the interests of private actors (in the case of public bodies). In such cases, one should apply a different kind of analysis: the level of review should be that of the body that takes the concrete decision affecting competition.

If it is the executive that has acted, review should be soft but somewhat less deferential than that applied to legislation. One should assess whether the means are *adequate* to achieve their public interest aim (*adequacy test*). Review is more strict than the 'reasonableness test' applied to the legislator. But still it is more deferential than a strict proportionality review (less restrictive option) that would encroach excessively on the margin of appreciation of States' executives.

If the relevant public measures were taken by municipalities, State administrative bodies or agencies, or if the legislation involves an *open delegation* of powers leaving such bodies enough leeway to take regulatory decisions affecting competition, there should be less deference, unless the act of delegation itself imposed a particular form of conduct. Review should be more stringent, because these administrative bodies probably are more prone to capture than legislatures or executives, and in any case they lack the democratic legitimacy that justifies deference. If the open delegation is to private parties, then the competition rules should apply directly with full force—as in *BNIC*. The behaviour of undertakings, in such cases, could be justified on public interest grounds—within the State action doctrine, without having recourse to Article 81(3)—but a strict proportionality test should be applied.[103] One should then examine whether an option less restrictive of competition was available to achieve the public end aimed at by the act of delegation (*less restrictive option test*). Otherwise it could be presumed that they have used the delegated powers for their own benefit, in breach of the principles of competition. They are immune from the competition rules only when they have no autonomy whatsoever as to their behaviour in the market because of the State's regulation. This immunity has been rather narrowly construed by the Court.[104]

Only in this particular case should the Court adopt a substantive test similar to those proposed by Luc Gyselen or Advocate General Jacobs in *Pavlov*.

The proposed analysis thus appears as a sliding scale. The steps of the scale start at the legislator and go down to undertakings, covering executive action, administration, agencies, mixed private-public bodies, etc. In this analysis, more weight is given to competition considerations the lesser the democratic legitimacy of the author of the public measure under review; conversely, less relative weight is given to competition considerations the higher the democratic legitimacy of the author of the measure. Thus, the standards of review and deference are adapted to each situation. The various forms that the Court has been giving to the principle of proportionality would no doubt ease the adoption of the approach proposed here.

---

[103] This approach is similar to that recently adopted by the Court in Case C–309/99 *Wouters* [2002] ECR 000, analysed above pp 151–153.

[104] See Case T–513/93 *CNSD v Commission* [2000] ECR II–1807, paras 57–72; and Joined Cases C–359/95 P and C–379/95 P *Ladbroke Racing* [1997] ECR I–6265, para 33.

9

Final Thoughts

THIS WORK IS nearly at its end. I have tried to examine the relationship between competition and free movement, the two main elements of the economic constitutional law of the European Community. The examination has been put in the context of the constitutional law of the Community, highlighting the intimate relationship between the constitutional structure and the substantive content of such law, between the supranational political process established by the Treaty and the economic orientation of its provisions.

The study required a conception of the constitution and its relationships with the economy. I have opted, in contrast to other approaches, for a conception of Community constitutionalism that stays as close as possible to traditional constitutionalism. The projection of such a conception on to the Community reality has shown a series of scattered constitutional materials which are not held together in a complete constitution. These materials deserve a proper constitutional approach and interpretation.

Competition and free movement are part of these constitutional materials. The relationship between both normative groups has been analysed in the light of the proposed framework of analysis. Special attention has been paid to the gaps between their respective scopes of application.

Other issues related to the present work have only received cursory treatment in this work, in view of the limitation of its object.

Some are part of the economic constitutional law of the Community: reverse discrimination and internal measures in free movement law, the *de minimis* issue in competition law and its relationship with free movement law, the specific problems of Article 86 EC, or the contribution of the Community legislator to the filling of gaps between competition and free movement. All these issues, while being very important, would have demanded separate chapters overstepping the acceptable length of a work of this nature. Besides, the issues analysed in chapters 5 to 8 have explored a series of questions which are representative of the economic constitutional law of the Community.

Other themes are of a general character: constitutional or judicial review and constitutional interpretation. Throughout this work, constitutional interpretation has been seen as distinct from the interpretation of other infraconstitutional norms. This remains an axiom in want of further justification and elaboration, critically so in relation to Community law. Concerning constitutional review, this work has recurrently referred to the problems it may raise from the point of view of democratic theory, and has acknowledged the need for a specific theory of constitutional review that takes into account the peculiar political structure of the Community.

Beyond these limitations, the analysis of the oldest and best established layer of the Community constitution, and of a series of structural relationships and interpretive approaches that obtain in it, may not be without interest and usefulness for the analysis of a foreseeable constitution or constitutional treaty of the European Union that will give shape to and complete the currently existing constitutional materials.

Works Cited

B Ackerman, 'The Storrs Lectures: Discovering the Constitution', (1984) *Yale Law Journal*, 1013

——, *We the People: Foundations* (Harvard University Press, Cambridge, Mass 1991)

E Albertí Rovira, *Autonomía política y unidad económica* (Civitas, Madrid, 1995)

R Alexy, *Theorie der Grundrechte* 3rd edn (Suhrkamp, Frankfurt a M., 1986)

——, *A Theory of Legal Argumentation: the Theory of Rational Discourse as Theory of Legal Justification* (tr by R Adler and N MacCormick, Clarendon Press, Oxford, 1989)

G Amato, *Antitrust and the Bounds of Power: the Dilemma of Liberal Democracy in the History of the Market* (Hart, Oxford, 1999)

P Areeda and H Hovenkamp, *Antitrust Law* (vols 1 and IA Aspen Law & Business, New York, 1997)

A Bach, *Wettbewerbsrechtliche Schranken für staatliche Maßnahmen nach europäischem Gemeinschaftsrecht* (Mohr, Tübingen, 1992)

——, 'Annotation on *Reiff, Meng* and *OHRA*', (1994) *Common Market Law Review*, 1357

P Badura, 'Grundprobleme des Wirtschaftsverfassungsrechts', (1976) *Juristische Schulung*, 205

J Baquero Cruz, 'Disintegration of the Law of Integration in the External Economic Relations of the European Community', (1997) *Columbia Journal of European Law*, 257

——, 'La protección de los derechos sociales en la Comunidad Europea tras el Tratado de Amsterdam', (1998) *Revista de Derecho Comunitario Europeo*, 639

——, 'Free Movement and Private Autonomy', (1999) *European Law Review*, 603

—— and F Castillo de la Torre, 'A Note on *PreussenElektra*', (2001) *European Law Review*, 489

M Bassols Coma, *Constitución y sistema económico* (2nd edn, Tecnos, Madrid, 1988)

C A Beard, *An Economic Interpretation of the Constitution of the United States* (The Free Press, New York, 1986)

N Bernard, 'La libre circulation des marchandises, des personnes et des services dans le Traité CE sous l'angle de la compétence', (1998) *Cahiers de droit européen*, 11

A M Bickel, *The Least Dangerous Branch: The Supreme Court at the Bar of Politics* (Bobbs-Merrill, Indianapolis, 1962)

R Bieber, R Dehousse, J Pinder and J H H Weiler (eds), *1992: One European Market?* (Nomos, Baden-Baden, 1988)

A von Bogdandy and M Nettesheim, 'Ex Pluribus Unum: Fusion of the European Communities into the European Union', (1996) *European Law Journal*, 267

G Bognetti, *La costituzione economica italiana* (Giuffrè, Milano, 1993)

F Böhm, W Eucken and H Grossmann-Doerth, 'The Ordo Manifesto of 1936', in A Peacock and H Willgerodt (eds), *Germany's Social Market Economy: Origins and Evolution* (MacMillan, London, 1989)

G de Búrca, 'The Institutional Development of the EU: A Constitutional Analysis', in P Craig and G de Búrca (eds) *The Evolution of EU Law* (OUP, Oxford, 1999)

F Capotorti, M Hilf, FG Jacobs and J-P Jacqué, *The European Union Treaty* (Clarendon Press, Oxford, 1986)

M Cappelletti and D Golay, 'The Judicial Branch in the Federal and Transnational Union: Its Impact on Integration', in M Cappelletti *et al* (eds), *Integration Through Law: Europe and the American Experience* (vol 1, Book 2 (de Gruyter, Berlin-New York, 1986)

C Chung, 'The Relationship Between State Regulation and EC Competition Law: Two Proposals for a Coherent Approach', (1995) *European Competition Law Review*, 87

F Cocozza, 'Riflessioni sulla nozione di "costituzione economica"', (1992) *Il diritto dell'economia*, 71

L-J Constantinesco, 'La spécificité du droit communautaire', (1966) *Revue trimestrielle de droit européen*, 1

——, 'La constitution économique de la CEE', (1977) *Revue trimestrielle de droit européen*, 244

F Dehousse, 'Les résultats de la Conférence intergouvernamentale', (1997) *Cahiers du CRISP*, No 1565–1566, 4

P Delannay, Annotation on *Walrave*, (1976) *Cahiers de droit européen*, 209

M Dorf, 'Integrating Normative and Descriptive Constitutional Theory: The Case of Original Meaning', (1997) *Georgetown Law Journal*, 1765

P Eleftheriadis, 'The Direct Effect of Community Law: Conceptual Issues', (1996) *Yearbook of European Law*, 205

J H Ely, *Democracy and Distrust: A Theory of Judicial Review* (Harvard University Press, Cambridge, Mass 1980)

B van der Esch, 'Loyauté fédérale et subsidiarité: à propos des arrêts du 17 novembre 1993 dans les affaires C–2/91 (Meng), C–245/91 (Ohra) et C–185/91 (Reiff)', (1994) *Cahiers de droit européen*, 523

J Eule, 'Laying the Dormant Commerce Clause to Rest', (1982) *Yale Law Journal*, 425

European Commission, *Second Survey on State Aids in the European Community in the Manufacture and Certain Other Sectors* (ECSC-EEC-EAEC, Brussels-Luxembourg, 1990)

European University Institute, *Basic Treaty of the European Union: Draft* (European Communities, Italy, 2000)

——, *A Basic Treaty for the European Union: A Study of the Reorganisation of the Treaties: Report Submitted on 15 May 2000 to Mr Romano Prodi, President of the European Commission* (European Communities, Italy, 2000)

J Fischer, *From Confederacy to Federation—Thoughts on the Finality of European Integration* (http://www.auswartiges-amt.de/6_archiv/2/r/r000512b.htm/, visited on 15 September 2000)

Y Galmot and J Biancarelli, 'Les réglementations nationales en matière de prix au regard du droit communautaire', (1985) *Revue trimestrielle de droit communautaire*, 269

E García de Enterría, *La Constitución como norma y el Tribunal Constitucional* (3rd edn, Civitas, Madrid, 1983)

M García Pelayo, 'Consideraciones sobre las cláusulas económicas de la Constitución', in Manuel Ramírez (ed) *Estudios sobre la Constitución española de 1978* (Libros Pórtico, Zaragoza, 1979)

D J Gerber, 'Constitutionalizing the Economy: German Neo-liberalism, Competition Law and the 'New' Europe', (1994) *American Journal of Comparative Law*, 25

J Gerkrath, *L'émergence d'un droit constitutionnel pour l'Europe* (Éditions de l'Université de Bruxelles, Brussels, 1997)

J J Gomes Canotilho, *Direito Constitucional* (5th edn, Almedina, Coimbra, 1992)

L W Gormley, *Prohibiting Restrictions on Trade within the EEC* (North Holland, Amsterdam, 1985)

D Grimm, 'Does Europe Need a Constitution?', (1995) *European Law Journal*, 282

G Gunther and K M Sullivan, *Constitutional Law* (13th edn, Foundation Press, New York, 1997)

L Gyselen, 'State Action and the Effectiveness of the EEC Treaty's Competition Provisions', (1989) *Common Market Law Review*, 33

——, 'Anti-Competitive State Measures Under the EC Treaty: Towards a Substantial Legality Standard', (1993) *European Law Review*, Competition Checklist, CC55

B E Hawk, 'The American (Anti-trust) Revolution: Lessons for the EEC?', (1988) *European Competition Law Review*, 53

F A Hayek, *The Constitution of Liberty* (Routledge & Kegan Paul, London, 1960)

V Hatzopoulos, 'Recent Developments of the Case Law of the ECJ in the Field of Services', (2000) *Common Market Law Review*, 43

T Hobbes, *Leviathan* (Cambridge University Press, Cambridge, 1991)

M Jaensch, *Die unmittelbare Drittwirkung der Grundfreiheiten: Untersuchung der Verpflichtung von Privatpersonen durch Art 30, 48, 52, 59, 73b EGV* (Nomos, Baden-Baden, 1997)

C Joerges and J Neyer, 'From Intergovernmental Bargaining to Deliberative Political Processes: The Constitutionalisation of Comitology', (1997) *European Law Journal*, 273

——, 'The Impact of European Integration on Private Law: Reductionist Perceptions, True Conflicts and a New Constitutional Perspective', (1997) *European Law Journal*, 378

——, ''Deliberative Supranationalism'—A Defence', *European Integration online Papers*, 2001 (http://eiop.or.at/eiop/texte/2001–008a.htm)

R Joliet, 'National Anti-Competitive Legislation and Community Law', in B Hawk (ed) *1987 Fordham Corporate Law Institute*, (1988) 16

—— with D T Keeling, 'Trade Mark Law and the Free Movement of Goods: The Overruling of the Judgment in *Hag I*', (1991) *International Review of Industrial Property and Copyright law* (IIC), 303

——, 'Derecho de la competencia desleal y libre circulación de mercancías', (1995) *Revista General de Derecho*, 493

T M Jorde, 'Antitrust and the New State Action Doctrine: A Return to Deferential Economic Federalism', (1987) *California Law Review*, 227

O de Juan Asenjo, *La Constitución económica española* (Centro de Estudios Constitucionales, Madrid, 1984)

T Kingreen, *Die Struktur der Grundfreiheiten des Europäischen Gemeinschaftsrechts* (Duncker & Humblot, Berlin, 1999)

W Kluth, 'Die Bindung privater Wirtschaftsteilnehmer an die Grundfreiheiten des EG-Vertrages', (1997) *Archiv des öffentliches Rechts*, 557

L D Kramer, 'Putting the Politics Back into the Political Safeguards of Federalism', (2000) *Columbia Law Review*, 215

K Lenaerts, 'Constitutionalism and the Many Faces of Federalism', (1990) *American Journal of Comparative Law*, 205

—— and A Verhoeven, 'Towards a Legal Framework for Executive Rule-Making in the EU? The Contribution of the New Comitology Decision', (2000) *Common Market Law Review*, 645

P Lindseth, 'Democratic Legitimacy and the Administrative Character of Supranationalism: The Example of the European Community', (1999) *Columbia Law Review*, 628

K Loewenstein, *Political Power and Governmental Process* (University of Chicago Press, Chicago, 1957)

M López Escudero, 'Intervencionismo estatal y Derecho comunitario de la competencia en la jurisprudencia del TJCE', (1989), *Revista de instituciones europeas* 725

——, 'Las reglamentaciones nacionales anticompetitivas (Comentario a las sentencias del TJCE de 17 de noviembre de 1993, asuntos Meng, Ohra y Reiff)', (1994) *Revista de instituciones europeas*, 917

J-V Louis, *L'ordre juridique communautaire* (OPOCE, Luxembourg, 1993)

——, 'Droit communautaire et droit national', in *Commentaire Mégret—Le droit de la CE* (2nd edn, Presses de l'Université libre de Bruxelles, Brussels, 1995)

——, 'Le modèle constitutionnel européen: de la Communauté à l'Union', in P Magnette and E Remacle (eds), *Le nouveau modèle européen* (vol 1, Éditions de l'Université de Bruxelles, Brussels, 2000)

N MacCormick, 'Beyond the Sovereign State', (1993) *Modern Law Review*, 1

——, *Questioning Sovereignty: Law, State and Nation in the European Commonwealth* (OUP, Oxford, 1999)

I Maher, 'Competition Law and Intellectual Property Rights: Evolving Formalism', in P Craig and G de Búrca (eds), *The Evolution of EU Law* (OUP, Oxford, 1999)

G Majone, *Regulating Europe* (Routledge, London, 1996)

G Marenco, 'Effets des règles communautaires de concurrence (art 85 et 86) sur l'activité des États membres', in J Schwarze (ed), *Discretionary Powers of the Member States in the Field of Economic Policies and their Limits under the EEC Treaty* (Nomos, Baden-Baden, 1988)

——, 'Competition Between National Economies and Competition Between Business— A Response to Judge Pescatore', (1987) *Fordham International Law Journal*, 420

D Martin, '«Discriminations», «entraves» et «raisons impérieuses» dans le Traité CE: trois concepts en quête d'identité', (1998) *Cahiers de droit européen*, 261

K Marx, 'Critique of the Gotha Programme', in K Marx and F Engels, *Collected Works* (vol 24, London, 1989)

A P van der Mei, 'Cross-Border Access to Medical Care within the European Union— Some Reflections on the Judgments in *Decker* and *Kohll*', (1998) *Maastricht Journal of European Law*, 277

A Menéndez, *Constitución, sistema económico y Derecho mercantil* (UAM, Madrid, 1982)

G R Milner-Moore, *The Private Accountability of Private Parties under the Free Movement of Goods Principle* (Harvard Jean Monnet Working Paper 9/95)

A Moravcsik and K Nicolaïdis, 'Keynote Article: Federal Ideals and Constitutional Realities in the Treaty of Amsterdam', (1998) 36 *Journal of Common Market Studies*, Annual Review, 13

W F Murphy, 'Constitutions, Constitutionalism and Democracy', in D Greenberg *et al* (eds), *Constitutionalism and Democracy* (OUP, Oxford, 1993)

W J Nardini, 'Passive Activism and the Limits of Judicial Self-Restraint: Lessons for America from the Italian Constitutional Court', (1999) *Seton Hall Law Review*, 1

U B Neergaard, *Competition & Competences: The Tensions between European Competition Law and Anti-Competitive Measures by the Member States* (DJØF Publishing, Copenhagen, 1998)

——, 'State Action and European Competition Rules: A New Path?', (1999) *Maastricht Journal of European Law*, 380

K W Nörr, 'Economic Constitution: On the Roots of a Legal Concept', (1993) *Journal of Law and Religion*, 343

P Oliver, *Free Movement of Goods in the European Community* (3rd edn, Sweet & Maxwell, London, 1996)

——, 'Some Further Reflections on the Scope of Articles 28–30 (ex 30–36) EC', (1999) *Common Market Law Review*, 783

C F Ophüls, 'Grundzüge europäischer Wirtschaftsverfassung', (1962) *Zeitschrift für Handelsrecht*, 136

H W O Okoth-Ogendo, 'Constitutions without Constitutionalism: Reflections on an African Political Paradox', in D Greenberg *et al* (eds), *Constitutionalism and Democracy* (OUP, Oxford, 1993)

W H Page, 'Interest Groups, Antitrust and State Regulation: *Parker* v *Brown* in the Economic Theory of Legislation', (1987) *Duke Law Journal*, 618

Ph E-Partsch, comment on Article 56 EC, in Ph Léger (ed) *Commentaine article pour article des traités EU et CE* (Helbing and Lichtenhaln Basle 2000) 478

E B Pashukanis, *Law and Marxism: A General Theory* (Pluto Press, London, 1989)

E Paulis, 'Coherent Application of EC Competition Law in a System of Parallel Competences', in C-D Ehlermann (ed) *European Competition Law Annual 2000: The Modernisation of EC Antitrust Policy* (Hart, Oxford, 2001)

E Paz Ferreira, 'A Constituição Economica de 1976: "Que reste-t-il de nos amours?"', in J Miranda (ed), *Perspectivas Constitucionais nos 20 Anos da Constituição de 1976* (vol I, Coimbra Editora, 1996)

I Pernice, 'Multilevel Constitutionalism and the Treaty of Amsterdam: European Constitution-Making Revisited?', (1999) *Common Market Law Review*, 703

P Pescatore, 'La notion du marché commun dans les traités instituant l'Union économique belgo-luxembourgeoise, le Benelux et les Communautés européennes', in *En hommage à Victor Gothot* (Faculté de Droit de Liège, Liège, 1962)

——, 'La Cour en tant que juridiction fédérale et constitutionnelle' in *Dix ans de jurisprudence de la Cour de Justice des Communautés européennes* (Institut du Droit des Communautés Européennes de l'Université de Cologne, Carl Heymanns Verlag, Cologne, 1965)

——, 'Les objectifs de la Communauté européenne comme principes d'interprétation dans la jurisprudence de la Cour de Justice', in *Miscellanea WJ Ganshof van der Meersch* (vol 2, Bruylant, Brussels, 1972)

——, *The Law of Integration: Emergence of a New Phenomenon in International Relations Based on the Experience of the European Communities* tr C Dwyer, (Sijthoff, Leiden, 1974, first published in French, 1972)

——, 'The Doctrine of 'Direct Effect': An Infant Disease of Community Law' (1983) *European Law Review*, 155

——, 'Public and Private Aspects of Community Competition Law', in B Hawk (ed) *US and Common Market Antitrust Policies: 1986 Corporate Law Institute*, (1987) 381

P Pescatore, 'Guest Editorial: Nice—Aftermath', (2001) *Common Market Law Review*, 265

M Poiares Maduro, *We the Court The European Court of Justice and the European Economic Constitution* (Hart, Oxford, 1998)

——, 'Striking the Elusive Balance Between Economic Freedoms and Social Rights in the EU', in P Alston (ed), *The EU and Human Rights* (OUP, Oxford, 1999)

A Pubusa, in G Branca (ed) *Commentario della Costituzione: Le regioni, le province, i comuni, Tomo I, Art 114–120* (Zanichelli, Bologna, 1985)

H Putnam, 'The Meaning of Meaning', in *Mind, Language and Reality, Philosophical Papers* (vol 2, Cambridge University Press, Cambridge, 1975)

H Rabault, 'La constitution économique de la France', (2000) *Revue française de Droit constitutionnel*, 707

J Raz, 'On the Authority and Interpretation of Constitutions: Some Preliminaries', in L Alexander (ed), *Constitutionalism: Philosophical Foundations* (Cambridge University Press, Cambridge, 1999)

N Reich, 'The 'November Revolution' of the European Court of Justice: *Keck, Meng* and *Audi* Revisited', (1994) *Common Market Law Review*, 459

——, 'A European Union for Citizens: Reflections on the Rethinking of Union and Community Law', (1997) *European Law Journal*, 131

G C Rodríguez Iglesias and A Valle Gálvez, 'El Derecho comunitario y las relaciones entre el Tribunal de Justicia de las Comunidades Europeas, el Tribunal Europeo de Derechos Humanos y los Tribunales Constitucionales nacionales', (1997) *Revista de Derecho comunitario europeo*, 329

W-H Roth, 'Drittwirkung der Grundfreiheiten?', in O Due *et al* (eds), *Festschrift für Ulrich Everling* (Nomos, Baden-Baden, 1995)

F Rubio Llorente, *La forma del poder* (Centro de Estudios Constitucionales, Madrid, 1997)

E W Said, *Beginnings: Intention & Method* (Columbia University Press, New York, 1985)

R Sally, *Classical Neoliberalism and International Economic Order* (Routledge, London, 1998)

F de Saussure, *Cours de linguistique générale* (published by C Bally and A Sechehaye, Payot, Paris, 1983)

W Sauter, *Competition Law and Industrial Policy in the EU* (Clarendon Press, Oxford, 1997)

——, 'The Economic Constitution of the European Union', (1998) *Columbia Journal of European Law*, 27

D Schaefer, *Die unmittelbare Wirkung des Verbots der nichttarifären Handelshemmnisse (Art 30 EWGV) in den Rechtsbeziehungen zwischen Privaten: Probleme der horizontalen unmittelbaren Wirkung des Gemeinschaftsrechts, gezeigt am Beispiel des Art 30 EWGV* (Lang, Frankfurt a M, 1987)

R Schmidt, 'Staatliche Veranwortung für die Wirtschaft', in J Isensee and P Kirchhof (eds), (1988) *Handbuch des Staatsrechts des Bundesrepublik Deutschland* (vol III, Müller, Heidelberg)

C Schmitt, *Verfassungslehre* (Duncker & Humblot, Berlin, 1970, first published in 1928)

——, *The Concept of the Political* (University of Chicago Press, Chicago, 1996, first published in 1932)

——, *Political Theology: Four Chapters on the Concept of Sovereignty* (MIT Press, Cambridge, Mass 1988, first published in 1922)

B H Siegan, *Economic Liberties and the Constitution* (University of Chicago Press, Chicago, 1980)

D Simon, *Le système juridique communautaire* (PUF, Paris, 1997)

R Smend, 'Verfassung und Verfassungsrecht' [1928], in *Staatsrechtliche Abhandlungen* (Duncker & Humblot, Berlin, 1968)

F Snyder, 'General Course on Constitutional Law of the European Union', (1998) *Collected Courses of the Academy of European Law*, vol VI Book 1, 41

Spaak Report, Comité intergouvernemental créé par la conférence de Messine, *Rapport des Chefs de Délégation aux Ministres des Affaires Étrangères* (Bruxelles, 21 avril 1956)

E Steindorff, *EG-Vertrag und Privatrecht* (Nomos, Baden-Baden, 1996)

J Stuyck, 'Libre circulation et concurrence: les deux piliers du marché commun', in M Dony (ed), *Mélanges en hommage à Michel Waelbroeck* (vol II, Bruylant, Brussels, 1999)

C R Sunstein, 'Lochner's Legacy', (1987) *Columbia Law Review*, 873

——, 'The Beard Thesis and Franklin Roosevelt', (1987) *George Washington Law Review*, 114

——, 'The Supreme Court 1995 Term: Foreword: *Leaving Things Undecided*', (1996) *Harvard Law Review*, 6

——, *One Case at a Time: Judicial Minimalism on the Supreme Court* (Harvard University Press, Cambridge, Mass 1999)

J B Thayer, 'The Origin and Scope of the American Doctrine of Constitutional Law', (1893) *Harvard Law Review*, 6

P VerLoren van Themaat, 'Zum Verhältnis zwischen Artikel 30 und Artikel 85 EWG-Vertrag', in H Gutzlen *et al* (eds) *Wettbewerb im Wandel: Eberhard Günther zum 65 Geburtstag* (Nomos, Baden-Baden, 1976)

—— and L W Gormley, 'Prohibiting Restriction of Free Trade within the Community: Articles 30–36 of the EEC Treaty', (1981) *Northwestern Journal of International Law & Business*, 577

G Vico, *La scienza nuova* (P Rossi, ed, BUR, Milano, 1996, originally published in 1744)

M Waelbroeck, 'Droit des marques et règles du Traité de Rome: au terme d'une évolution?' 1977 *Revue critique de jurisprudence belge*, 219

——, 'Les rapports entre les règles sur la libre circulation des marchandises et les règles de concurrence applicables aux entreprises dans la CEE', in Capotorti *et alii* (eds) *Liber Amicorum Pescatore* (Nomos, Baden-Baden, 1987)

—— and A Frignani, *Commentaire Mégret vol 4, Concurrence,* (2nd edn, Presses de l'Université libre de Bruxelles, Brussels, 1997)

J Waldron, "Transcendental Nonsense' and System in the Law', (2000) *Columbia Law Review*, 16

S Weatherill, Annotation on *Bosman*, (1996) *Common Market Law Review*, 991

M Weber, *Economy and Society: An Outline of Interpretive Sociology* ed by G Roth and C Wittich (University of California Press, Berkeley, 1978)

H Wechsler, 'The Political Safeguards of Federalism: the Rôle of the States in the Composition and Selection of the National Government', (1954) *Columbia Law Review*, 543

——, 'Toward Neutral Principles of Constitutional Law', in *Principles, Politics and Fundamental Law: Selected Essays* (Harvard University Press, Cambridge, Mass 1961)

J H H Weiler, *The Constitution of Europe* (Cambridge University Press, Cambridge, 1999)

J H H Weiler, 'Epilogue: 'Comitology' as Revolution—Infranationalism, Constitutionalism and Democracy', in C Joerges and E Vos (eds), *EU Committees: Social Regulation, Law and Politics* (Hart, Oxford, 1999)

R Von Weizsäcker, J-L Dehaene and D Simon, *The Institutional Implications of Enlargement*, Report presented to the European Commission on 18 October 1999, published in *Europe*, 20 October 1999, Documents No 2159

S Wernicke, *Die Privatwirkung im Europäischen Gemeinschaftsrecht: Strukturen und Kategorien der Pflichtenstellungen Privater aus dem primären Gemeinschaftsrecht unter besonderer Berücksichtigung der Privatisierungsfolgen* (Nomos, Baden-Baden, 2002)

K C Wheare, *Modern Constitutions* (OUP, Oxford, 1966)

B de Witte, 'Direct Effect, Supremacy, and the Nature of the Legal Order', in P Craig and G de Búrca (eds), *The Evolution of EU Law* (OUP, Oxford, 1999)

L Wittgenstein, *Über Gewißheit / On Certainty* (eds G E M Anscombe and G K V Wright, Harper & Row, New York, 1972)

Index